The
CONCISE ATLAS
of GERMAN
WINES

INTRODUCED BY HUGH JOHNSON
CONSULTANT EDITOR IAN JAMIESON

The Concise Atlas of German Wines
Edited and designed by Mitchell Beazley International Ltd., Artists House,
14–15 Manette Street, London W1V 5LB, for the German Wine Institute
Copyright © Mitchell Beazley Publishers 1986
Text copyright © Hugh Johnson and Mitchell Beazley Publishers 1986
Touring maps copyright © Hallwag AG, Bern 1986 and © Mairs
Geographischer Verlag, Stuttgart 1986
Wine maps copyright © Stabilisierungsfonds für Wein 1986
All rights reserved

ISBN 0 85533 655 2

The introductions to the wine regions in this Atlas are based on text in *Hugh
Johnson's Wine Companion (Hugh Johnson's Modern Encyclopedia of Wine)*
published in 1983 and as *Der Grosse Johnson* in 1984.

Although the information in this Atlas is the most up to date available at the
time of going to press and all reasonable care has been taken in the
preparation of the Atlas, neither the author and publishers nor the German
Wine Institute can accept any liability for any consequences arising from the
use thereof or from the information contained herein.

Filmsetting by Servis Filmsetting Ltd., Manchester, England
Reproduced by Gilchrist Bros. Ltd., Leeds, England
Printed and bound in West Germany by Neue Stalling GmbH & Co. KG,
Oldenburg

Front cover: Castle Pfalz near Kaub on the Rhine, with Burg Gutenfels
in the background

CONTENTS

**This Atlas divides Germany's winelands into four zones.
A key to these zones appears on page 9.**

NORTHWEST ZONE

CENTRAL ZONE

EASTERN ZONE

SOUTHERN ZONE

FOREWORD

Soil, climate and grape varieties are the three basic factors for growing fine wines, combined by human skill and the dedication of wine growers to centuries of tradition. Soil and climate are the blessed gifts of nature, which give the individual and distinctive character and quality to wines. And nature cannot be changed by man – it is the creation of God, created to last until the end of time. Nature is the reason – not commercial inventions – why the geography of vineyards, with all its elements from soil to climate, is so important for the definition of wine.

This is not the case with other products of human endeavour: in almost any industry, raw materials, equipment and labour can be moved to almost anywhere they may be needed to manufacture a certain product. Agricultural commodities can be produced in many places without much difference in quality or character. A vine, too, can be planted in many places on earth, but the quality and character, the aroma and bouquet, the style and finesse will be different, depending on where the vine is grown. Human intelligence can move almost anything, but never a vineyard. Therefore, there is scarcely any other product in the world for which the birthplace, the place of origin, is as important as it is for noble wines. This is the philosophy behind labelling a wine with its appellation of geographical origin – in contrast to the industrial concept of a trade-mark.

This philosophy is less relevant for winegrowing countries in warm latitudes, where climate and soil may not change over large areas of flat surface; where wine is mostly produced in quantity as a commodity without any individual significance. The appellation of origin is most relevant in countries or regions where individual wines of distinctive character and quality are produced. In Germany, the wine-producing regions along the Rhine and the Mosel are extremely sensitive to geographical designations, because at the latitude of 50 degrees – the same latitude as Labrador – climate and soil often change within a mere hundred metres or so. Germany's winegrowing regions are mostly concentrated in the narrow valleys of the Rhine, Mosel and their tributaries, which twist and turn through mountainous, mainly wooded regions in basin-shaped land areas. The variations in soil structure stem directly from the earth's history: slaty on deep inclines, fertile, alluvial land at the foot of hills; other areas have lime deposits or volcanic rocks. The micro-climate of a vineyard depends on whether it faces south or west, on the steepness of its incline, the intensity of the sun's reflection from the surface of the river, the proximity of sheltering forests or mountain peaks, the altitude and the soil humidity. Therefore, reaching back for centuries in history, every single hill or section of a valley has a different name, is a geographical origin with individual characteristics, is a "Lage" (site) explicitly named on the wine label.

In the 2,000-year-old winegrowing landscapes of Germany, everything is on a small scale. Distances between villages are short. About 90,000 families own mostly small parcels of vineyards in different localities. Most winegrowing communities have several vineyards within their boundaries. Historically, there have been more than 25,000 individual vineyard names in use for centuries; this number was reduced to less than 3,000 in the early 1970s – an important amendment of the wine law. Still this immense variety of natural and historical conditions with so many names makes German wine labels look complicated. But as soon as you understand the philosophy behind such names, labels for German wines tell a fascinating story. As the famous German playwright Carl Zuckmayer said: "Reading a German wine list with imagination is as joyful as having drunk each wine."

The philosophy of German geographical origins is in principle the same as the system of the *Appellation d'Origine Contrôlée* in France. But there is one fundamental difference: in France the appellation of origin simultaneously decides and defines the quality grading. The appellations, for example, *Grand Cru*, *Premier Cru* and *Deuxième Cru*, once determined, are forever kept. The birth-place determines the nobility. If wine is grown in an area without an *appellation d'origine* it cannot be labelled with its birth-place, even if the winegrower makes an excellent quality wine.

Such a system does not fit for Germany. Here, the geography designates the origin, but not necessarily the quality of a wine. In good years, with special endeavour and dedication, the winegrower can produce the highest classified wines. Under less propitious circumstances his best produce is just a normal quality wine from a specified region. Therefore, German winegrowers even from the most famous vineyards are challenged every year to produce high qualities to justify their reputation. They can never rest on a good name. The "human factor" is still essential for the taste and style of wine. German wines are individuals, as are the men who make them.

God made nature, man makes wine. The cultural history of winegrowing landscapes and their inhabitants is reflected in their wine and its geography. One must travel along the narrow river valleys, through the picturesque historical villages, enjoy the local Gasthaus, see the winegrowers' families, grandparents and children included, working in the vineyard, breathe the incomparable smell of young wine coming from the door of old, vaulted wine cellars, to understand the secret of German wines. What would have been the life-style, art and culture in German wine country without wine? Symphonies from Beethoven, sculptures from Riemenschneider or poems from Goethe have all been inspired by the spirit of German wine.

Germany's legal requirements for wine sound very academic and complicated. But they become simpler as you study the labels, or better, when you travel through the wine country. This *Concise Atlas of German Wines* is a guide to both. It opens the door to wonderful experiences for the wine connoisseur, for the traveller and for the lover of wine culture.

DR. FRANZ WERNER MICHEL
CO-DIRECTOR OF THE GERMAN WINE INSTITUTE

INTRODUCTION BY HUGH JOHNSON

German wine is a category far more distinct and homogeneous than French or Italian: distinct but various in itself as water-colour is among paintings, or woodwind among the sounds of the orchestra.

Its distinctiveness is relatively easy to describe; its variety almost impossible. How does German wine differ from French, or any other within Europe or beyond? Transparency is the word that always comes to my mind first: transparency of texture that makes the intricacies of aroma and flavour more readily discernible than in other wines. A relatively low alcohol content is partly responsible: the sheer winey weight, the warmth in the mouth known as "vinosity", is generally missing. Its place is taken, or should be taken, by a sort of tension between incipient richness and fruity acidity. This tension, or balance, is the hallmark of all the best German wines and is the reason for their astonishing longevity: they continue to mature with benefit for longer than any other white wines except those that are very sweet.

There is another reason, however, for thinking of modern German wines as homogeneous, and that is the powerful tendency of the consumer to settle for a common denominator rather than to exploit the available variety. The tendency is much more pronounced outside Germany, where the German language of the label seems to present a barrier few are prepared to tackle. A regional blend is probably the most characteristic German wine the majority of foreign wine drinkers have ever tasted.

Happily, German wine drinkers are more than equal to the challenge, and revel in the variety at their disposal. Nobody knows how, when and where to enjoy their wine better than the Germans – especially the inhabitants of the wine villages themselves. The contrast with France could hardly be more complete. What friendly corner does the Médoc provide for a visitor to sit and sip and discuss Pauillac or Margaux with the locals? But try to find a German wine village without its Weinstube. By definition it is the people who make the wine in Germany who appreciate it most. While there are great estates (and great cooperatives) that specialize in exports, most German growers at least give the impression that they are making wine primarily for themselves, their friends, and the guests at their fireside in winter, and in their flowery courtyard in summer. It is central to the experience of German wine to be guided, barrel by barrel or bottle by bottle, through the range of qualities, of different grape varieties and ages of wine that even a small farmer of the Rhine or Mosel will have in his cellar. Few will have less than a dozen sorts to pour, to justify or criticize or just to enjoy with a craftsman's pride.

This is the romantic side of German wine. The full picture may contain more steel vats and industrial-looking premises than pretty half-timbered farmhouses. Yet in Germany the romantic imposes itself. It cannot be ignored, any more than the serpentine gorges of the rivers, the eagle's-nest castles, the blackness of the forest or the tender green of spring in the vineyards. The true Germany is here, and not in the airports and autobahns, the city centres and supermarkets. German wines express the essence of these matchless landscapes – at least for their fortunate inhabitants. Happily both are easily accessible for visitors, too.

If sensual enjoyment is the first aim and object of wine, it is followed, qualified and amplified by aesthetic interest. Like any species of thing that is consistent yet alterable, similar yet various, all wines invite analysis and comparison.

With its clear family resemblance, yet its widely various character, German wine appeals to the discriminating mind more than any other, except perhaps claret. It is the most analytically labelled wine on earth, and anyone with the leisure and the capacity could progress logically through each harvest noting and comparing the gradations of quality by categories. Indeed the official government wine-tasting and -approving machinery does just that, systematically controlling every barrel or tank of wine in Germany, setting standards that the conscientious achieve and the curious can follow.

The heart of Germany's systematic approach to wine is a simple measurement; a measurement that every winegrower the world over makes before the vintage: the sugar content of the grapes. In warmer climates ripe grapes are taken for granted; in Germany it is only certain privileged sites that reach the necessary sugar-level with any degree of regularity. It could be done more easily, with grape varieties that ripen early in the autumn. But it is a hard fact of life that the best varieties take a long time to reach maturity. Precocious grapes never develop the concentrated fruity acidity that makes wine lively, vigorous and refreshing when young, and gives it the potential to mature; to develop depth and harmony.

The archetypal late grape is the Riesling: with very few exceptions all Germany's best wines are made from it. But it is only worth planting Riesling in warm soils on sheltered south- and east-facing slopes. On flatter, colder land the overwhelming favourite is the early ripening Müller-Thurgau. The two grapes between them account for almost half of the total vineyard of Germany.

The other half is largely composed of such traditional varieties as Silvaner and Ruländer, whose qualities on certain soils, and in certain local climates, ensure their continued use; of the red grapes, led by the Spätburgunder or Pinot Noir, that together make up about ten per cent of Germany's vineyards, and of a dozen or so new vine varieties, led by the Kerner, which have been bred in a continuing effort to achieve Riesling quality without its concomitant drawbacks: uncertain ripening, and (by German standards) less than spectacular crops. (For the grapes of Germany, *see* page 112.)

The German word for vineyard is "Weinberg", literally "winehill". There are flat Weinbergs, even a few very good flat Weinbergs; but the word forcefully expresses the innate superiority of a hill as a place to grow grapes. If it is true on the "Côtes" of France (true even in Italy: it was Vergil who said "vines love an open hill"), it becomes even truer as you go further north. The angle of the sun in the sky gets lower, the shadows longer. With cooler temperatures the grapes start ripening later – so late in the autumn that the vines cast long shadows for most of the day, and mist often wreathes the vineyards all morning long before the sun finds the power to burn it off.

At these latitudes every degree of warmth lasting an hour longer is precious to the ripening fruit. Where everything is marginal the microclimate is crucial – microclimate in the most intimate vine-by-vine detail, as wall or tree or tilt of hill casts shade or gives protection. What is the balance in calories (as the measure of heat) if one vine shades another all morning, but towards dusk prevents accumulated warm air lying in the vine-row from being flushed out by the evening breeze?

One simple rule prevails: a south slope has the edge. A slope at 45 degrees to the sky theoretically (although perhaps not effectively) has the sun straight overhead. Its rays hit the ground perpendicularly, shadows are minimized, and at least one of the consequences of a high latitude is eliminated. The south slope of most German hills is the only one it is worth planting with vines.

In foggy districts a westerly tilt can be an added advantage: there is less fog in the afternoon so the sun has better access. In the majority of districts, though, in Germany as in France (think of Alsace, the Côte d'Or, the Champagne Côte de Blancs), it is better to incline to the east from south for the sake of the early sun that warms the ground, warmth that lingers in a sheltered vineyard even after the afternoon casts shadows between the vines.

The maps in this Atlas make it crystal clear just how far these considerations have shaped the landscapes of Germany. In map after map the vineyards fall exactly as the hill-shadows would if the world were upside down and the sun shining from the north.

Since geology and soil structure is far less consistent and predictable than sunshine it is equally clear that they must be secondary considerations in deciding where to cultivate the vine. Soils change rapidly and often within a district, yet the vines hug each south slope. Certainly there will be differences in fertility, in drainage, in mineral make-up of the soil that will make it yield bigger or smaller crops, ripen them more (or less) regularly, and give hints of flavour to the fruit, and eventually to the wine.

Important though these variations are, the matter for endless earnest discussion over a glass, and certainly the cause of considerable differences in price between one wine and another, in Germany they are not considered central to the question of essential quality. Only the ripeness of the grapes is taken into official account. Theoretically at least any vineyard in Germany can produce top-quality wine: it only needs to conjure the grape-sugar from the elusive sun. Differences between vineyards are officially considered to be questions of style, and therefore in the final analysis subjective.

The German philosophy is thus the precise opposite of the French, which classifies land, and only land. The proprietor of a Burgundy Grand Cru vineyard may add as much sugar as necessary to his wine (within the law) and still sell it as Grand Cru; thus in the highest quality category. Whereas the owner of Germany's noblest plot may find himself, in a year of terrible weather, with nothing but ordinary wine.

The difference is fundamental, and well worth thinking about. Can both the German and the French philosophies be right in their contexts? It seems to one observer at least that logic and natural justice are truly on the side of the German.

So, in German law, the land is neutral. Quality begins each vintage with the sugar content of the grapes. The vital reading of the "degree Oechsle" – the specific gravity of the must – decides once for all whether the wine will be graded as "quality wine" or not; even more significant, whether it will be allowed as natural quality wine, and if so at what quality level. These distinctions need spelling out in detail. The law is complex and easily misunderstood.

The crop, let us say, is a wash-out. The autumn has turned cold and wet, the grapes are only half-ripened, and with rot beginning and no prospect of better weather the grower is obliged to pick. The specific gravity of the juice from one vineyard is barely enough to convert to 5% of natural alcohol. This is the minimum figure to qualify as even the humblest form of wine, Tafelwein – and to make wine at all it needs a huge addition of non-grape sugar. Whatever the grower does he cannot sell this as his own wine,

identified by its vineyard or even district name. He will probably do best to sell it as base-wine to be converted by some big concern into sparkling Sekt.

Three days later in a better-sited vineyard the same grower measures his "must-weight" again, and discovers to his satisfaction that these grapes have a specific gravity of 1.060 (or an "Oechsle-degree" of 60). This means 7.5% potential alcohol, the minimum allowed for a quality wine from a specific region (Qualitätswein bestimmter Anbaugebiete). While the wine still requires the addition of non-grape sugar to increase its alcohol content to a satisfactory level of between 9 and 11 per cent, it is legally acknowledged as the wine of his vineyard. In many cases such "QbA" wines have distinct and satisfying characters – just as their French counterparts from under-ripened grapes helped by chaptalization would do.

It is up to the grower to decide whether the character of the wine emerges best if he leaves it in its natural state after fermentation, which is completely dry, or "trocken", or adds some unfermented (and therefore sweet) must to make it either "halbtrocken" – often a very satisfying compromise – or distinctly sweet. His decision will be influenced by the balance of the wine: if the acidity is very high some "Süssreserve" (the unfermented must) can balance it to make a wine of verve and character. It will also be influenced by his clients' taste; more and more Germans are asking for drier wines to drink with meals. They tend to choose trocken or halbtrocken. Wine with less than 4 grams per litre of sugar can even be labelled as "safe for diabetics".

Another year in the same vineyard the picture is very different. The summer has been glorious, the autumn is golden, and the grapes are fully ripe in early October. The Oechsle reading gives a minimum "must-weight" of 75, which in potential alcohol means 9.8%. In this district (let us say we are in the Rheingau) an Oechsle degree of 73 or over moves the wine into the top category: natural quality wine that needs no additional sugar. The German term, Qualitätswein mit Prädikat, translates clumsily as "quality wine with specific attributes". The "specific attributes" in question are those of Kabinett, Spätlese, Auslese or even later-gathered and more luscious wines.

QmP wines are generally listed as though it was their quality that rose with each step of the ladder of richness; as though Kabinett wines are mere footsoldiers, Spätlesen the non-commissioned officers, while only Auslesen and above are the true officer-class. On the contrary, though, we are talking about style. A Kabinett wine can be as perfect in its way as an Auslese: what is different is the level of natural sugar, therefore strength and impressive flavour.

A week later our grower is picking grapes from different parts of his vineyards at Oechsle degrees ranging from 85 to 95. At 85 degrees the wine has a potential alcohol content of 11.4 per cent; it qualifies as a Spätlese or "Late-Picked". At 95 it qualifies as an Auslese, or "Selection"; its potential alcohol – seldom realized, as the wine will remain sweet to balance its strength – is 13 per cent; the same as an average white burgundy.

In a great vintage as much as half the crop in good sites may be ripe enough to fall into the Auslese category. When this happens the grower gauges his chances of making super-Auslesen; either Beerenauslese by selecting only the ripest berries to achieve an Oechsle degree of 125 or more, or, with patience and good fortune, a Trockenbeerenauslese. The last, a "dry berry selection",

6

depends on the same noble rot as Sauternes to shrivel the bunches into a powder-coated, wizened concentration of sweetness and intense flavour. A good autumn, when morning mists alternate with sunny afternoons, will set off a degree of botrytis, or noble rot, throughout the vineyard. It is at the discretion of the grower whether he seeks it all out to make a quintessence, a Trockenbeerenauslese in a minute quantity, or leaves "nobly rotten" berries and the occasional bunch to give his best Auslesen an extra richness and dimension of flavour. There are miracle vintages, one in a decade or less, when he can do both.

Sometimes at the end of a merely average vintage there are good-looking bunches of grapes left in the vineyard which the grower is reluctant to pick: they give him the sporting chance of making an "Eiswein". The principle of "ice-wine" is that if the grapes can be kept in good condition (which usually means shielding them with plastic sheets) until the first really hard frost, they can be picked at dawn in a deep-frozen state. Pressed while their water content is still solid ice they yield a juice incredibly high in flavour and acidity as well as sugar. (The ice is thrown away.) Eiswein has none of the luscious complexity of a Trockenbeerenauslese made by noble rot. For years it tastes as though it were in suspended animation: stiff and dumb, sweet and acid, scarcely vinous, in fact, at all. Long years of ageing, however, eventually thaw the mastodon. A mature Eiswein can be one of Germany's most spectacular specialities.

All the above categories of ripeness and quality are set forth on all German wine labels in a fashion which, once mastered, leaves no room for doubt.

The true key, inevitably, to the quality and probity of the wine in any bottle, whatever its official status, is the name of the maker. This fact simplifies at a stroke most of the intricacies and ambiguities of any set of wine laws. There are many labels in Germany whose very design, once recognized, gives one the certain hope of an excellently made wine, of whatever category, vineyard, grape or vintage.

How best, then, is the huge range of Germany's production to be explored, and how is it to be enjoyed? The ideal way, without a doubt, is to set off on a leisurely tour, preferably walking, with this Atlas in your pack. The short distances between villages would only lend vigour to the thirst, and zest to the appetite. A month could be spent exploring the Mosel in this way; another month the Rheingau . . . a lifetime of summer holidays could go by without exhausting the variety of every Gemeinde in every Gebiet.

Lacking the leisure to drink in Germany this way, we can quite easily arrange an armchair tour, either in macro-focus, ranging wines of contrasting regions, grapes, categories and ages, or micro-focus, concentrating even on one village, or one producer, and tasting for smaller and more subtle distinctions. Either course will reveal at once how German wine is infinitely various; a unique cultural heritage worth a lifetime of study.

HOW TO USE THIS ATLAS

This Atlas is divided into four geographical zones, **North-west**, **Central**, **Eastern** and **Southern**, each identified throughout the Atlas by its own colour (see page 9). Each zone is subdivided into the quality-wine regions in that zone. However, for clarity, Baden – the most diffuse of the wine regions – has been divided in this Atlas into north and south, with a general introduction to the area on page 89.

Touring Maps are grouped into the four colour-coded geographical zones shown on page 9. The zones are indicated both by name and by the coloured bar at the top of each page. The broad pink bands on the touring maps are the outlines of the vineyard maps, and at the outer edge of each touring map is printed the name of the wine region(s) covered, followed by the page number where the relevant vineyard map can be found. At the corners of each touring map, arrows with page numbers indicate where to find adjacent maps.

Placenames are frequently abbreviated on German maps. The most common of these are, for example: Veitshöchhm = Veitshöchheim; St. Goarshsn = St. Goarshausen; Idar-Oberstn = Idar-Oberstein; Gr.-Umstadt = Groß-Umstadt.

Vineyard Maps show every registered vineyard (Einzellage) in West Germany, its official number and the Großlage to which it belongs. Each number can be traced from the maps to the lists accompanying the maps to find the name of the Einzellage as well as the village, Großlage and Bereich under which it is classified. The Großlage names and their boundaries are marked on the map in red. The vineyards within each Großlage are colour-coordinated to make them easily identifiable.

The Location Map beside each vineyard map cross-refers to the touring maps. It shows the outline of the vineyard map and main towns in the area. The colour of the outline follows the colour-coding of the four zones and the strip across the top of the location map gives the touring map page numbers.

Vineyard Lists: accompanying each vineyard map are lists of all the vineyards (Einzellagen) shown on the map, followed by their official numbers. Headings denote the Bereich, Großlage, Gemeinde and (frequently) Ortsteil to which the vineyards belong. These terms are explained on pages 110–111.

"P" (for Part) following the number indicates that an Einzellage extends over more than one parish (Ortsteil) or village (Gemeinde).

An asterisk following the number means that this vineyard lies outside the area covered by the map.

An a, b, c, d, e, f or g following the number simply means that a vineyard has been subdivided into two or more separate Einzellagen (using an additional letter instead of renumbering all the vineyards avoids confusion).

All the villages, Großlagen and Bereiche in the vineyard lists are indexed at the back of the Atlas, on pages 114–116.

The German Wine Institute is always happy to provide information about German wines. Contact them at: Deutsches Weininstitut GmbH, Gutenbergplatz 3–5, 6500 Mainz 1 (Tel: 06131-28290). Office hours are usually 9–12 a.m. and 2–5p.m. Monday to Friday.

TOURING MAP LEGEND

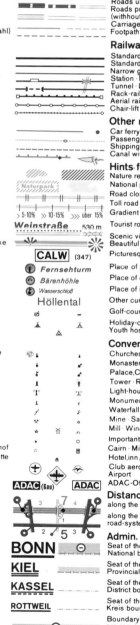

Straßen und Wege	Roads and tracks
Autobahn mit Anschlußstelle und Nummer	Motorway with access point and number
Rasthaus mit Übernachtung	Road house (with night accommod.)
Raststätte · Erfrischungsstelle	Restaurant · Snackbar
Tankstelle · Parkplatz mit/ohne WC	Filling station · Parking places ·
Bedarfsumleitung an der Autobahn	By-pass if required
Autobahn in Bau mit baldiger Verkehrsübergabe und Datum	Motorway under construction with early expected completion date
Autobahn in Bau und geplant	Motorway under construction/project.
Zweibahnige Straße (4-spurig)	Dual carriage-way
Sonstige Kfz.-Straße	Road for motorvehicles only
Bundesstraße · Straßennummern	Federal road · Road numbers
Wichtige Hauptstraße	Important main road
Hauptstraße · Tunnel · Brücke	Main road · Tunnel · Bridge
Nebenstraße	Minor road
Straßen in Bau	Roads under construction
Straßen in Planung (ohne Farbe und Anschluß)	Roads projected (without colour and junction)
Fahrweg · Fußweg	Carriage-way · Footpath
Bevorzugter Wanderweg (Auswahl)	Footpath (selection)

Bahnen	Railways
Vollspurbahn mit Fernverkehr	Standard gauge,long-distance traffic
Vollspurbahn ohne Fernverkehr	Standard gauge,short-distance traffic
Kleinbahn	Narrow gauge
Bahnhof · Bahnbrücke	Station · Bridge
Tunnel · Niveaukreuzung	Tunnel · Level crossing
Zahnradbahn,Standseilbahn	Rack-railway,Funicular
Kabinenschwebebahn	Aerial railway
Sessellift	Chair-lift

Sonstige Verkehrswege	Other means of communic.
Autofähre	Car ferry
Personenfähre	Passenger ferry
Schiffahrtslinie	Shipping route
Kanal mit Schleuse · Staudamm	Canal with lock · Dam

Touristische Hinweise	Hints for tourists
Naturschutzgebiet · Sperrgebiet	Nature reserve · Milit.training ground
Naturpark · Wald	National park · Forest
Straße für Kfz.gesperrt	Road closed to motor-traffic
Straße für Kfz.gegen Gebühr	Toll road
Steigungen in Pfeilrichtung	Gradient
Touristenstraße · Paß	Tourist route · Pass
Schöner Ausblick · Rundblick	Scenic view · Panoramic view
Landschaftlich bes.schöne Strecke	Beautiful scenery
Malerisches Stadtbild · Ortshöhe	Picturesque town · Elevation
Besonders sehenswertes Objekt	Place of particular interest
Sehenswertes Objekt	Place of considerable interest
Beachtenswertes Objekt	Place of interest
Sonstige Sehenswürdigkeit	Other curiosity
Golfplatz · Schwimmbad	Golf-course · Swimming pool
Ferienzeltplatz · Zeltplatz	Holiday-camp · Transit-camp
Jugendherberge	Youth hostel

Signaturen	Conventional signs
Kirche im Ort,freistehend · Kapelle	Churches · Chapel
Kloster · Klosterruine	Monastery · Monastery ruin
Schloß,Burg · Schloß-,Burgruine	Palace,Castle · Ruin
Turm · Funk-,Fernsehturm	Tower · Radio or TV tower
Leuchtturm · Feuerschiff	Light-house · Light-ship
Denkmal · Feldkreuz	Monument · Calvary
Wasserfall · Kraftwerk	Waterfall · Power station
Bergwerk · Sägewerk	Mine · Saw mill
Mühle · Windmühle · Höhle	Mill · Windmill · Cave
Bauwerk · Marktplatz,Areal	Important building · Market place etc.
Hünen- · Hügelgrab · Soldatenfriedhof	Cairn · Military cemetery
Hotel,Wirtshaus,Berggasthaus,-hütte	Hotel,inn,refuge
Landeplatz · Segelfluggelände	Club aerodrome · Gliding field
Verkehrsflughafen	Airport
ADAC-Geschäftsstellen	ADAC-Offices

Entfernungen	Distances
auf der Autobahn	along the motorway
auf dem übrigen Straßennetz	along the other road-system

Verwaltung	Admin. organization
Sitz der Bundesregierung Staatsgrenze · Grenzübergang	Seat of the Federal Government National boundary · Custom house
Sitz der Landesregierung Landesgrenze	Seat of the Provincial Government Provincial boundary
Sitz der Bezirksverwaltung Verwaltungsbezirksgrenze	Seat of the District Administration District boundary
Sitz der Kreisverwaltung Kreisgrenze	Seat of the Kreis Administration Kreis boundary
Grenze,zu deren Überschreiten besondere Ausweise erforderlich sind,mit Übergang	Boundary where special licences are required for crossing Check point

KEY TO TOURING MAPS

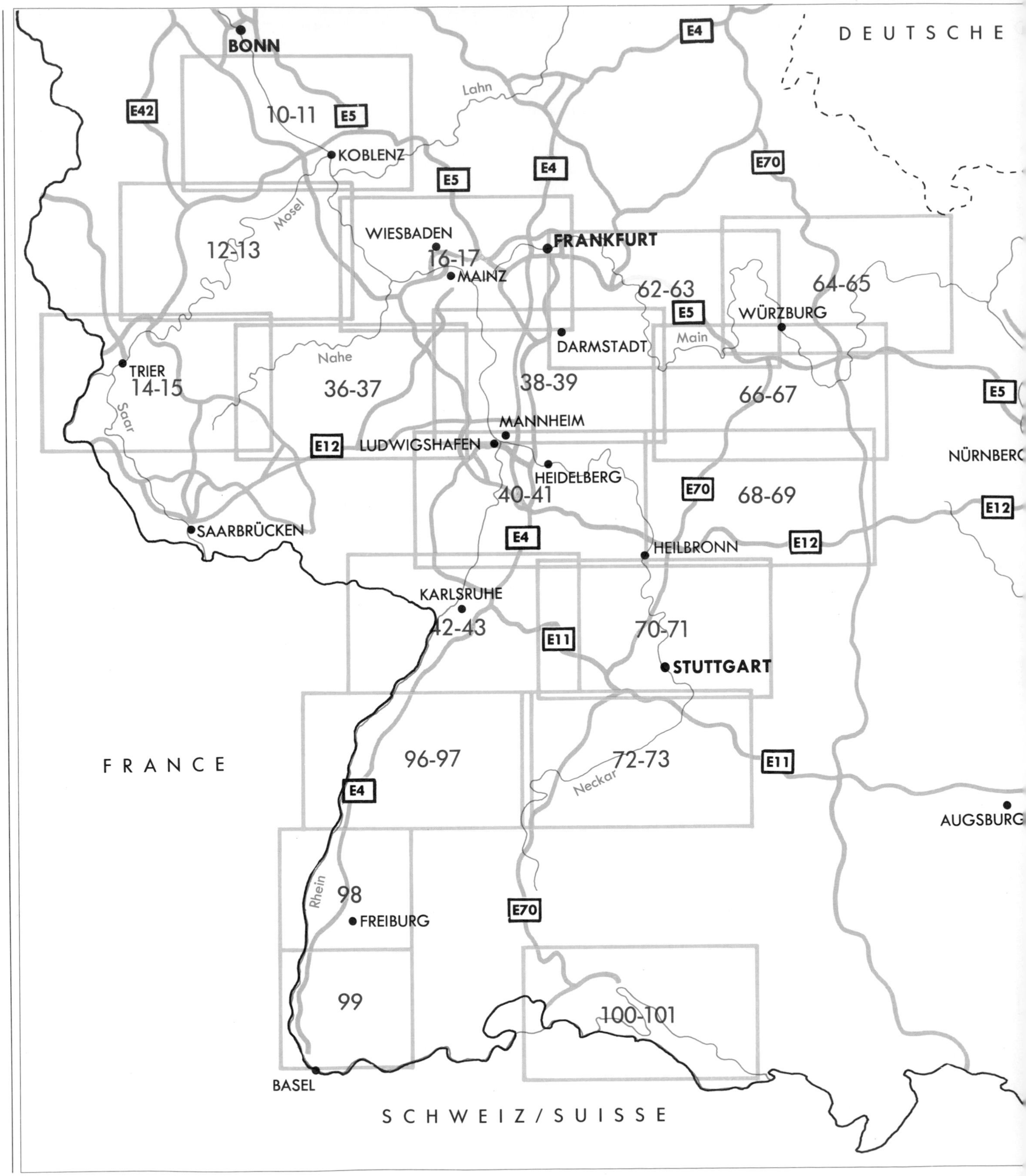

DEUTSCHE

E4

BONN

E42

10-11

E5

Lahn

E5

E4

KOBLENZ

E5

E4

E70

Mosel

12-13

WIESBADEN

FRANKFURT

16-17

62-63

64-65

MAINZ

E5

WÜRZBURG

Main

Nahe

DARMSTADT

38-39

TRIER

14-15

36-37

66-67

Saar

MANNHEIM

E5

E12 LUDWIGSHAFEN

NÜRNBERG

40-41

HEIDELBERG

E70

68-69

E12

SAARBRÜCKEN

E4

HEILBRONN

E12

KARLSRUHE

E11

70-71

42-43

STUTTGART

F R A N C E

96-97

72-73

E11

Neckar

E4

AUGSBURG

Rhein

98

E70

• FREIBURG

99

100-101

BASEL

S C H W E I Z / S U I S S E

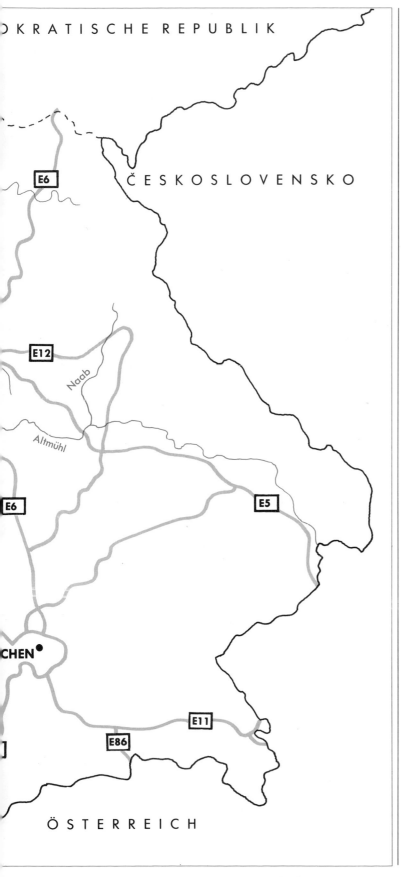

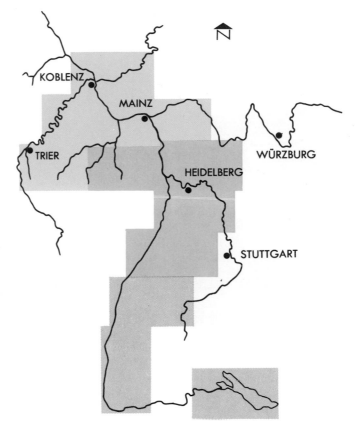

OKRATISCHE REPUBLIK

ČESKOSLOVENSKO

E6

E12

Naab

Altmühl

E6

E5

CHEN •

E11

E86

ÖSTERREICH

NORTHWEST ZONE:

Ahr
Mosel-Saar-Ruwer
Mittelrhein
Rheingau

CENTRAL ZONE:

Nahe
Rheinhessen
Rheinpfalz
Hessische Bergstraße

EASTERN ZONE:

Franken
Württemberg
North Baden

SOUTHERN ZONE:

South Baden

100-101

Touring Map page number

E11 ⎯⎯⎯⎯ Motorway (autobahn)

NORTHWEST ZONE

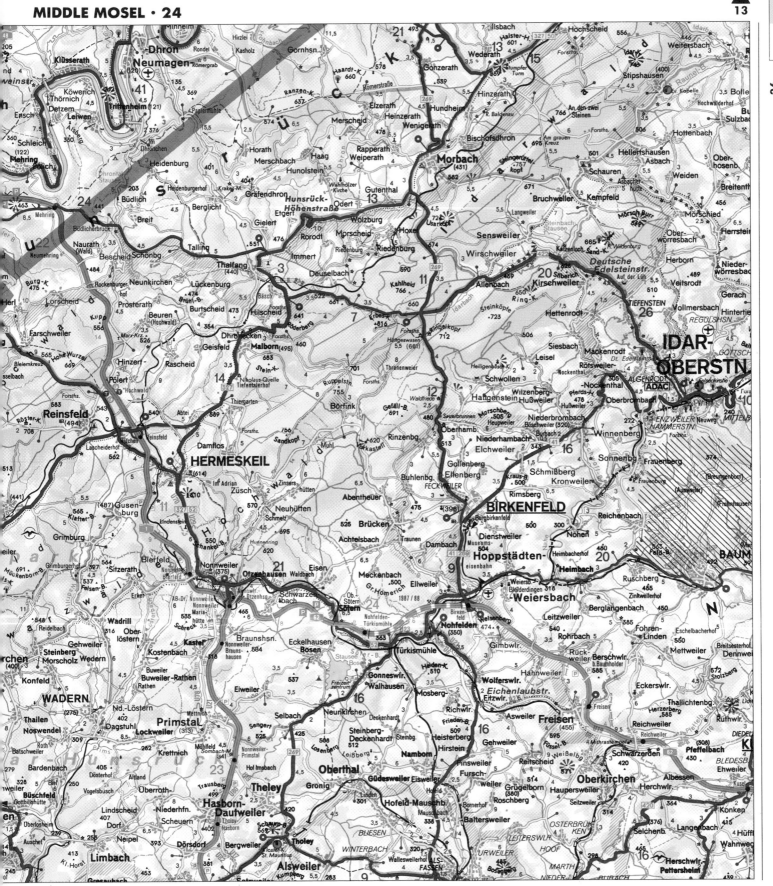

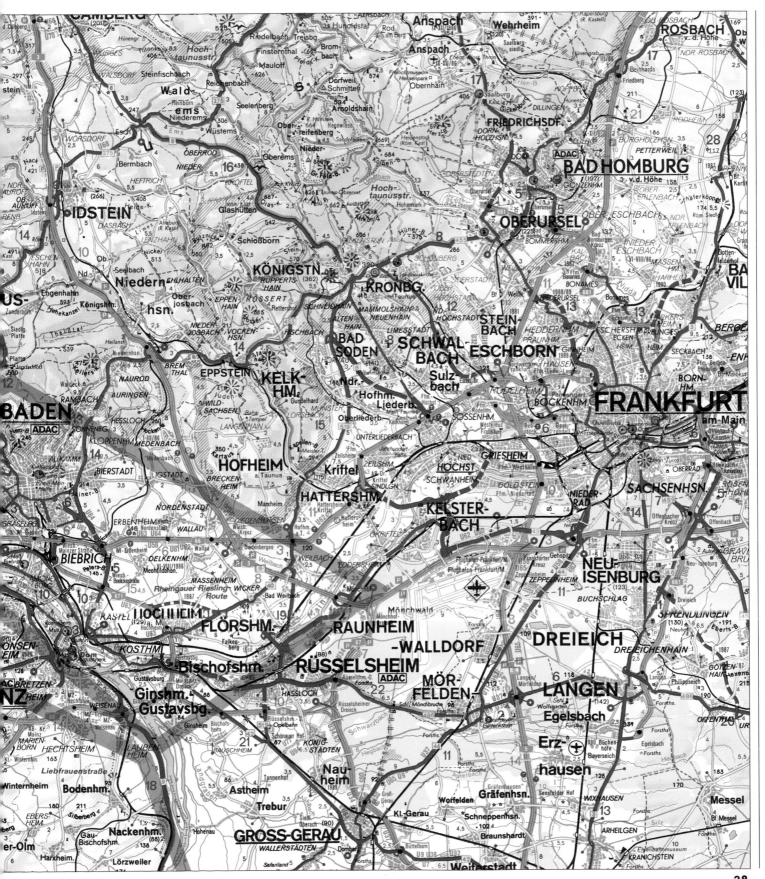

AHR

Red grapes in general need more sunshine and warmth to ripen than white, so it may seem surprising that the Ahr, Germany's northernmost wine region, should be so well known in Germany for its red wine. But the volcanic origin of the region, and the benign effect of the narrow river that twists and turns through the beautiful little valley, combine to provide the conditions necessary for growing the red-wine grapes that are the speciality of the Ahr.

The River Ahr is a western tributary of the Mittelrhein, rising in the Eifel mountains and flowing into the Rhine not far south of Bonn. The steep valley sides are clothed almost continuously in vines for 16 kilometres (10 miles): some 400 hectares, of which a third is Spätburgunder, a third Portugieser and other red grapes, and the balance is mainly Riesling and Müller-Thurgau.

The white wines can have a distinct lilt that is very attractive. The red wines are generally light, sometimes sweet, and much enjoyed by the many tourists who visit the valley to walk among the woods and vineyards, and relax in the evening in one of the snug little restaurants that have found a place between the river and the steep vineyard slopes, eating country food and drinking the proprietor's wine.

The capital of the Ahr, Bad Neuenahr, is also a spa with healing waters: a useful excuse for tired politicians from nearby Bonn to escape the town and rejuvenate the spirit.

The Ahr vineyards have a long history: winegrowing there goes back to Roman times. The Spätburgunder vine came to the valley in the late 17th or early 18th century. Today no less than 900 small growers till the soil, most of them banded into seven cooperatives, but a hundred or so making and selling their own wine. The Ahr growers claim to have founded Germany's first cooperative cellar in 1868. At this time the valley was considered remote, and the area under vine was in decline until quite recently. Very little of the wine they produce leaves the district, and still less is exported, so the best place to enjoy it is in the valley itself.

There is one Bereich and only one Großlage name: Klosterberg, covering the 11 villages and 43 Einzellagen.

▲ Autumn in the Ahr: the vineyard path provides a pleasant and instructive stroll: signs give information about the vineyards.

TRAVEL INFORMATION

The Ahr Valley is highly organized for wine tourism, with plenty of inns, signposted paths and the benefit of scenic towns. It can get quite crowded at weekends, especially in summer.

The north–south autobahn A61 crosses the valley at Heppingen: the autobahn brings the Ahr within 15 minutes' driving time of Bonn. The junction is Bad Neuenahr, with a spur autobahn (A573) running down the valley and rejoining the main A61 at Löhndorf. The B267 runs the length of the valley.

A branch railway leaves the Köln–Frankfurt line at Remagen and runs up the valley, through the wine district and beyond to Adenau.

The *Rotweinwanderweg* – red wine path – runs for 30km between Altenahr and Lohrsdorf through woods and vineyards, with side-paths into the villages, which are conveniently close together. The path is signposted with a symbol of a red grape in a white background. A map is available locally.

The *Rotweinstraße* starts at Sinzig and covers the length of the valley. The signpost is a stylized valley. There are many parking places provided.

Places to visit
Altenahr: romanesque church and ruins of a castle.
Mayschoß: wine cooperative with cellar open for visits at most times, art treasures (such as marble monuments) in the parish church.

Rech: typical wine village with cellars to visit and an ancient bridge.
Dernau: baroque church. Kloster Marienthal State Domain is nearby.
Bad Neuenahr-Ahrweiler: old town walls, a church (in Heimersheim) with the oldest windows in Germany; castle ruins. Both towns are replete with inns, wine cellars and other amenities. Bad Neuenahr is a spa.

Food and drink
Specialities include *Rauchfleisch* (smoked meats), mushrooms, *Schinken* (ham) from the Eifel mountains and local trout from the river.

There are more restaurants than hotels – most visitors are day-trippers. The inns of the valley – *Stuben* – are notoriously *gemütlich*.

Regional Wine Information Office
Gebietsweinwerbung Ahr
Marktplatz 11
5483 Bad Neuenahr-Ahrweiler
Tel: 02641–5555

AHR · VINEYARDS

▲ Picking in the Kloster Marienthal vineyards. An Augustinian convent from the 12th to the 19th centuries, Kloster Marienthal is now a model Ahr estate, producing prestigious red wines.

ROAD MAP

BEREICH WALPORZHEIM/ AHRTAL

GROSSLAGE KLOSTERBERG

Ehlingen
(Ortsteil of Bad Neuenahr-Ahrweiler)
Kapellenberg 1

Heimersheim
(Ortsteil of Bad Neuenahr-Ahrweiler)
Landskrone 2 P
Burggarten 3 P

Lohrsdorf
(Ortsteil of Bad Neuenahr-Ahrweiler)
Landskrone 2 P

Heppingen
(Ortsteil of Bad Neuenahr-Ahrweiler)
Burggarten 3 P
Berg 4

Neuenahr
(Ortsteil of Bad Neuenahr-Ahrweiler)
Sonnenberg 5
Schieferley 6
Kirchtürmchen 7

Bachem
(Ortsteil of Bad Neuenahr-Ahrweiler)
Karlskopf 8
Sonnenschein 9
Steinkaul 10

Ahrweiler
(Ortsteil of Bad Neuenahr-Ahrweiler)
Daubhaus 11
Forstberg 12
Rosenthal 13
Silberberg 14
Riegelfeld 15
Ursulinengarten 16

Walporzheim
(Ortsteil of Bad Neuenahr-Ahrweiler)
Himmelchen 17
Kräuterberg 18
Gärkammer 19
Alte Lay 20
Pfaffenberg 21
Domlay 22

Marienthal
(Ortsteil of Bad Neuenahr-Ahrweiler)
Rosenberg 23
Jesuitengarten 24
Trotzenberg 25
Klostergarten 26
Stiftsberg 27

Dernau
Hardtberg 28
Pfarrwingert 29
Schieferlay 30
Burggarten 31
Goldkaul 32

Rech
Hardtberg 33
Blume 34
Herrenberg 35

Mayschoß
Mönchberg 36
Schieferlay 37
Burgberg 38
Silberberg 39
Laacherberg 40
Lochmühlerley 41

Altenahr
Eck 42 P
Übigberg 43 P

– Ortsteil Reimerzhoven
Eck 42 P

– Ortsteil Kreuzberg
Übigberg 43 P

Ahrbrück Ortsteil Pützfeld
Übigberg 43 P

MOSEL-SAAR-RUWER · LOWER MOSEL

One regional (Gebiet) name covers the long and tortuous route of the Mosel from Luxembourg to the Rhine and both its winegrowing tributaries. It is justified by the wine. To a surprising degree the wines of the Mosel (Upper, Middle and Lower), of the Saar and the Ruwer are homogenous in style. They are the brightest, briskest, most aromatic and yet most hauntingly subtle of all the fruits of the Riesling. This is essentially Riesling country – well over half the vines of the Mosel-Saar-Ruwer are Riesling, and many villages grow nothing else. Müller-Thurgau is the next most widely planted grape, with almost a quarter of the vineyard area, followed by Elbling and Kerner. Few of the vineyards are out of sight of the water; the valley sides, more or less steep, form the vineyard sites. The determinants of wine quality are the soil – slate is best, and occurs most frequently in the Middle Mosel – and microclimate. In this northern region, the angle and exposure of each slope makes a difference to the amount of sun it receives, and the consequent ripeness of the grapes it produces.

THE LOWER MOSEL begins – or rather ends – at Koblenz, where the river makes a majestic confluence with the Rhine. The Mosel follows a fairly straight northeasterly course for the last few kilometres before Koblenz, with most of the vineyards on the southeast-facing left bank. But above Cochem the characteristic swinging bends begin.

The Mosel vineyards start within the Koblenz city boundaries, with two small sites at Metternich and Güls. Once outside the city, the river valley soon takes on its characteristic steepness, with well placed vineyards in villages such as Winningen.

Zell is the best-known wine community (and the Bereich name) of the Lower Mosel, due in some measure to its memorable Großlage name Schwarze Katz and the inevitable black cat on the label. Zell and Zell-Merl, immediately downstream, both have steep slopes with slaty soil capable of producing very tempting, light but aromatic and flowery wines. The other Großlagen are Grafschaft, Rosenhang, Goldbäumchen and Weinhex.

▼ The dramatic bend of the Mosel at Bremm encircles the ruins of a medieval convent. The almost flat vineyards around it are the Abtei Kloster Stuben and Stubener Klostersegen.

BEREICH ZELL/MOSEL

GROSSLAGE WEINHEX

Metternich
(Ortsteil of Koblenz)
Marienberg 1 P

Güls
(Ortsteil of Koblenz)
Marienberg 1 P
Bienengarten 2
Königsfels 3
Im Röttgen 4 P

Moselweiß
(Ortsteil of Koblenz)
Hamm 5 P

Lay
(Ortsteil of Koblenz)
Hamm 5 P
Hubertusborn 6

Winningen
Im Röttgen 4 P
Brückstück 8
Domgarten 9
Hamm 10
Uhlen 11

**Kobern-Gondorf
Ortsteil Kobern**
Uhlen 11 a
Fahrberg 12
Weißenberg 13
Schloßberg 14 P

– Ortsteil Gondorf
Schloßberg 14 P
Gäns 15
Fuchshöhle 16
Kehrberg 17

Dieblich
Heilgraben 18

Niederfell
Fächern 19
Kahllay 20
Goldlay 21

Lehmen
Lay 22
Klosterberg 23
Würzlay 24
Ausoniusstein 25

Oberfell
Goldlay 26
Brauneberg 27
Rosenberg 28

Moselsürsch
(Ortsteil of Lehmen)
Fahrberg 29 P

Kattenes
(Ortsteil of Löf)
Fahrberg 29 T
Steinchen 30

Alken
Bleidenberg 31
Burgberg 32
Hunnenstein 33

Brodenbach
Neuwingert 34

Löf
Goldblume 35
Sonnenring 36

Hatzenport
(Ortsteil of Löf)
Stolzenberg 37
Kirchberg 38
Burg Bischofstein 39

Burgen
Bischofstein 40

GROSSLAGE GOLDBÄUMCHEN

Moselkern
Rosenberg 41
Kirchberg 42
Übereltzer 43

Müden
Funkenberg 44
Leckmauer 45
Sonnenring 46
St. Castorhöhle 47
Großlay 48

**Treis-Karden
Ortsteil Karden**
Dechantsberg 49
Münsterberg 50
Juffermauer 51

Pommern
Zeisel 52
Goldberg 53
Sonnenuhr 54
Rosenberg 55

Klotten
Rosenberg 55 a
Burg Coreidelsteiner 56
Sonnengold 57
Brauneberg 58

Cochem
Herrenberg 59
Pinnerkreuzberg 60
Schloßberg 61

**Cochem
Ortsteil Sehl**
Hochlay 62
Klostergarten 63
(Ebernach)

Sonnenberg 64
(Ebernach)
Bischofstuhl 65
(Ebernach)

Ernst
Feuerberg 66
Kirchlay 67

Bruttig-Fankel
Götterlay 68

Ellenz-Poltersdorf
Kurfürst 69
Altarberg 70
Rüberberger Dom-
herrenberg 71 P

Briedern
Rüberberger Dom-
herrenberg 71 P

**Senheim
Ortsteil Senhals**
Rüberberger Dom-
herrenberg 71 P
Römerberg 73

Coch

116
118 a Ell
Bremm 103 104
119
120 124
125
St. Aldegund
Großlage
126
Grafschaft
128 129
131 130
132 Alf 133

VINEYARDS

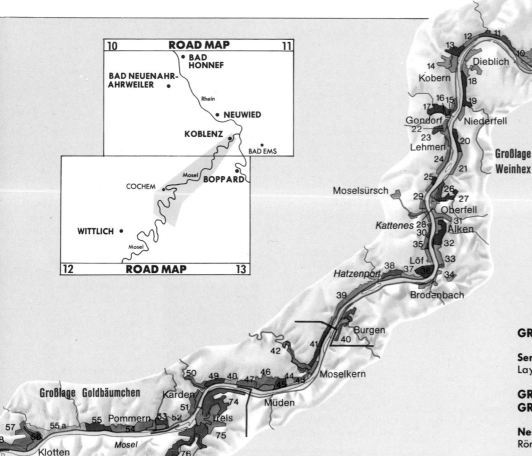

Metternich

Moselweiß

Koblenz

Güls

Lay

Dieblich

Kobern

Winningen

Gondorf

Niederfell

Lehmen

Großlage Weinhex

Moselsürsch

Oberfell

Kattenes

Alken

Löf

Hatzenport

Brodenbach

Burgen

Moselkern

Müden

Großlage Goldbäumchen

Karden

Pommern

Treis

Klotten

Mosel

Valwig

Ernst

Großlage Rosenhang

Bruttig

Ebernach

Fankel

Briedern

Ellenz

Beilstein

Poltersdorf

Senheim

Großlagenfrei

Großlage Rosenhang

Großlage Schwarze Katz

Zell

ROAD MAP

10 · 11

BAD HONNEF

BAD NEUENAHR-AHRWEILER

Rhein

NEUWIED

KOBLENZ

BAD EMS

COCHEM

Mosel

BOPPARD

WITTLICH

Mosel

12 **ROAD MAP** 13

Alf
Kapellenberg 127
Katzenkopf 128
Herrenberg 129
Burggraf 130
Kronenberg 131
Arrasberg-
  Schloßberg 132
Hölle 133

Beuren
Pelzerberger 133 a*

Bullay
Graf Beyßel-
  Herrenberg 134
Brautrock 135
Kroneberg 136
Kirchweingarten 137
Sonneck 138

Also vineyards not
registered as Einz. in
Zell, Ortsteil Merl

GROSSLAGE SCHWARZE KATZ

Zell
Ortsteil Merl
Sonneck 139
Adler 140
Königslay-Terrassen
  141
Stephansberg 142
Fettgarten 143
Klosterberg 144

Zell
Nußberg 145
Burglay-Felsen 146
Petersborn-
  Kabertchen 147
Pommerell 148
Kreuzlay 149
Domherrenberg 150
Geisberg 151

Zell
Ortsteil Kaimt
Marienburger 153
Rosenborn 154
Römerquelle 155

GROSSLAGENFREI

Senheim
Lay 105

GROSSLAGE GRAFSCHAFT

Nehren
Römerberg 106

Ediger-Eller
Ortsteil Ediger
Osterlämmchen 107
Hasensprung 108
Elzhofberg 109
Pfaffenberg 110
Feuerberg 111

– Ortsteil Eller
Pfirsichgarten 112
Kapplay 113
Bienenlay 114
Höll 115
Engelströpfchen 116
Schützenlay 117
Calmont 118

Bremm
Calmont 118 a
Schlemmertröpfchen
  119
Laurentiusberg 120
Frauenberg 121 P

Neef
Frauenberg 121 P
Petersberg 122
Rosenberg 123

St. Aldegund
Himmelreich 124
Palmberg Terrassen
  125
Klosterkammer 126

Ellenz-Poltersdorf
Woogberg 89
Silberberg 90

Beilstein
Schloßberg 91

Briedern
Herrenberg 92
Kapellenberg 93
Servatiusberg 94
Römergarten 95

Mesenich
Abteiberg 96
Goldgrübchen 97
Deuslay 98

Senheim
Wahrsager 99
Bienengarten 100
Vogteiberg 101
Rosenberg 102

Bremm
Abtei Kloster
  Stuben 103

Ediger-Eller
Ortsteil Eller
Stubener
  Klostersegen 104

GROSSLAGE ROSENHANG

Treis-Karden
Ortsteil Treis
Kapellenberg 74
Greth 75
Treppchen 76

Cochem
Ortsteil Cond
Arzlay 77
Rosenberg 78
Nikolausberg 79

Valwig
Schwarzenberg 80
Palmberg 81
Herrenberg 82

Bruttig-Fankel
Ortsteil Bruttig
Pfarrgarten 83
Rathausberg 84
Kapellenberg 85 P

– Ortsteil Fankel
Kapellenberg 85 P
Martinsborn 86
Layenberg 87
Rosenberg 88

TRAVEL INFORMATION

22

The Lower Mosel is easily accessible from Koblenz and makes a fascinating side-trip to a journey along the Rhine.

The north–south A61 autobahn crosses the Mosel southwest of Koblenz. There is a junction (Koblenz/Dieblich) on the south side with a spur road leading down into the valley. This gives access to the south bank: to reach the Moselweinstraße on the north bank, leave the autobahn at the A61/A48 junction and head for Koblenz or (to the west) Kobern.

Cochemer Krampen – a great 24km-bend – in the Kaiser Wilhelm tunnel. River boats of the KD and other lines run from Koblenz to Cochem, with a train connection to the start of the upper Mosel service at Bernkastel.

Southeast from the river, the wooded Hunsrück hills offer walking, hunting and peaceful villages. The Eifel hills to the northwest have spectacular volcanic lakes.

Bridges are scarce on the Mosel: there is one at Koblenz, another at Löf and a third at Kerden, where the south bank road is interrupted by steep slopes.

A railway runs along the north bank as far as Cochem, where it tunnels through the neck of the

Places to visit
Kobern-Gondorf: historical wine museum; the oldest German timbered building (1321) is in Kirchstraße. Burg Eltz: castle dating from 11th to 17th centuries: frescoes, tapestries, furniture and views. Access via Moselkern.
Cochem: small riverside town with dramatic, heavily restored castle. Chairlift to the Pinnerkreuz for a notable view.
Bruttig-Fankel: beautiful Renaissance houses in both villages, and a splendid parish church in Fankel.
Beilstein: picturesque half-timbered town, less busy than Cochem.

▶ Merl, near Zell, a village on the right bank which the twists and turns of the river gives an unusual southerly exposure.

Bad Bertrich: spa in a side valley 10km from the river, 1780 Kurhaus, castle.
Zell: busy wine centre with Roman origins.

Wine roads
The Moselweinstraße runs the length of the river, switching banks periodically. Well signposted: look for the stylized "M".

Wine festivals
Cochem (mid-June), Ellenz (Jul & Aug), Ediger (Jul, Aug & Oct), Mesenich (1st w/e in Aug), Winningen (last w/e in Aug to 1st in Sept), Moselkern (1st w/e in Sept).

Wine trails
Wine trails at Mesenich, Senheim-Senhals, Valwig & Winningen. Wine tasting everywhere in grower's cellars, wine centres at Bruttig-Fankel, Ellenz-Poltersdorf, Kobern-Gondorf. One-day seminars in Senheim every Mon (Jul–Oct).

Food and drink
Mosel specialities include pork marinated in local wine, snails cooked with grapes, *Weincräwes* – rib of pork with sauerkraut, pickled pork tongues with cream and mustard sauce, and "vintner's breakfast": liver sausage, mustard and onion rings on wholemeal bread.
All the historic towns have characterful restaurants and hotels.

Tourist Information Offices
The tourist office in Koblenz (tel: 0261–31304) opposite the main station will book rooms, as will the information office by the bridge in Cochem (tel: 02671-39710).

Regional Wine Information Office
Weinwerbung Mosel-Saar-Ruwer e.V.
Gartenfeldstraße 12a
5500 Trier
Tel: 0651-76621/ 45967

MOSEL WEIN STRASSE

MIDDLE MOSEL

The Bereich Bernkastel, still known to old-timers by its pre-1971 name of Mittelmosel (Middle Mosel), contains most of the best vineyard sites of the main stream, now slowed and broadened by locks to make it a noble river, winding in matchless beauty through alternating cliffs of vineyard to the right and left. Whichever side confronts the river with a high hill and makes it bend, offers vines the inclination they need towards the sun.

The river's banks here would be better called cliffs: in many places they rise, almost sheer, in 200-metre (700-feet) precipices. The geology gives the Middle Mosel a structure and a soil of pure slate, which is both highly porous and an efficient reflector of heat. The porosity allows the rain to run straight through the soil, keeping it stable on the steep slopes. The heat reflecting from the slate lets the Riesling make the most of every ray of sun.

Here, as throughout the length of the Mosel, the exposure of the slope is central to the quality of its wine. The river bends provide perfect south- and southeast-facing vineyards and also half-shaded northerly ones. Many of the villages own land on both sides of the river. Some, like Brauneberg, restrict themselves to the south bank, leaving the sun-facing north bank entirely to the vines.

Authors differ on where the villages of noteworthy quality upstream and downstream begin and end. The conservative view limits the classic Middle Mosel to the stretch from Trittenheim to Ürzig. But excellent estates extend much farther upstream and downstream in the best sites. Those on the extremities are more dependent, like the Saar and Ruwer, on exceptional seasons. But lovely, lively, classic Riesling is within their grasp and they should be remembered along with the more familiar Piesport, Bernkastel and Wehlen.

Trittenheim occupies the centre of a splendid oxbow bend, with equally fine sites on both sides of the river. Piesport lies in the middle of the biggest south-facing horseshoe of the steepest vineyards on the river, producing wines that unite ripeness and a touch of spice with the underlying "nerve" that gives lasting power and style.

Bernkastel-Kues is the hub of the Middle Mosel: Kues, the larger town, on the left bank; Bernkastel across the bridge, crammed up against its precipitous vineyards, with the most famous of them, the Doctor, apparently on the point of sliding straight into its streets. Bernkastel's best wines bring together all the qualities of the Mosel: delicacy and drive, force and grace, honey and earth.

Bernkastel melts into Graach, Graach into Wehlen and Wehlen into Zeltingen along the eight-kilometre (five-mile) hill of uninterrupted vines that starts with the Doctorberg. It rises over 200 metres above the river, hardly deviating from its ideal vertiginous tilt or its steady orientation south-southwest. It may well be the largest vineyard of sustained superlative quality in the world.

TRAVEL INFORMATION

The Middle Mosel has the greatest vineyards and many of the most well-known estates. Many growers accept visitors, and there are plenty of opportunities to taste the wines.

Places to visit
Bernkastel, with its spectacular site and old buildings, is a well-known tourist town and worth visiting, particularly for the wine museum, the St. Nikolaus Hospital, founded in the 15th century by the great theologian Nicolaus Cusanus, and the Cusanus library, and for the view from the nearby Burg Landshut. Bernkastel apart, Piesport, Wintrich, Graach and the other villages familiar from wine lists provide tasting cellars and superb views of the vineyards. It is worth following side-roads such as those above Trarbach and Graach in order to enjoy the dramatic prospects along the river.

Wine roads
The *Moselweinstraße* follows the river. There are vineyard paths in Ensch, Enkirch, Kröv, Leiwen, Reil, Schleich, Schweich and Trittenheim.

Wine seminars
Weekend wine courses are held in Traben-Trarbach, Senheim and Bernkastel.

Wine festivals
Alf (1st Sunday in Aug), Bernkastel-Kues (1st w/e in Sept), Burg (Sept), Enkirch (Whitsun and Aug), Kröv (1st w/e in Oct), Traben-Trarbach (end of June & last w/e in July), Zeltingen-Rachtig (Aug).

Food and drink
See page 22.

Tourist Information Offices
Bernkastel and its suburb Kues have several hotels, and guest houses and private rooms are numerous — consult the tourist office beside the river (tel: 06531-4023). Traben-Trarbach's tourist office will also find rooms (Bahnhofstraße 22).

Regional Wine Information Office
Weinwerbung Mosel-Saar-Ruwer e.V.
Gartenfeldstraße 12a
5500 Trier
Tel: 0651-76621/45967

VINEYARDS

Bullay

Großlage 168 Pünderich
vom heißen Stein
208 a
164
Zel

165
Reil 169
166 171 Briedel

167 170
Burg
172

173
174 175

176

Springiersbach

Olkenbach
Flußbach 211 210 209
213 212 Bausendorf Bengel

Großlage
Nacktarsch
227 226 223
228

214
215
217 216 208 206 204 201
Hupperath 219 218 Großlage 205 200 Kröv 225 Kövenig 177
Schwarzlay 199 198 178 Enkirch
Ürzig Erden 203 202 Kinheim 197 196 Wolf 179
Wittlich 207 229 230 Lösnich 199a 194 191 180
230 Rachtig 199a Mosel 195 181
234 Zeltingen 231 193 183 182
222 235 232 233a 242 Starkenburg
Platten 236 233 239 190 184
237 Wehlen **Großlage** 240 241 185 **Großlage**
221 267 **Münzlay** 238 186 187 **Schwarzlay**
268 271 Graach 189 188
283 277 269 258 Lieser Kues 244
284 Maring- 250 249 245 251 245
282 Noviand 279 277 248 256 255 251 246 **Großlage Badstube**
Osann 281 278 263 252 247
Monzel 285 266 260 261 Mülheim Andel **Bernkastel-**
Kesten 286 288 Brauneberg 275 259 252 253 **Kues**
Sehlem 287 276 263
322 Krames 302 301 Filzen 266 264
322a 300 297 299 276 272 265 Veldenz
303 298 Piesport 289 274 273
Rivenich 304 293 Wintrich 276 Burgen
320 307 294 **Großlage**
Hetzerath 321 318 319 296 299 295 **Kurfürstlay**
Niederemmel
Bekond 328 305 Dhron Minheim 292
326 308 306 289
329 327 309 Neumagen 305 289 291
330 331 Klüsserath 310
328 333 311
Thörnich Köwerich 312 310 306
332 325 313
Ensch 336 324 314 315 317 **Großlage**
335 334 Detzem 323 315 Trittenheim 317 **Michelsberg**
Schweich 350 Schleich 337 Leiwen 315 314
352 338 339 341
351 Longuich 349 Longen 343 342 316
353 Lörsch 344 Pölich **Großlage**
Kenn 354 348 340 **St. Michael**
Fastrau Riol Mehring 343
347 346
Fell
347 **Großlage**
Probstberg
347

| 12 | **ROAD MAP** | 13 |

BOPPARD
COCHEM

WITTLICH
Mosel

SCHWEICH

TRIER
IDAR-OBERSTEIN

| 14 | **ROAD MAP** | 15 |

BEREICH BERNKASTEL

GROSSLAGE VOM HEISSEN STEIN

Briedel
Weisserberg 156
Schäferlay 157
Herzchen 158
Nonnengarten 159
Schelm 160

Pünderich
Goldlay 161
Rosenberg 162
Nonnengarten 163
Marienburg 164

Reil
Goldlay 165
Falklay 166
Moullay-Hofberg 167
Sorentberg 168

GROSSLAGE SCHWARZLAY

Burg
Wendelstück 169
Hahnenschrittchen 170
Thomasberg 171
Falklay 172
Schloßberg 173

Enkirch
Edelberg 174
Monteneubel 175
Steffensberg 176
Weinkammer 177
Herrenberg 178
Zeppwingert 179
Batterieberg 180
Ellergrub 181

Starkenburg
Rosengarten 182

Traben-Trarbach Ortsteil Traben
Gaispfad 183
Zollturm 184
Königsberg 191
Kräuterhaus 192
Würzgarten 193

– Ortsteil Trarbach
Burgberg 185
Schloßberg 186
Ungsberg 187
Hühnerberg 188
Kreuzberg 189
Taubenhaus 190

Wolf
(Ortsteil of Traben-Trarbach)
Schatzgarten 194

Sonnenlay 195
Klosterberg 196
Goldgrube 197
Auf der Heide 198

Kinheim
Rosenberg 199
Römerhang 199 a
Hubertuslay 200

Lösnich
Försterlay 201
Burgberg 202

Erden
Busslay 203
Herrenberg 204
Treppchen 205
Prälat 206

Ürzig
Würzgarten 207
Goldwingert 208

Bengel Ortsteil Springiersbach
Klosterberg 208 a

Bausendorf Ortsteil Olkenbach
Herzlay 209
Hubertuslay 210

Flußbach
Reichelberg 211

Wittlich
Kupp 212
Lay 213
Bottchen 214
Felsentreppchen 215
Rosenberg 216
Portnersberg 217
Klosterweg 218
Klosterweg 219 P

Hupperath
Klosterweg 219 P

Dreis
Johannisberg 220

Platten
Klosterberg 221
Rotlay 222

GROSSLAGE NACKTARSCH

Kröv
Steffensberg 225
Letterlay 226
Kirchlay 227
Paradies 228

– Ortsteil Kövenig
Burglay 223
Herrenberg 224

GROSSLAGE MÜNZLAY

Zeltingen-Rachtig (Zeltingen)
Deutschherrenberg 229
Himmelreich 230
Schloßberg 231
Sonnenuhr 232

Wehlen
(Ortsteil of Bernkastel-Kues)
Sonnenuhr 233
Rosenberg 233 a
Hofberg 234
Abtei 235
Klosterhofgut 236
Klosterberg 237
Nonnenberg 238

Graach
Domprobst 239
Himmelreich 240
Abtsberg 241
Josephshöfer 242

GROSSLAGE BADSTUBE

Bernkastel-Kues Ortsteil Bernkastel
Lay 243
Matheisbildchen 244
Bratenhöfchen 245
Graben 246
Doctor 247

Lieser
Süßenberg 248
Niederberg-Helden 249
Rosenlay 250
Schloßberg 252 P

GROSSLAGE KURFÜRSTLAY

Bernkastel-Kues Ortsteil Bernkastel
Johannisbrünnchen 251
Schloßberg 252 P
Stephanus-Rosen-gärtchen 253

Andel
(Ortsteil of Bernkastel-Kues)
Schloßberg 252 P

Bernkastel-Kues Ortsteil Kues
Rosenberg 254
Kardinalsberg 255
Weisenstein 256

Mülheim
Elisenberg 259 P

Sonnenlay 260
Helenenkloster 261
Amtgarten 262

Veldenz
Elisenberg 259 P
Kirchberg 263
Mühlberg 264
Grafschafter Sonnenberg 265
Carlsberg 266

Maring-Noviand
Honigberg 267
Klosterberg 268
Römerpfad 269
Sonnenuhr 271

Burgen
Römerberg 272
Kirchberg 273
Hasenläufer 274

Brauneberg
Mandelgraben 275 P
Klostergarten 276
Juffer 277
Juffer Sonnenuhr 278
Kammer 279

– Ortsteil Filzen
Mandelgraben 275 P

Osann-Monzel Ortsteil Monzel
Paulinslay 281
Kätzchen 282

– Ortsteil Osann
Kirchlay 283
Rosengarten 284

Kesten
Paulinshofberger 285
Herrenberg 286
Paulinsberg 287

Wintrich
Stefanslay 288
Großer Herrgott 289
Ohligsberg 291
Geierslay 292

GROSSLAGE MICHELSBERG

Minheim
Burglay 293
Kapellchen 294
Rosenberg 295
Günterslay 299 P

Piesport
Treppchen 296 P
Falkenberg 297
Goldtröpfchen 298 P
Günterslay 299 P
Domherr 300
Schubertslay 303

Grafenberg 304 P

– Ortsteil Niederemmel
Treppchen 296 P
Goldtröpfchen 298 P
Gärtchen 301
Kreuzwingert 302
Hofberger 305 P

Neumagen-Dhron Ortsteil Dhron
Goldtröpfchen 298 P
Grafenberg 304 P
Hofberger 305 P
Roterd 306
Großer Hengelberg 307
Häs'chen 308

– Ortsteil Neumagen
Nußwingert 309
Engelgrube 310
Laudamusberg 311
Rosengärtchen 312
Sonnenuhr 313

Trittenheim
Altärchen 314
Apotheke 315
Felsenkopf 316
Leiterchen 317

Rivenich
Niederberg 318
Geisberg 319
Rosenberg 320
Brauneberg 321 P

Hetzerath
Brauneberg 321 P

Sehlem
Rotlay 322

Klausen Ortsteil Krames
Vineyard not registered as Einz. 322 a

GROSSLAGE ST. MICHAEL

Leiwen
Klostergarten 323
Laurentiuslay 324

Köwerich
Laurentiuslay 324 a
Held 325

Klüsserath
Bruderschaft 326
Königsberg 327

Bekond
Schloßberg 328
Brauneberg 329

Thornich
Enggaß 330
Ritsch 331
Schießlay 332

Ensch
Mühlenberg 333
St. Martin 334
Sonnenlay 335

Detzem
Würzgarten 336
Maximiner Klosterlay 337

Schleich
Sonnenberg 338
Klosterberg 339

Pölich
Held 340
Südlay 341

Mehring
Blattenberg 342
Goldkupp 343
Zellerberg 344 P

Lörsch
(Ortsteil of Mehring)
Zellerberg 344 P

Longen
Zellerberg 344 P

GROSSLAGE PROBSTBERG

Riol
Römerberg 346

Fell
(incl. Ortsteil Fastrau)
Maximiner Burgberg 347

Longuich
Hirschlay 348
Maximiner Herrenberg 349
Herrenberg 350 P

Schweich
Herrenberg 350 P
Annaberg 351
Burgmauer 352

Kenn
Held 353
Maximiner Hofgarten 354

UPPER MOSEL

The Mosel wears its first tentative vineyards in France, flows through the little Grand-Duchy of Luxembourg festooned with them, then enters Germany near the ancient Roman capital of Trier to be joined by the rivers Saar and Ruwer. It is their side-valleys, rather than the main stream, that boast the first great Mosel vineyards. Upper Mosel ("Obermosel") wines at their best are gentle. A good deal of the pleasantly neutral, often somewhat sharp Elbling grape is still planted – one of the oldest grape varieties growing in Germany, it has apparently given yeoman service since the Roman origins of the vineyard. Vines were well established here by the first century.

Germany's first vineyards face those of Luxembourg across the still-narrow river. Schloß Thorn at Perl still operates a 16th-century press, said to be the oldest in Germany still to be doing its annual duty. The little town of Wincheringen is the busiest centre in the district, with a press-house out-station of the giant Mosel-Saar-Ruwer cooperative (whose headquarters is at Kues, opposite Bernkastel).

Two Großlage names cover the Obermosel: Gipfel, for the major portion of the district on the east bank of the river opposite Luxembourg, and Königsberg for the few vineyards around Mesenich on the west bank, clustered near the confluence of the Mosel and the Saar.

In the Saar valley the Riesling takes a giant stride to greatness. On the best slopes here and the neighbouring valley of the Ruwer, the results are unsurpassable anywhere on earth: quintessential Riesling, clean as steel, haunting with the qualities of remembered scents or distant music.

A scattering of sites in these two pleasantly pastoral valleys must be listed among the very greatest in Germany, or in the world, for white wines of the greatest finesse, "breed", and, curiously enough, longevity. It seems strange that such pale and apparently insubstantial wines should share this quality with, for example, vintage port. But this is the magic of the Riesling: equilibrium which seems everlasting.

The uppermost vineyards of the Mosel are within the Bereich Moseltor, which has one Großlage: Schloß Bübinger. Just north of the village of Palzem the Bereich Obermosel takes over with its two Großlagen Gipfel and Königsberg.

The vineyards of the Saar and Ruwer, plus one or two on the main river around Konz and Trier, belong in the Bereich Saar-Ruwer, with its two Großlagen Scharzberg (Saar) and Römerlay (Ruwer). Wiltingen is the hub of the Saar region, surrounded by major vineyards and giving its name to most Saar Großlage wines ("Wiltinger Scharzberg"). Kasel, tiny as it is, is the "capital" of the Ruwer. Its Nies'chen site performs wonders of delicacy, perfume and utter charm. Usefully for the student, there is a short gap between the Ruwer vineyards and the first sites of the Middle Mosel around Schweich.

▼ Saarburg, the capital of the Saar, is hardly a metropolis. With its castle, church and setting of woods and meadows it epitomizes the gentle charm of the region.

TRAVEL INFORMATION

▲ Steep slopes and slippery slate make the picker's job a hard one. A glass is always welcome.

The gentle landscape of the Upper Mosel is not obvious tourist country and is hence uncrowded.

Places to visit
Trier: a Roman town with many relics surviving, also many Renaissance and baroque buildings. Information at the Porta Nigra Roman gate (tel: 0651-75440).
Konz: town at Mosel-Saar confluence, baroque *Karthause* – monastery.
Saarburg: pretty small town, one of the oldest in Germany. Medieval buildings include castle, town walls, church. A wine centre for the Saar (see wine festivals below).
The Ruwer: Kasel, Waldrach and Eitelsbach are small, old and charming wine villages.

Wine festivals
Ockfen (1st w/e in June), Trier (3rd w/e in June), Saarburg (1st w/e in July), Serrig (last w/e in July), Wiltingen (last w/e in July), Olewig-Trier (1st w/e in Aug), Saarburg (2nd w/e in Aug), Ayl (3rd w/e in Aug), Saarburg: Saar Wine Festival (1st w/e in Sept).

Food and drink
See page 22.

Regional Wine Information Office
See page 22.

VINEYARDS

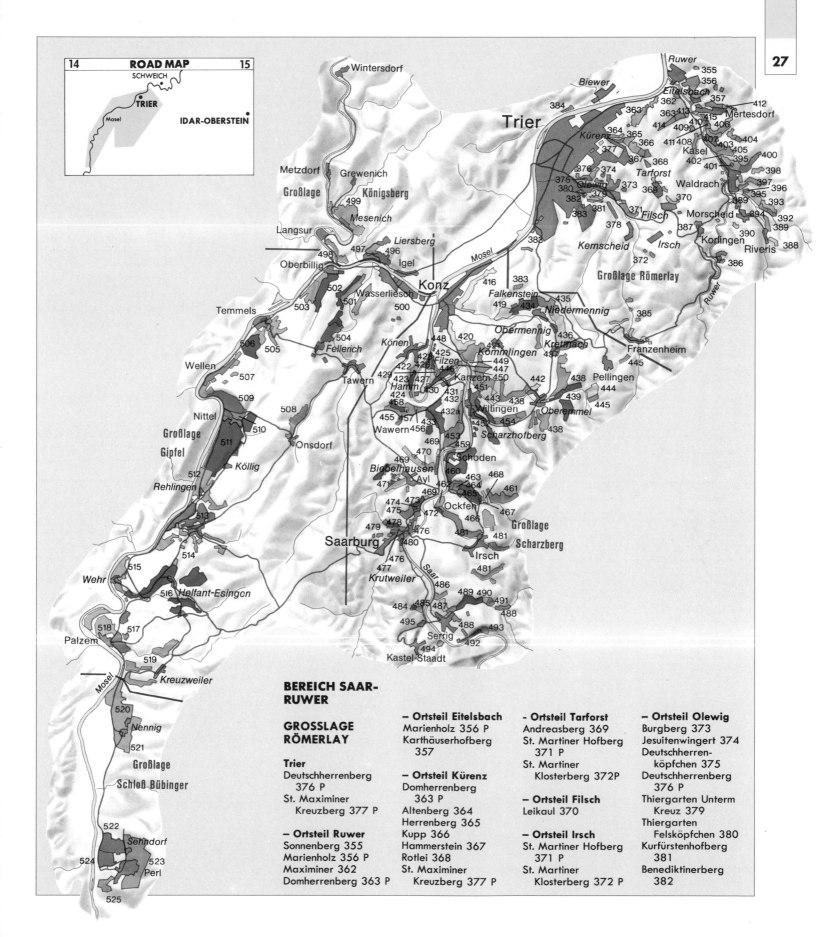

ROAD MAP 14 15
SCHWEICH
TRIER
Mosel
IDAR-OBERSTEIN

Wintersdorf
Ruwer 355
356
Biewer
362
Eitelsbach
363 357
384
Trier 363 413 412
364 365 414 410 415 Mertesdorf
Kürenz 366 409 406
Metzdorf Grewenich 411 408 407 403 404
377 367 368 402 405 395 400
Großlage 376 374 Kasel
Königsberg 375 Tarforst 401 398
499 380 Olewig 373 369 370 397 396
Mesenich 382 379 395 393
383 381 371 Filsch Waldrach 389
Langsur 378 Morscheid 394 392
498 497 496 387 389
Liersberg Mosel Kernscheid 372 Korlingen 390
Oberbillig Igel 383 Irsch Riveris 388
502 416 Großlage Römerlay 386
Wasserliesch Konz Falkenstein
503 501 500 419 434 435
Temmels 500 Niedermennig 385
504 420 Obermennig 436
506 505 Fellerich Könen 448 421 Kretinach 437
Wellen 425 Kommlingen
507 428 Filzen 449 Franzenheim
422 426 446 447 445
Tawern 429 423 427 Kanzem 450 442 438 Pellingen
509 430 431 451 444
424 432 443 438 439
508 Nittel 458 432a Wiltingen Oberemmel 445
Großlage 510 455 457 433 452 454
Gipfel 511 Wawern 456 453 Scharzhofberg 438
Köllig 469 459
512 470 Schoden
Rehlingen 469
Biebelhausen 460
471 Ayl 463 468
Onsdorf 474 473 462 464 461
475 469 465
513 472 Ockfen 467
479 478 476 466 Großlage
514 480 481 481 Scharzberg
Saarburg Irsch
515 476 481
Wehr 477 Saar
516 Helfant-Esingen Krutweiler 486
489 490
484 485 487 491
518 517 495 488
Palzem 488 493
519 Serrig 492
494
Kreuzweiler Kastel-Staadt
Mosel
520
Nennig
521
Großlage
Schloß Bübinger
522
Sehndorf
524 523
Perl
525

28

**– Ortsteil
Kernscheid**
St. Petrusberg 378

– Ortsteil Matthias
St. Matheiser 383

– Ortsteil Biewer
Augenscheiner 384

Franzenheim
Johannisberg 385

Sommerau
Schloßberg 386

Korlingen
Laykaul 387

Riveris
Kuhnchen 388
Heiligenhäuschen
389 P

Morscheid
Heiligenhäuschen
389 P
Dominikanerberg
390

Waldrach
Heiligenhäuschen
389 P
Hubertusberg 392
Sonnenberg 393
Jungfernberg 394
Krone 395
Laurentiusberg 396
Ehrenberg 397
Doktorberg 398
Meisenberg 400
Jesuitengarten 401
Kurfürstenberg 402

Kasel
Herrenberg 403
Dominikanerberg
404
Kehrnagel 405
Hitzlay 406
Nies'chen 407
Paulinsberg 408
Timpert 409

Lorenzhof
(Ortsteil of
Mertesdorf)
Mäuerchen 410
Felslay 411

Mertesdorf
Johannisberg 412
Herrenberg 415 P

Maximin Grünhaus
(Ortsteil of
Mertesdorf)
Bruderberg 413
Abtsberg 414
Herrenberg 415 P

Also vineyards not
registered as Einz.
in the parishes
of Hockweiler,
Franzenheim and
Plowig

**GROSSLAGE
SCHARZBERG**

Konz
Karthauser
Klosterberg 416
Euchariusberg 420

Kommlingen
(Ortsteil of Konz)
Auf der
Wiltingerkupp
421

Falkenstein
(Ortsteil of Konz)
Hofberg 419
Herrenberg 434 P

Könen
(Ortsteil of Konz)
Fels 422
Kirchberg 423

Filzen
(Ortsteil of Konz)
Urbelt 425
Pulchen 426
Unterberg 427
Herrenberg 428
Steinberger 429
Altenberg 430 P

Hamm
(Ortsteil of Konz)
Liebfrauenberg 424
Altenberg 430 P

Kanzem
Altenberg 430 P
Hörecker 431
Schloßberg 432
Sonnenberg 433
Ritterpfad 455 P

Niedermennig
(Ortsteil of Konz)
Herrenberg 434 P
Sonnenberg 435
Euchariusberg 436 P

Obermennig
(Ortsteil of Konz)
Euchariusberg 436 P

Krettnach
(Ortsteil of Konz)
Euchariusberg 436 P
Altenberg 437

Oberemmel
(Ortsteil of Konz)
Karlsberg 438

Altenberg 439
Hütte 440
Raul 441
Agritiusberg 442
Rosenberg 443

Pellingen
Jesuitengarten 444
Herrgottsrock 445

Wiltingen
Schloßberg 432 a
Rosenberg 443 a
Sandberg 446
Hölle 447
Kupp 448
Braune Kupp 449
Gottesfuß 450
Klosterberg 451
Braunfels 452
Schlangengraben
453

Scharzhofberg
(Ortsteil of
Wiltingen)
Vineyards not
registered as Einz.

Wawern
Ritterpfad 455 P
Jesuitenberg 456
Herrenberger 457
Goldberg 458

Schoden
Saarfeilser
Marienberg 459
Herrenberg 460
Geisberg 461

Ockfen
Kupp 462
Herrenberg 463
Heppenstein 464
Bockstein 465
Zickelgarten 466
Neuwies 467
Geisberg 468

Ayl
(incl. Ortsteil
Biebelhausen)
Kupp 469
Herrenberger 470
Scheidterberg 471

Saarburg
Klosterberg 472
Fuchs 473
Stirn 479
(Niederleuken)
Kupp 475
Schloßberg 476
Rausch 477
Antoniusbrunnen 478
Bergschlößchen 479
Laurentiusberg 480
(Krutweiler)

Irsch
Sonnenberg 481

Serrig
König Johann Berg
484
Antoniusberg 485
Schloß Saarsteiner
486
Schloß Saarfelser
Schloßberg 487
Kupp 488
Vogelsang 489
Heiligenborn 490
Hoeppslei 491
Würtzberg 492
Herrenberg 493

Kastel-Staadt
König Johann Berg
494
Maximiner Prälat
495

**BEREICH
OBERMOSEL**

**GROSSLAGE
KÖNIGSBERG**

Igel
Dullgärten 496

Liersberg
(Ortsteil of Igel)
Pilgerberg 497

Langsur
Brüderberg 498

Mesenich
(Ortsteil of Langsur)
Held 499

Also vineyards not
registered as Einz. in
Igel (incl. Ortsteil of
Liersberg),
Grewenich and
Metzdorf (Ortsteile
of Langsur), Edingen,
Godendorf and
Wintersdorf
(Ortsteile of
Ralingen)

**GROSSLAGE
GIPFEL**

Wasserliesch
Reinig auf der Burg
500
Albachtaler 501

Oberbillig
Hirtengarten 502
Römerberg 503

Fellerich
(Ortsteil of Tawern)
Schleidberg 504

Temmels
St. Georgshof 505
Münsterstatt 506

Wellen
Altenberg 507

Onsdorf
Hubertusberg 508 P

Nittel
Hubertusberg 508 P
Leiterchen 509
Blümchen 510
Rochusfels 511 P

Köllig
(Ortsteil of Nittel)
Rochusfels 511 P

Rehlingen
(Ortsteil of Nittel)
Kapellenberg 512

Wincheringen
Burg Warsberg 513
Fuchsloch 514

Wehr
(Ortsteil of Palzem)
Rosenberg 515

Helfant & Esingen
(Ortsteile of Palzem)
Kapellenberg 516

Palzem
Carlsfelsen 517
Lay 518

Kreuzweiler
(Ortsteil of Palzem)
Schloß Thorner Kupp
519

Also vineyards not
registered as Einz. in
Fisch, Kirf (incl.
Ortsteil of Meurich),
Porz (Ortsteil of
Merzkinschen),
Tawern, Bilzingen
and Soest (Ortsteile
of Wincheringen)

**BEREICH
MOSELTOR**

**GROSSLAGE
SCHLOSS
BÜBINGER**

Nennig
(Ortsteil of Perl)
Schloßberg 520
Römerberg 521

Sehndorf
(Ortsteil of Perl)
Klosterberg 522
Marienberg 523

Perl
Quirinusberg 524
Hasenberg 525

Also vineyards not
registered as Einz.
in the parishes of
Besch, Tettingen
and Wochern.

MITTELRHEIN

Amore logical name for this spectacular but dwindling wine region would be the Lower Rhine. It is exactly analogous to the Lower Mosel – the part of the river downstream from the classic sites, where custom (and extraordinary effort) maintain a narrow necklace of vineyards on the immediate riverside slopes – and sometimes cliffs. The very steep valley sides provide pockets of slaty soil with the crucial south or southwest exposure.

There are 760 hectares of vines – a declining total – along some 100 kilometres (60 miles) of river. Moving from north to south, the vines start on the east bank at Königswinter, opposite Bonn. From Koblenz southward the vineyards line both banks, ending at Trechtingshausen on the left bank, almost opposite Assmannshausen, the last of the Rheingau. The chief towns are Bacharach, St. Goarshausen, Boppard, Koblenz, Neuwied, Bad Honningen and Unkel. The great sights are the Rhine gorge, the Loreley rock and dozens of perching medieval castles, and the confluence with the Mosel at Koblenz. The entire valley reverberates with the legends of the German past: the Nibelung treasure is said to be in the keeping of "Father Rhine".

Another little tributary, the Lahn, flowing from the east through the spa town of Bad Ems, also has a few vines which are included in the Mittelrhein region.

Riesling is the principal grape of the morsels of vineyard that cling to the hills. It makes good, even very good, but usually austere wine and excellent sparkling wine. Some Müller-Thurgau is also grown and a little Kerner.

The region is divided into three Bereiche and 11 Großlagen. The Bereich Siebengebirge – Seven Mountains – consists of just one Großlage, Petersberg. The Bereich Rheinburgengau takes in everything from Großlage Burg Hammerstein south of Königswinter to Großlage Herrenberg, opposite the town of Bacharach. Bereich Bacharach includes two Großlagen: Schloß Stahleck and Schloß Reichenstein. The town of Bacharach is the centre of the wine trade, such as it is. It was once an important entrepot for all Rhine wines; a good harbour just downstream of the treacherous rapids at Bingen.

TRAVEL INFORMATION

The federal capital, Bonn, marks the northern limit of the region. It is also a university town and a musical centre: Beethoven's birthplace at Bonngasse 20 is now a museum, and Schumann lived and died in the city.

The Rhine gorge begins at Bonn, with the most spectacular section starting south of Koblenz. The gorge has castles both romantic and forbidding, ruined and inhabited. Many can be visited. Some are hotels. At Bingen the river's abrupt bend marks the southern limit of the Mittelrhein.

The gorge is a great north–south route, with major roads and railways on each bank. There is much river traffic, both cargo barges and passenger steamers.

The many villages are well used to tourists, and are amply equipped with taverns, restaurants and tasting cellars.

Autobahns run parallel to the Rhine on both banks, but at some distance. For the best view of the river, follow the B9 on the right bank, or take the quieter B42 on the other shore. Note that there are no bridges between Koblenz and Mainz, but several ferries. The railway offers fine views, but to see the Rhine Gorge at its best, take a steamer. Many services start at Koblenz. Combined train/steamer tickets can be had.

Places to visit
Bonn: see above.
Bad Ems: spa in the pretty side-valley of the Lahn.

Braubach: fine well-preserved medieval castle.
Boppard: old houses, castle, several hotels.
Königswinter, close to Bonn, is a river and forest resort. Information tel: 02223-21048.
St. Goarshausen: close by is the Loreley rock, a giant cliff over the Rhine. The *Loreleyburgstraße* runs from the village to the summit and on, past imposing castles, back to the river at Kaub.
St. Goar: ferry from its twin across the river. Fine view of the Loreley.
Bacharach: the steep, scenic *Rheingoldstraße* runs from here to St. Goar through hill villages and past castles. The town has good shops – antiques especially. Tourist information: Heerstraße 120 (tel: 06741-383).
Die Pfalz: island castle in the

river, a medieval customs post for extracting river tolls. Open for visits.

Wine festivals
Kaub (1st week in Sept), Rhens (2nd w/e in Sept), Boppard (last week in Sept), Koblenz (last w/e in Sept), Dattenberg (1st week in Oct), Leubsdorf (2nd w/e in Oct).

Regional Wine Information Office
Mittelrhein Burgen & Wein e.V.
Am Hafen 2
5407 St. Goar
Tel: 06741-7644

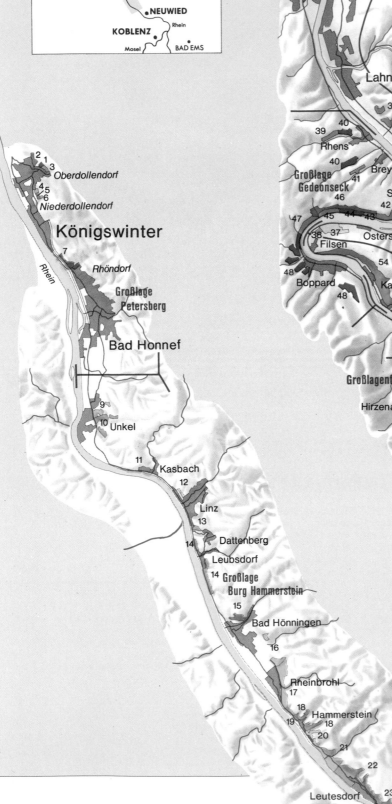
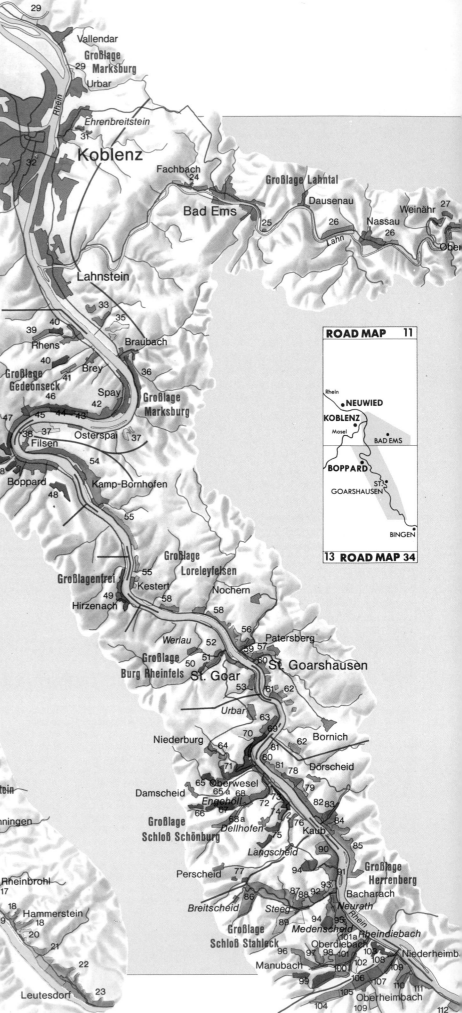

BEREICH SIEBENGEBIRGE

GROSSLAGE PETERSBERG

Oberdollendorf
(Ortsteil of Königswinter)
Rosenhügel 1
Laurentiusberg 2
Sülzenberg 3

Niederdollendorf
(Ortsteil of Königswinter)
Goldfüßchen 4
Longenburgerberg 5
Heisterberg 6

Königswinter
Drachenfels 7 P

Rhöndorf
(Ortsteil of Bad Honnef)
Drachenfels 7 P

BEREICH RHEINBURGEN-GAU

GROSSLAGE BURG HAMMERSTEIN

Unkel
Berg 9
Sonnenberg 10

Kasbach
(Ortsteil of Kasbach-Ohlenberg)
Stehlerberg 11

Linz
Rheinhöller 12

Dattenberg
Gertrudenberg 13

Leubsdorf
Weißes Kreuz 14

Bad Hönnigen
Schloßberg 15

Rheinbrohl
Monte Jup 16
Römerberg 17

Hammerstein
In den Layfelsen 18
Hölle 19
Schloßberg 20

Leutesdorf
Forstberg 21
Gartenlay 22
Rosenberg 23

GROSSLAGE LAHNTAL

Fachbach
Vineyard not registered as Einz.

Bad Ems
Hasenberg 25 P

Dausenau
Hasenberg 25 P

Nassau
Schloßberg 26

Weinähr
Giebelhöll 27

Obernhof
Goetheberg 28

GROSSLAGE MARKSBURG

Vallendar
Rheinnieder 29 P

Urbar
Rheinnieder 29 P

Koblenz
Ortsteil Ehrenbreitstein
Kreuzberg 31

Koblenz
Schnorbach
Brückstück 32

Lahnstein
Koppelstein 33 P

Braubach
Koppelstein 33 P
Mühlberg 35
Marmorberg 36

Osterspai
Liebeneck-Sonnenlay 37

Filsen
Pfarrgarten 38

GROSSLAGE GEDEONSECK

Rhens
König Wenzel 39
Sonnenlay 40

Brey
Hämmchen 41

Spay
Engelstein 42 P

Boppard
Ortsteil Bopparder Hamm
Engelstein 42 P
Ohlenberg 43
Feuerley 44
Mandelstein 45
Weingrube 46
Fässerlay 47
Elfenley 48

GROSSLAGENFREI

Hirzenach
(Ortsteil of Boppard)
Probsteiberg 49

GROSSLAGE BURG RHEINFELS

St. Goar
Ortsteil Werlau
Rosenberg 50
Frohwingert 51 P
Ameisenberg 52 T

St. Goar
Frohwingert 51 P
Ameisenberg 52 P
Kuhstall 53

GROSSLAGE LORELEYFELSEN

Kamp-Bornhofen
Pilgerpfad 54
Liebenstein-Sterrenberg 55 P

Kestert
Liebenstein-Sterrenberg 55 P

Nochern
Brünnchen 56

Patersberg
Teufelstein 57

St. Goarshausen
Ortsteile Wellmich & Ehrental
Burg Maus 58

St. Goarshausen
Hessern 59
Burg Katz 60
Loreley Edel 61

Bornich
Rothenack 62

GROSSLAGE SCHLOSS SCHÖNBURG

Urbar
(Ortsteil of Oberwesel)
Beulsberg 63

Niederburg
Rheingoldberg 64
Bienenberg 65

Damscheid
Frankenhell 66
Sonnenstock 67
Goldemund 68

Oberwesel
Bienenberg 65 a
Goldemund 68 a
Sieben Jungfrauen 69
Ölsberg 70
St. Martinsberg 71
Römerkrug 73

— Ortsteil Engehöll
Bernstein 72

Dellhofen
(Ortsteil of Oberwesel)
Römerkrug 74
St. Werner-Berg 75

Langscheid
(Ortsteil of Oberwesel)
Hundert 76

Perscheid
Rosental 77

GROSSLAGE HERRENBERG

Dörscheid
Wolfsnack 78
Kupferflöz 79

Kaub
Roßstein 80
Backofen 81
Rauschelay 82
Blüchertal 83
Burg Gutenfels 84
Pfalzgrafenstein 85

BEREICH BACHARACH

GROSSLAGE SCHLOSS STAHLECK

Bacharach
Ortsteil Breitscheid
Schloß Stahlberg 86 P

— Ortsteil Steeg
Schloß Stahlberg 86 P
Lennenborn 87
St. Jost 88
Hambusch 89

Bacharach
Hahn 90
Insel Heylesen Werth 91
Wolfshöhle 92
Posten 93

— Ortsteile Medenscheid & Neurath
Mathias Weingarten 94
Kloster Fürstental 95

Manubach
Langgarten 96
St. Oswald 97
Mönchwingert 98
Heilgarten 99

Oberdiebach
Bischofshub 100
Fürstenberg 101 P
Kräuterberg 102

Rheindiebach
(Ortsteil of Oberdiebach)
Fürstenberg 101 P
Rheinberg 103

Also vineyards not registerd as Einzellagen

Schloß Fürstenberg
(Ortsteil of Oberheimbach)
Rebflächen 101 a

GROSSLAGE SCHLOSS REICHENSTEIN

Oberheimbach
Römerberg 104
Klosterberg 105
Wahrheit 106
Sonne 107

Niederheimbach
Froher Weingarten 108
Schloß Hohneck 109
Reifersley 110
Soonecker Schloßberg 111

Trechtingshausen
Morgenbachtaler 112

RHEINGAU

The winegrowing Rhine reaches its undisputed climax where the broad body of its waters, hurrying northwards in a perpetual turmoil of eddies and islands, barge-traffic and wheeling birds, meets the bulk of the Taunus mountains, rising to their forested heights three or four kilometres (two or three miles) back from the river.

These three or four kilometres are given entirely to the vine. The river, balked by the rising ground, turns and dashes westward below the vineyards for a space of thirty kilometres (twenty miles) – thirty kilometres of monoculture that link the words Rheingau and Riesling like a rallying cry.

The English name for all Rhine wine comes from the Rheingau: specifically the village of Hochheim that extends the scope of the Rheingau eastward towards Frankfurt. Hochheim's vineyard hill looks down on the tributary river Main, with the broad bend of the Rhine dim in the distance to the south. From Hochheim came the original "hock": wine of a soft vigorous earthiness that could mature as long as claret, the other English favourite.

It is 50-odd kilometres (30 miles) from Hochheim to Rüdesheim, the western end of the Rheingau. Sixteen of these kilometres (10 miles) are occupied by the sprawl of Wiesbaden, but where the vineyards start again at Niederwalluf they start in earnest, and fill every unurbanized cranny through the succession of a dozen riverside and hillside villages that constitute the heart of the Rheingau.

Riesling is the predominant grape in area as well as quality, planted over three-quarters of the whole vineyard and almost without exception in all the best sites. The soils of the Rheingau vary widely with the altitude and exposure of the vineyards; in general lighter, more recently weathered soils on the higher ground grading to heavier loess, loam and finally clay in the valleylands. The steeper and higher the vineyards the more sunshine they enjoy (as mists form closer to the river), but higher, more exposed sites are also subject to cooling winds. The soil/sunshine/shelter equation is never simple, and the best sites of the Rheingau seem to be scattered almost at random, from the surprisingly low-lying suntrap of Marcobrunn to the extremely exposed, almost cliff-like south slopes of the Rüdesheimer Berg. All, however, are said to benefit from the effect of the Rhine flowing by, 800 metres wide (875 yards), as both a stabilizing factor for temperature and, as it were, a vast mirror for solar radiation.

These conditions allow the Riesling to achieve wine with all the force, the cut, the drive and follow-through that makes its finest Rheingau wines among the best of the Rhine.

To some the purest magic is when all this vitality is captured in the relative delicacy and miniature scale of a Kabinett wine. It is not so difficult to be impressive with forceful late-gathered Spätlesen and Auslesen. It is when the region is judged on what it can pack into the lightest category of top quality wine that the Rheingau asserts its supremacy.

Other grape varieties of the Rheingau include Müller-Thurgau and some Silvaner, and a small proportion (about five per cent) of red-wine grapes, mainly Spätburgunder.

The entire region has only one Bereich name: Johannisberg, with ten Großlagen: Daubhaus (for the Hochheim extension), Steinmächer for the eastern vineyards as far west as Kiedrich (which also has a small Großlage, Heiligenstock), Deutelsberg for Erbach and Hattenheim, Mehrhölzchen (and also the smaller

▲ The Rhine, with the Mäuseturm (Mouse Tower Island), from the Rüdesheimer Berg Schloßberg.

Gottesthal) for Hallgarten and Oestrich, Erntebringer (and also Honigberg) for Mittelheim, Winkel, Johannisberg and Geisenheim. Rüdesheim, part of Geisenheim, Lorch and Lorchhausen have the Großlage name of Burgweg, and Großlage Steil takes in Assmannshausen and Aulhausen.

Officially the Rheingau rounds the river bend past Rüdesheim to include the red-winegrowing village of Assmannshausen and the Riesling village of Lorch. Assmannshausen is a special case, hotly defended by the State Domain. Lorch and Lorchhausen might be more realistically classed with the other good Riesling sites of the Mittelrhein.

▼ Below: Lorch is in the Rheingau, but the west bank opposite (the Rheinberg, in Großlage Schloß Stahleck) is in the Mittelrhein.

TRAVEL INFORMATION

The landscape of the Rheingau is more gentle than the Rhine gorge, but the wine is of far greater renown. Many ancient villages, castles and wine estates provide interest.

Wine roads

The *Rheingauer Riesling Route* follows the right bank of the river from Lorch through Assmannshausen, opposite Bingen, and then weaves east through the undulating vineyard country to Hochheim and Wicker, close to the River Main. The signposts are green and white, showing a large goblet. A footpath follows a similar route.

Places to visit

Lorch: wine village, painted medieval houses.
Assmannshausen: red wines are the local speciality.
Rüdesheim: dozens of wine taverns, especially in the famous Drosselgasse. Wine museum in the ancient Brömsersburg, west of the town. Tourist office: Rheinstraße 16 (tel: 06722-2962).
Geisenheim: home of the famous wine teaching and research college, also the Rheingauer Dom (cathedral).
Schloß Johannisberg: former Benedictine monastery, now a great wine estate.
Winkel: the Graues Haus is the oldest wine tavern in Germany.
Kloster Eberbach: 12th C. church, ancient monastery, now base of the Rheingau State Domain and the German Wine Academy, which runs wine courses. The famous Steinberg is a monastic walled vineyard, first planted in the 12th C. and still part of the Eberbach estate.
Kiedrich: wine village with a Gothic church and especially fine timbered houses.
Eltville: Prince Elector's castle, church and old mansions of the wine estates are worth a visit.
Wiesbaden: major spa, casino, many sports facilities and a cultural festival in May.
Hochheim: at the eastern end of the Rheingau, isolated among busy towns, an island of Riesling. The Taunus: wooded hills that bound the Rheingau to the north. Nature reserves, walks, hunting, scenic farms and villages.

Historic hotels

It is possible to stay in some very ancient buildings such as castles and monasteries which have been converted into hotels. Contact the Gast im Schloß (guests in castles) organization at Postfach 40, Vor der Burg, D 3526 Trendelburg 1.

Wine festivals

Wicker, near Winkel, has cellar open days (end Apr), Assmannshausen, red-wine festival (early May), Niederwalluf & Kiedrich (3rd w/e in June), Eltville, sparkling wine festival (last w/e in June), Hochheim (1st w/e in July), Flörsheim, winetasting festival (end July), Hallgarten (1st w/e in Aug), Wiesbaden, Rheingau Wine Week (2nd week in Aug), Rüdesheim & Rauenthal (3rd w/e in Aug), Hattenheim (4th w/e in Aug), Martinsthal & Aulhausen (last w/e in Aug), Oestrich (1st w/e in Sept), Oberwalluf (2nd w/e in Sept), Johannisberg, cellar open day (last w/e in Sept).

Wine tasting

There are plenty of opportunities to buy local wine in taverns and cafés. Many wine estates offer tasting facilities and an opportunity to buy bottles of the wine made there. Some have a Weinstube on the premises. Kloster Eberbach (see Places to visit) offers tastings.

Food and drink

The superlative wines of the Rheingau, especially the Kabinetts and drier Spätlesen, are well complemented by the cuisine. This is a prosperous region and the gastronomic traditions are well developed.

Fruit other than grapes thrives in the gentle climate: almonds are grown, figs and even lemons can be coaxed to crop in warm corners, and fruit finds its way into several savoury dishes. *Rheinischer Sauerbraten*, a pot roast of marinated beef, is, typically, often served with stewed dried fruit.

Forest game – *Wild* – is a frequent component of Rhineland menus. You are likely to come across *Fasan* (pheasant), *Hase* (hare) and *Reh* (venison).

Regional Wine Information Office

Der Rheingau – Der Weingau Weinwerbung e.V.
Im Alten Rathaus
6225 Johannisberg
Tel: 06722-8117

VINEYARDS

BEREICH JOHANNISBERG

Lorchhausen
(Ortsteil of Lorch)
Rosenberg 1
Seligmacher 2

Lorch
Schloßberg 3
Kapellenberg 4
Krone 5
Pfaffenwies 6
Bodental-Steinberg 7

GROSSLAGE STEIL
Einzellagen 8–10

Assmannshausen
(Ortsteil of Rüdesheim)
Frankenthal 8
Höllenberg 9 P
Hinterkirch 10

Aulhausen
(Ortsteil of Rüdesheim)
Höllenberg 9 P

GROSSLAGE BURGWEG
Einzellagen 1–7,
11–22, 24, 26, 27

Rüdesheim
Berg Kaisersteinfels 11
Berg Roseneck 12
Berg Rottland 13
Berg Schloßberg 14
Bischofsberg 15
Drachenstein 16
Kirchenpfad 17
Klosterberg 18
Klosterlay 19
Magdalenenkreuz 20
Rosengarten 21

Geisenheim
Rothenberg 22
Kläuserweg 23 P
Fuchsberg 24
Kilzberg 25 P
Mäuerchen 26
Mönchspfad 27
Schloßgarten 28
Klaus 29 P

GROSSLAGE ERNTEBRINGER
Einzellagen 23, 25,
30–35, 37, 44; A,
28, 29, 42, 43
(part)

Johannisberg
(Ortsteil of
Geisenheim)
Kläuserweg 23 P
Kilzberg 25 P
Klaus 29 P
Schwarzenstein 30
Vogelsang 31
Hölle 32
Hansenberg 33
Goldatzel 34
Mittelhölle 35
Schloß Johannisberg
(Ortsteil) A

GROSSLAGE HONIGBERG
Einz. 36, 38–40, B,
29, 42, 43, A

Winkel
(Ortsteil of Oestrich-
Winkel)
Klaus 29 P
Gutenberg 36 P
Dachsberg 37
Schloßberg 38
Jesuitengarten 39
Hasensprung 40
Schloß Vollrads
(Ortsteil) B

Mittelheim
(Ortsteil of Oestrich-Winkel)
Gutenberg 36 P
St. Nikolaus 42
Edelmann 43
Goldberg 44

GROSSLAGE GOTTESTHAL
Einzellagen 46, 47, C; 45 (part)

Oestrich
(Ortsteil of Oestrich-Winkel)
Klosterberg 45
Lenchen 46
Doosberg 47
Schloß
   Reichhartshausen
   (Ortsteil) C

GROSSLAGE DEUTELSBERG
Einzellagen 48–55 a, 60–65, 67, D; 58, 59, 66 (part)

Hattenheim
(Ortsteil of Eltville)
Mannberg 48
Nußbrunnen 49
Wisselbrunnen 50
Hassel 51
Heiligenberg 52
Schützenhaus 53
Engelmannsberg 54
Pfaffenberg 55
Rheingarten 55 a P
Jungfer 58 P
Hendelberg 59 P
Marcobrunn 60 P
Steinberg (Ortsteil) D

GROSSLAGE MEHRHÖLZCHEN
Einzellagen 56–57; 45, 58, 59 (part)

Hallgarten
(Ortsteil of Oestrich-Winkel)
Schönhell 56
Würzgarten 57
Jungfer 58 P
Hendelberg 59 P

Erbach
(Ortsteil of Eltville)
Rheingarten 55 a P
Marcobrunn 60 P
Schloßberg 61
Siegelsberg 62
Honigberg 63
Michelmark 64
Hohenrain 65
Steinmorgen 66 P
Rheinhell 67

GROSSLAGE HEILIGENSTOCK
Einzellagen 68–70; 66, 71 (part)

Kiedrich
Klosterberg 68
Gräfenberg 69
Wasseros 70
Sandgrub 71 P

GROSSLAGE STEINMÄCHER
Einzellagen 72–90, 92–97; 66, 71 (part)

Eltville
Steinmorgen 66 P
Sandgrub 71 P
Taubenberg 72
Langenstück 73
Sonnenberg 74
Rheinberg 75
Kalbspflicht 76

Rauenthal
(Ortsteil of Eltville)
Baiken 77
Gehm 78

Wülfen 79
Rothenberg 80
Langenstück 81
Nonnenberg 82

Martinsthal
(Ortsteil of Eltville)
Wildsau 83
Langenberg 84
Rödchen 85

Walluf
Ortsteil
Niederwalluf
Berg-Bildstock 86
Walkenberg 87
Oberberg 88
Gottesacker 88 a

– Ortsteil
Oberwalluf
Vitusberg 89
Langenstück 90

Wiesbaden
Neroberg 91
   (independent Einz.)

Schierstein
(Ortsteil of Wiesbaden)
Dachsberg 92
Hölle 93
Herrnberg 96 P

Frauenstein
(Ortsteil of Wiesbaden)
Marschall 94
Homberg 95
Herrnberg 96 P

Dotzheim
(Ortsteil of Wiesbaden)
Judenkirch 97

GROSSLAGE DAUBHAUS
Einzellagen 98–114 a

Kostheim
(Ortsteil of Mainz)
Reichesthal 98 P
Weiß Erd 99
Steig 100
St. Kiliansberg 100 a
Berg 101 P

Hochheim
Reichesthal 98 P
Berg 101 P
Kön. Victoriaberg 102
Hofmeister 103
Stielweg 104
Hölle 106
Domdechaney 107
Kirchenstuck 108
Stein 109
Herrnberg 110 P

Flörsheim
Herrnberg 110 P
St. Anna Kapelle 110 a

Wicker
(Ortsteil of Flörsheim)
Stein 111
Mönchsgewann 112
König-Wilhelmsberg 113
Nonnberg 114

Massenheim
(Ortsteil of Hochheim)
Schloßgarten 114 a

Frankfurt
Lohrberger Hang 115*

Böddiger
(Ortsteil of Felsberg/Schwalm-Eder-Kreis)
Berg 116*

Einz. Lohrberger Hanz in Frankfurt and Berg in Böddiger are not part of the Großlage or Bereich

CENTRAL ZONE

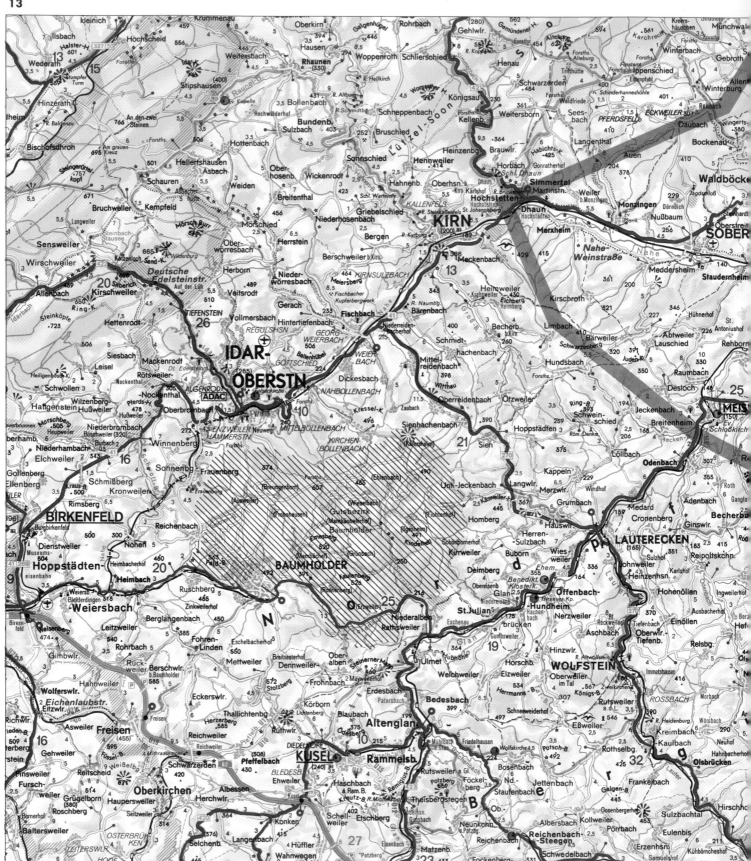

CENTRAL ZONE

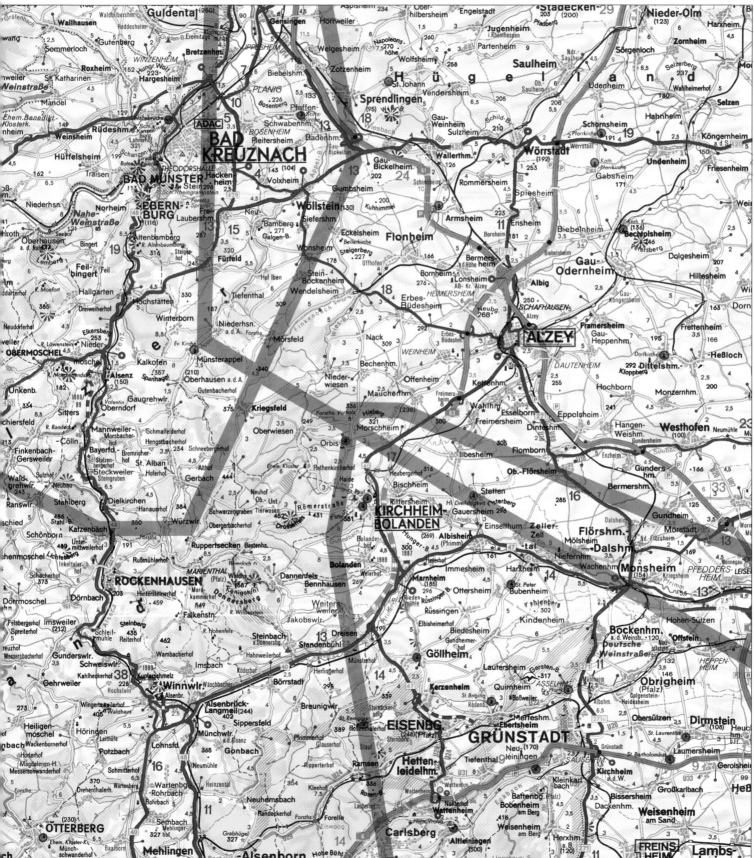

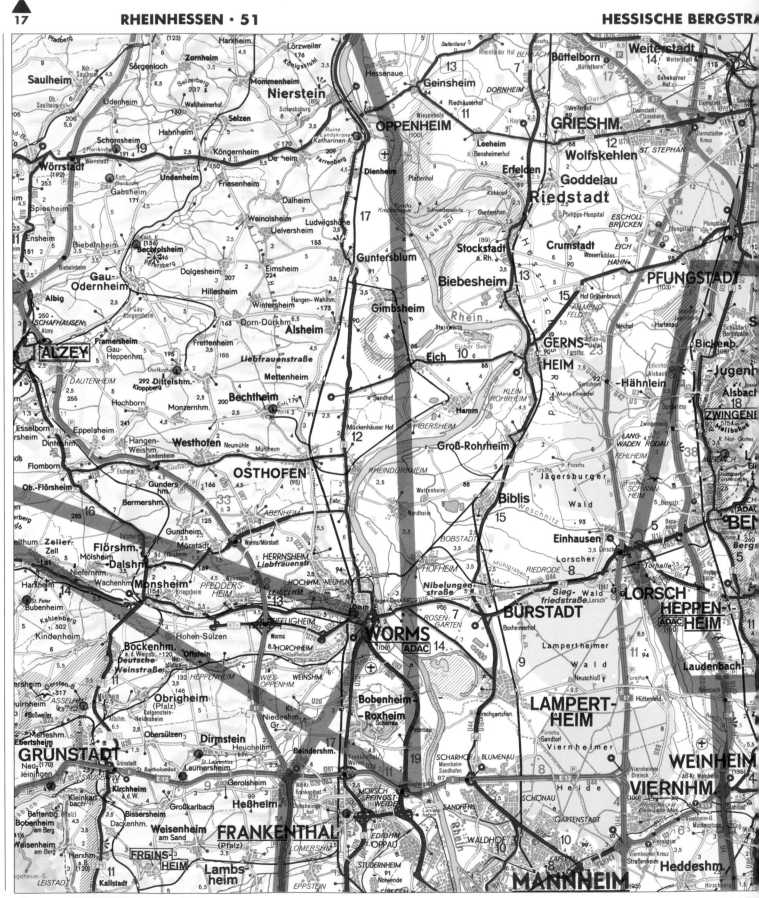

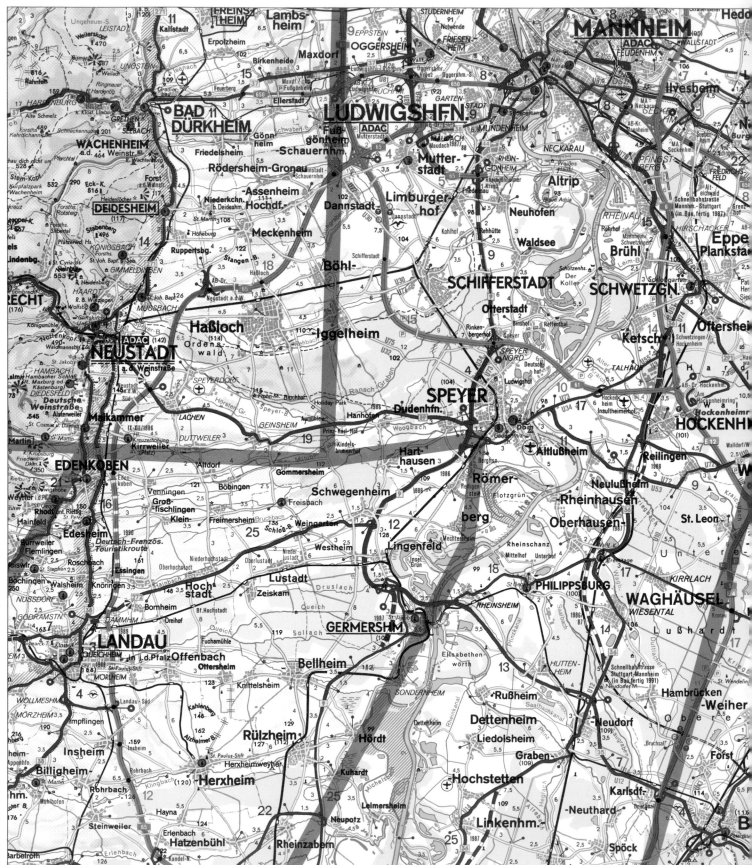

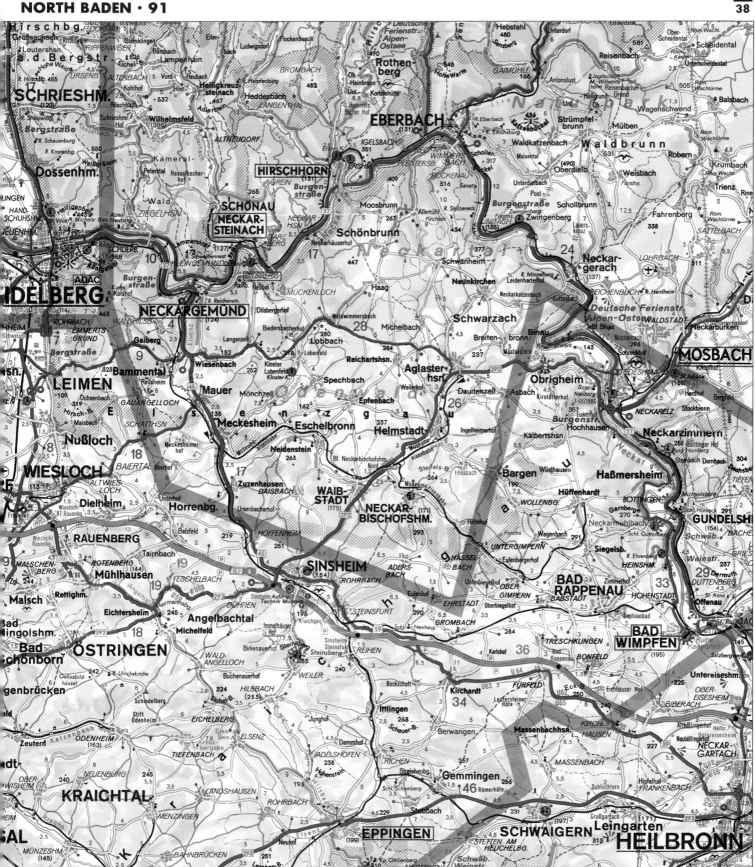

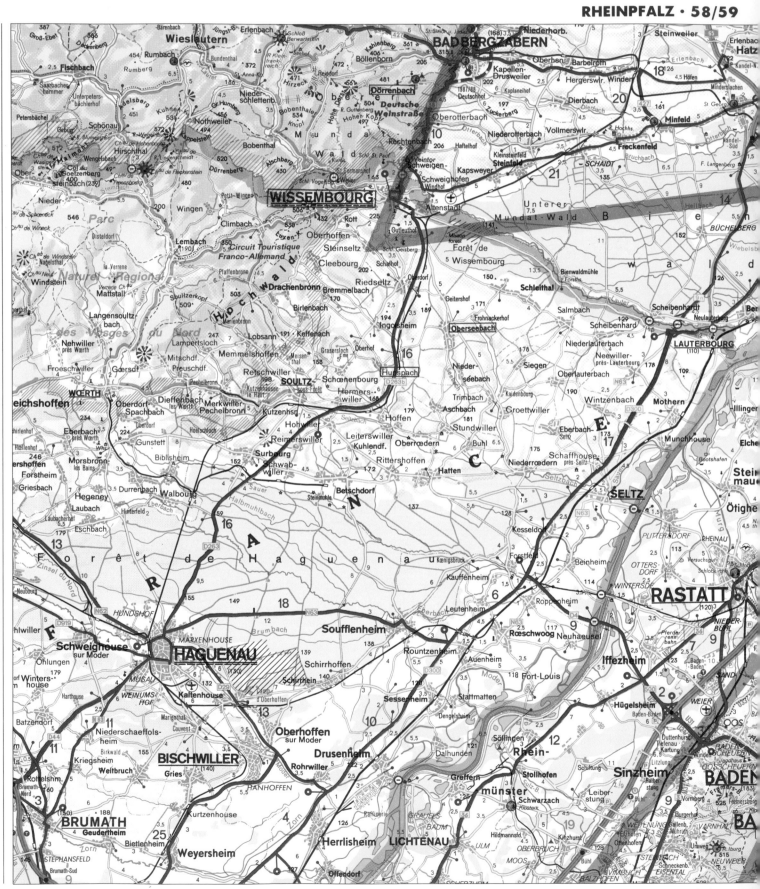

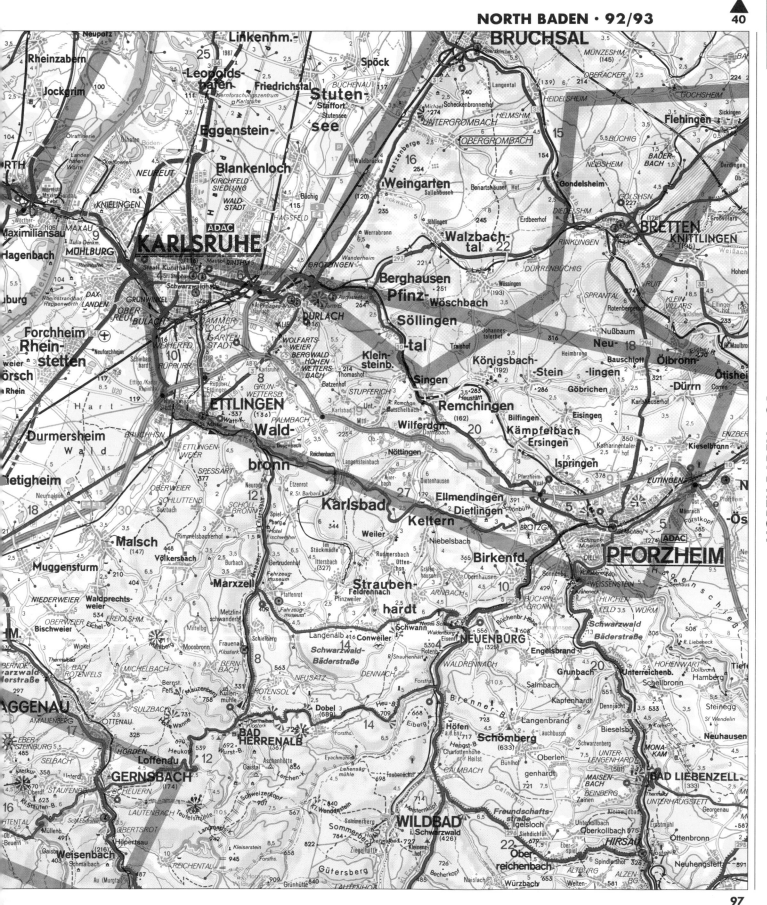

NAHE

44

The river Nahe (the "a" is long) is a minor tributary of the Rhine, joining its broad flood from the south at Bingen, opposite the vineyards of the Rheingau. Its vineyards are thus placed centrally between the Middle Mosel, the best of Rheinhessen, the Saar and the Rheingau. Its middle reaches have some of the most perfect vineyard sites in Germany. The whole region is not large, with some 4,500 hectares. Müller-Thurgau is the main grape with 28 per cent of the vineyard area, followed by Riesling (21 per cent) and Silvaner (15 per cent). Other white grapes include Kerner, Scheurebe, Ruländer and Weißburgunder. There is also a small proportion of Spätburgunder and Portugieser. The everyday wine is similar to that of neighbouring Rheinhessen. The outstanding wines come from a mere eight-kilometre (five-mile) stretch of the north bank of the upper river where it flows northeast into its capital town of Bad Kreuznach, and from singular spots on southern slopes abutting the river between Kreuznach and Bingen.

The conventional way of describing Nahe wines, not surprisingly, is as being transitional between Mosel and Rhine; some say specifically between Saar and Rheingau. This is true of the weight and balance, body and structure of the fine wines of the upper Nahe: they do have the "nerve", the backbone of the Saar with some of the meat of the weightier, more densely flavoured Rheingau. The soil, however, seems to add a certain singularity; the great Nahe wines often have a suggestion of ethereal Sancerre, a delicate hint of the blackcurrant leaf with a delicious mineral undertone. In their delicacy yet completeness they make hypnotic sipping, far into the night. The vineyards that most regularly produce wines that answer this description are most often found in three or four communes, of which Schloßböckelheim and Bad Kreuznach are the most famous, the first for its impeccable State Domain (which makes equally impeccable wines in neighbouring Niederhausen), the second for the very substantial area of

splendid vineyard in and around the town and the few but highly respected growers which exploit them.

Schloßböckelheim and Kreuznach are also the two Bereich names for the entire Nahe: Schloßböckelheim for the upper half, Kreuznach for the lower. Schloßböckelheim contains three Großlagen: Burgweg (the best and most restricted, containing the core of the riverside vineyards); Paradiesgarten, and Rosengarten (almost always associated with the village of Rüdesheim – one suspects in the hope of confusion with the famous Rüdesheim of the Rhine). Kreuznach contains four Großlagen: Kronenberg, Sonnenborn, Schloßkapelle and Pfarrgarten.

In contrast to the solid blocks of monoculture to the north, the extensive upper (southern) Nahe region is fragmented into scattered villages, with good sites at, for example, Kirschroth, Meddersheim, Monzingen and Alsenz.

▶ The picturesque old bridge over the river Nahe at Bad Kreuznach, formerly fortified, gives its name ("Brückes") to one of the best vineyard sites in this town of many small and excellent vineyards.

TRAVEL INFORMATION

The Nahe, between the twin magnets of the Rhine and the Mosel, tends to get overlooked. But the valley and the surrounding country has all the charm of rural Germany, and Bad Kreuznach, its capital, is a notable spa.

Wine roads
The *Naheweinstraße* runs in a long loop south down the valley from Bingen, past Bad Kreuznach and through the famous villages of the middle Nahe, then west upriver to Martinstein and back through the Rosengarten vineyards to Bingen. The signpost shows a glass with a letter N.

Wine trails
A network of footpaths or *Weinwanderwegen* leads through

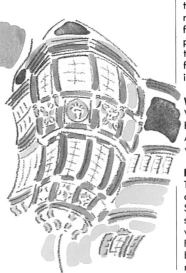

the Nahe countryside. The main route is 90km (55 miles) long and follows the Nahe valley. Side-paths, ranging from 3 to 30km (2 to 18 miles), branch off. Leaflet from the regional wine information office.

Wine seminars
Weekend seminars are held at Bad Kreuznach between May and August. Details from the regional wine information office.

Places to visit
The heart of the wine region, around Traisen and Schloßböckelheim, has spectacular scenery. The Alsenz valley to the south is gentler: Falkenstein is a small village buried in the forests beneath a ruined Hapsburg castle.

Bad Kreuznach and Bad Münster am Stein are splendid spas with thermal baths.

Regional Wine Information Office
Weinland Nahe e.V.
Brückes 6
6550 Bad Kreuznach
Tel: 0671–27563

VINEYARDS

▲ Road and rail hug the north bank of the river Nahe below the 180-metre (600-foot) porphyry precipice of the Rotenfels. At its foot fallen debris provides a superb little south-facing vineyard, Traiser Bastei. Its two hectares are 95% steep.

BEREICH KREUZNACH

GROSSLAGE SCHLOSSKAPELLE

Bingen
Ortsteil Bingerbrück
Hildegardis-
brünnchen 1
Klostergarten 2 P
Abtei Ruppertsberg
3 P
Römerberg 4 P

Weiler
Klostergarten 2 P
Abtei Ruppertsberg
3 P
Römerberg 4 P

Münster-Sarmsheim
Römerberg 4 a
Rheinberg 5
Kapellenberg 6
Dautenpflänzer 7
Trollberg 8
Pittersberg 9
Liebehöll 10
Steinkopf 11
Königsschloß 12

Rümmelsheim
(incl. Ortsteil Burg
Layen)
Steinköpfchen 13
Schloßberg 14
Hölle 15
Rothenberg 16
Johannisberg 17

Waldlaubersheim
Domberg 18
Altenburg 20
Lieseberg 22
Otterberg 23

Genheim
(Ortsteil of
Waldalgesheim)
Rossel 24

Eckenroth
Felsenberg 25
Hölle 26

Schweppenhausen
Steyerberg 27
Schloßgarten 28

Windesheim
Saukopf 29
Sonnenmorgen 30
Rosenberg 32
Römerberg 36

Guldental, Ortsteile Heddesheim and Waldhilbersheim
Apostelberg 38
Honigberg 39
St. Martin 40
Sonnenberg 41
Teufelsküche 42
Hölle 43
Hipperich 44
Rosenteich 45

Dorsheim
Burgberg 46
Honigberg 47
Goldloch 48
Pittermännchen 49
Klosterpfad 50
Laurenziweg 51
Jungbrunnen 52
Nixenberg 53
Trollberg 54

Laubenheim
Vogelsang 55
Karthäuser 56
St. Remigiusberg 57
Fuchsen 58
Junker 59
Hörnchen 60
Krone 61

GROSSLAGE SONNENBORN

Langenlonsheim
Löhrer Berg 62
Bergborn 63
Lauerweg 64
Königsschild 65
Rothenberg 66
Steinchen 67
St. Antoniusweg 68

GROSSLAGE PFARRGARTEN

Schöneberg
Schäfersley 69
Sonnenberg 70

Spabrücken
Höll 71

Dalberg
Schloßberg 72
Ritterhölle 73
Sonnenberg 74

Hergenfeld
Mönchberg 75
Sonnenberg 76
Herrschaftsgarten 77

Wallhausen
Felseneck 78
Hornchen 79
Mühlenberg 80
Johannisberg 81
Johannisweg 81 a

Kirschheck 82
Höllenpfad 83
Hasensprung 84
Pastorenberg 85
Backöfchen 86
Sonnenweg 87
Laurentiusberg 88

Sommerloch
Birkenberg 89
Steinrossel 90
Sonnenberg 91
Ratsgrund 92

Gutenberg
St. Ruppertsberg 93
Römerberg 94
Schloßberg 95
Schloß Gutenburg 96
Sonnenlauf 97
Felseneck 98

**GROSSLAGE
KRONENBERG**

Bad Kreuznach
Galgenberg 100 P
Tilgesbrunnen 101
Rosenberg 102
Kauzenberg-
    Oranienberg 103
Kauzenberg-
    Rosenhügel 104
Kauzenberg in den
    Mauern 105
Osterhöll 106
Hofgarten 107
Kahlenberg 108
Mollenbrunnen 110
Hinkelstein 111
Forst 112
Vogelsang 113
Kapellenpfad 115
Krötenpfuhl 116
Brückes 117
St. Martin 118
Gutental 120
Mönchberg 121
Narrenkappe 122
Steinberg 123
Hungriger Wolf 124

**– Ortsteil
Winzenheim**
In den siebzehn
    Morgen 125
Honigberg 126
Berg 127
Rosenheck 128

**– Ortsteil
Bosenheim**
Höllenbrand 99 P
Galgenberg 100 P
Hirtenhain 133
Paradies 135

– Ortsteil Ippesheim
Himmelgarten 129
Junker 130

– Ortsteil Planig
Höllenbrand 99 P
Römerhalde 131
Katzenhölle 132
Nonnengarten 134

Bretzenheim
Felsenköpfchen 137
Vogelsang 138
Hofgut 139
Pastorei 140
Schloßgarten 141

Hargesheim
Straußberg 142
Mollenbrunnen 143

**BEREICH
SCHLOSS
BÖCKELHEIM**

**GROSSLAGE
ROSENGARTEN**

Braunweiler
Michaeliskapelle 144
Wetterkreuz 145
Hellenpfad 146
Schloßberg 147

St. Katharinen
Fels 148
Klostergarten 149
Steinkreuz 150

Mandel
Alte Römerstraße 151
Schloßberg 152
Delichen 153
Palmengarten 154
Becherbrunnen 155

Roxheim
Berg 156
Hüttenberg 157
Sonnenberg 158
Höllenpfad 159
Mühlenberg 160
Birkenberg 161

Rüdesheim
Wiesberg 162
Goldgrube 163

Weinsheim
Katergrube 165
Kellerberg 166
Steinkaut 167

Sponheim
Mühlberg 168
Abtei 169
Grafenberg 170
Klostergarten 171
Schloßberg 172 P

Burgsponheim
Schloßberg 172 P
Höllenpfad 173
Pfaffenberg 174

Bockenau
Geisberg 175
Stromberg 176
Im Neuberg 177
Im Felseneck 178

Hüffelsheim
Mönchberg 179
Steyer 180
Gutenhölle 181

**GROSSLAGE
PARADIES-
GARTEN**

Auen
Kaulenberg 182
Römerstich 183

Martinstein
Schloßberg 184

Weiler/Monzingen
Herrenzehntel 185
Heiligenberg 186

Merxheim
Vogelsang 187
Römerberg 188
Hunolsteiner 189

Monzingen
Frühlingsplätzchen
    190
Rosenberg 191
Halenberg 192

Nußbaum
Sonnenberg 193
Höllenberg 194
Rotfeld 195

Kirschroth
Wildgrafenberg 196
Lump 197

Meddersheim
Liebfrauenberg 198
Rheingrafenberg 199
Präsent 200
Altenberg 201
Edelberg 202

Lauschied
Edelberg 203

Sobernheim
Marbach 204
Domberg 205

**Sobernheim
Ortsteil Steinhard**
Spitalberg 206
Johannesberg 207 P

Waldböckelheim
Johannesberg 207 P
Kastell 208 P

Oberstreit
Auf dem Zimmerberg
    209

Boos
Kastell 208 P
Herrenberg 210 P

Staudernheim
Herrenberg 210 P
Goldgrube 211

Odernheim am Glan
Kloster Disi-
    bodenberg 212
Heßweg 213
Montfort 214
Weinsack 215
Kapellenberg 216
Langenberg 216 a

Rehborn
Herrenberg 217
Schikanebuckel 218
Hahn 219

Raumbach/Glan
Schwalbennest 220
Schloßberg 221
Allenberg 222

Desloch
Vor der Hölle 223
Hengstberg 224

Meisenheim
Obere Heimbach 225

Lettweiler
Rheingasse 226
Inkelhöll 227

Unkenbach
Würzhölle 228
Römerpfad 229

Obermoschel
Sonnenplätzchen 230
Schloßberg 231
Langhölle 232
Geißenkopf 233 P
Silberberg 234 P

Niedermoschel
Geißenkopf 233 P
Silberberg 234 P
Hahnhölle 235
Layenberg 236

Feilbingert
Feuerberg 237
Königsgarten 238
Bocksberg 239
Kahlenberg 240
Höchstes Kreuz 241

Hochstätten
Liebesbrunnen 242

Kalkofen
Graukatz 243

Alsenz
Elkersberg 244
Pfaffenpfad 245
Falkenberg 246
Hölle 247

Oberndorf
Weißenstein 248
Feuersteinrossel 249
Aspenberg 250
Beutelstein 251

Mannweiler-Cölln
Weißenstein 248 a
Schloß Randeck 252
Seidenberg 253
Rosenberg 254

**Bayerfeld-
Steckweiler**
Adelsberg 255
Schloß Stolzenberg
    256
Aspenberg 257
Mittelberg 258

Gaugrehweiler
Graukatz 259

Oberhausen/Appel
Graukatz 259 a

Münsterappel
Graukatz 259 b

Niederhausen/Appel
Graukatz 259 c

Winterborn
Graukatz 260

**GROSSLAGE
BURGWEG**

Altenbamberg
Laurentiusberg 261
Treuenfels 262
Kehrenberg 263
Schloßberg 264
Rotenberg 265

**Bad Münster am
Stein-Ebernburg
Ortsteil Ebernburg**
Schloßberg 266
Erzgrube 267
Köhler-Köpfchen 268
Stephansberg 269
Feuerberg 270
Luisengarten 271
Götzenfels 272
Königsgarten 273

**– Ortsteil
Münster am Stein**
Steigerdell 274
Höll 275

**Rotenfelser im
    Winkel 276**
Felseneck 277

Traisen
Bastei 278
Kickelskopf 279
Rotenfels 280
Nonnengarten 281

Norheim
Götzenfels 282
Sonnenberg 283
Onkelchen 284
Oberberg 285
Kirschheck 286
Dellchen 287
Klosterberg 288
Kafels 289

Niederhausen/Nahe
Pfingstweide 290
Felsensteyer 291
Rosenberg 292
Rosenheck 293
Pfaffenstein 294
Steinwingert 295
Stollenberg 296
Kertz 297
Klamm 298

Hermannshöhle 299
Hermannsberg 300
Steinberg 301

Schloßböckelheim
Kupfergrube 302
Felsenberg 303
Mühlberg 304
In den Felsen 305
Heimberg 306
Königsfels 307 P

Waldböckelheim
Königsfels 307 P
Mühlberg 308
Muckerhölle 309
Kirchberg 310
Romerberg 311
Hamm 312
Kronenfels 313
Drachenbrunnen 314
Marienpforter
    Klosterberg 315

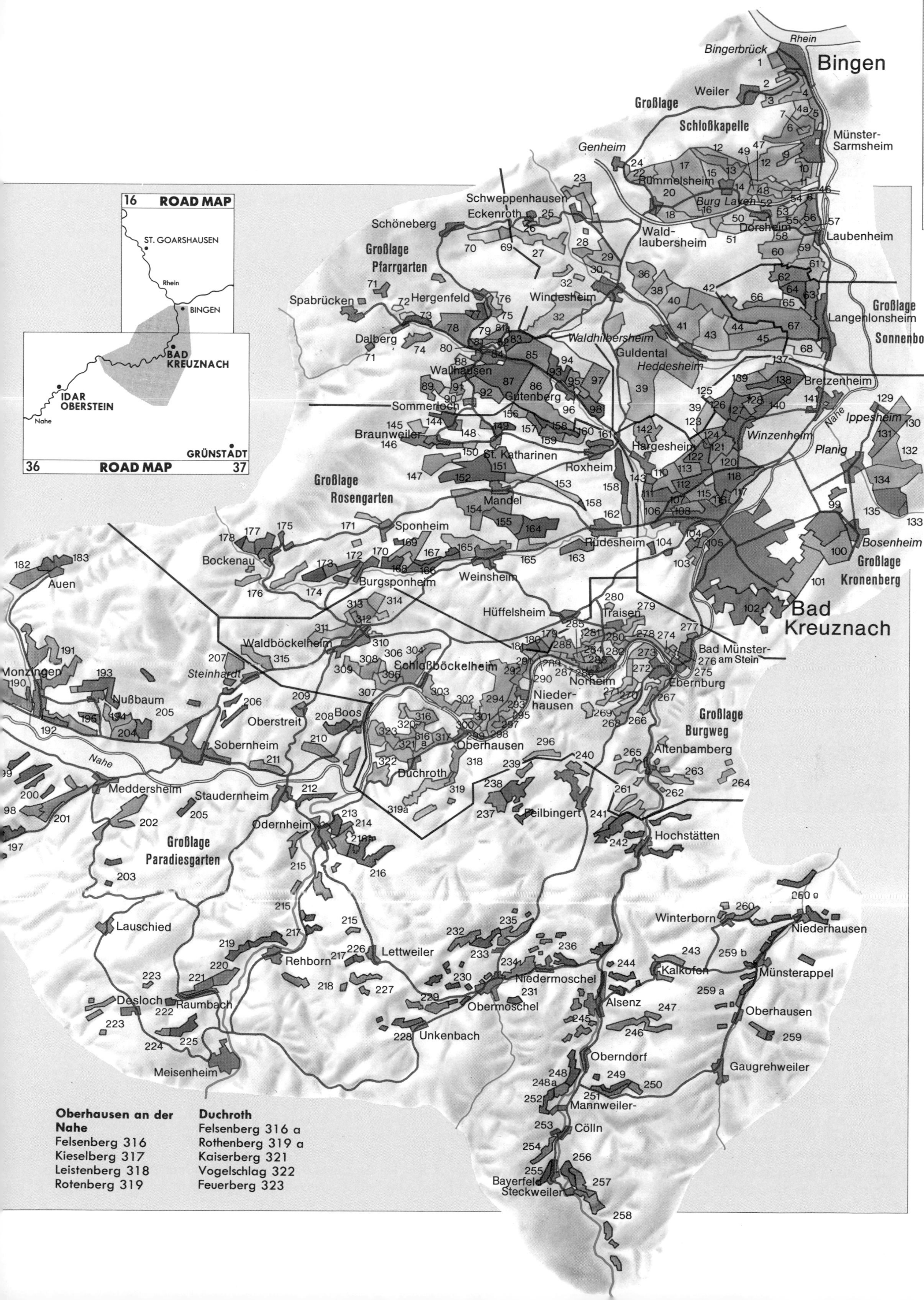

16 ROAD MAP
36 ROAD MAP 37

ST. GOARSHAUSEN

Rhein

BINGEN

BAD KREUZNACH

IDAR OBERSTEIN

Nahe

GRÜNSTADT

Rhein

Bingerbrück
1
Bingen
Weiler
2
3
4
4a 5
Großlage
Schloßkapelle
7 6
Münster-Sarmsheim
Genheim
12 49 47
9
24
17 15 13 12 10
22 Rümmelsheim 20 14 48 11
Schweppenhausen 23 18 16 Burg Layen 52 54 4a 8
Eckenroth 25 50 55 56 57
Schöneberg 26 51 Dorsheim 58 59
70 69 28 60 61 Laubenheim
Großlage 27 29 62
Pfarrgarten 30 36 42 64 66 63
71 32 38 40 66 65 67 Großlage
Spabrücken 72 Hergenfeld 76 Windesheim 41 44 45 68 Langenlonsheim
73 78 75 79 80 32 43 137 Sonnenborn
Dalberg 71 74 80 88 85 Waldhilbersheim 139 138
Wallhausen 87 94 Guldental 125 Bretzenheim
89 91 86 93 95 97 Heddesheim 126 140 141 129
90 92 Gutenberg 96 98 39 127 130
Sommerloch 156 160 39 124 Winzenheim Planig 131
145 144 149 157 158 161 123 121 132
Braunweiler 148 159 142 122 120 134
146 150 St. Katharinen 151 160 Hargesheim 113 118 99 135
147 152 153 143 110 112 115 117 133
Großlage 154 Mandel 155 158 111 106 107 108
Rosengarten 164 163 158 162 104 Bosenheim
171 Sponheim 165 Rüdesheim 104 105 100 Großlage
175 169 165 103 101 Kronenberg
178 177 172 170 167 166 Weinsheim 102 Bad
Bockenau 173 168 166 Hüffelsheim 280 279 277 Kreuznach
176 174 Burgsponheim 285 278 274 Bad Münster
313 314 Traisen 281 280 276 am Stein
182 183 311 312 310 184 179 288 284 273 275
Auen 207 315 308 304 180 289 290 287 286 272 Ebernburg
191 309 306 Schloßböckelheim 292 269 271 270 267
Monzingen 193 315 307 306 303 302 294 293 295 268 266 Großlage
190 206 209 Steinhardt 301 297 Niederhausen 265 Burgweg
195 194 205 208 Boos 316 300 299 298 Oberhausen 296 263 Altenbamberg
192 204 210 323 320 317 318 239 240 262 264
Nußbaum Oberstreit 321 319 261
Sobernheim 322 Duchroth 238 237 Feilbingert 241 242 Hochstätten
211 319 243
Meddersheim 212 319a 237
200 Staudernheim 213 214 238
201 205 Odernheim 215 216
202 216
197 Großlage 215 260
203 Paradiesgarten 215 235 Winterborn Niederhausen
Lauschied 217 232 236 243 259 b
219 217 226 233 234 244 Kalkofen Münsterappel
220 227 Lettweiler 230 231 259 a
223 221 218 229 Niedermoschel 245 247 Oberhausen
Desloch Raumbach 227 Obermoschel Alsenz 246 259
222 228 Unkenbach 231 Oberndorf 250
223 Meisenheim 248 248a 249 Gaugrehweiler
224 225 252 251 Mannweiler-
253 Cölln
254 256
255
Bayerfeld 257
Steckweiler 258

Oberhausen an der Nahe
Felsenberg 316
Kieselberg 317
Leistenberg 318
Rotenberg 319

Duchroth
Felsenberg 316 a
Rothenberg 319 a
Kaiserberg 321
Vogelschlag 322
Feuerberg 323

RHEINHESSEN

◄ The Rheinterrasse at Nierstein, looking south to the north-flowing Rhine. Nierstein hides behind the ridge of its best site, the Großlage Rehbach.
► Modern stained glass in Heinrich Seip's cellars captures an ageless vintage scene.

TRAVEL INFORMATION

The favourite adjective for Rheinhessen is "restful". This is farm country, sheltered and fertile, with vineyards as far as the eye can see and small, picturesque villages.

Places to visit
Mainz, the capital, is one of the great cities of Germany, and the cathedral and Gutenberg museum – printing began here – are well worth seeing. Nierstein and Oppenheim, twin centres of the Rheinterrasse district, are rewarding places to taste wine and visit cellars. Bingen, in the far northwest of the region, is at the mouth of the Rhine gorge and a stopping-place for river steamers. The Rheingau is paradoxically best seen from the Rheinhessen bank between Bingen and Mainz. The Hessische Schweiz is a wooded, hilly region to the west of the wine districts, with the usual amenities of forest paths and inns. Worms, apart from the vineyard which gave birth to Liebfraumilch, is an ancient city with a fine cathedral.

Wine tasting
In Mainz-Mombach the Rheinhessen wine office (address on p49) has a tasting cellar which offers many Rheinhessen wines (open by prior arrangement only). Worms has a similar cellar at Neumarkt 14 (tel: 06241-25045). Tastings, with a winegrower's supper, can be organized for groups of 10 or more in the Schloß at Alzey (tel: 06731-2061).

Wine seminars and trails
In Mainz, wine weekends; in Oppenheim, daily seminars in

The heart of the winegrowing Rhineland and the largest of the wine regions, Rheinhessen specializes in soft, flowery wine, much of it travelling the world under the *nom de verre* of Liebfraumilch (the name Liebfraumilch stems from an ecclesiastical vineyard in the cathedral city of Worms).

Müller-Thurgau is the most popular grape variety, with more than 6,200 out of a total of 24,000 hectares. Silvaner, the traditional grape of Rheinhessen – 40 per cent of all German Silvaner plantings are in Rheinhessen – comes second with nearly 3,400 hectares. At its best, particularly when made in the dryer, modern style, Silvaner here is capable of producing wines with a fine balance of fruit and acidity and unsuspected depths. Six of the "new" varieties between them account for more than 8,000 hectares. This, even more than the Rheinpfalz, is the land of the Scheurebe, Bacchus, Faberrebe, Kerner, Morio-Muskat and Huxelrebe. These aromatic grapes make up a large proportion of the Bereich Nierstein wines. They are allowed in Liebfraumilch, but only in small quantities. Riesling, with six per cent of the vineyard area, is concentrated in a few selected sites, particularly along the "Rheinterrasse", the riverside communities from Mettenheim to Bodenheim, with Oppenheim, Nierstein and Nackenheim at their centre.

A small amount of the red grape varieties Spätburgunder and Portugieser is also grown.

Frank Schoonmaker points out in his classic book *The Wines of Germany* that of the 160-odd villages producing wine in Rheinhessen no less than 120 have names ending in "heim" – home. They are scarcely a rarity anywhere in Germany, but this stress on domesticity seems especially fitting for Rheinhessen, an area of undulating, fertile farmland. The Rhine curls protectingly around its eastern and northern boundaries; the Nahe guards its western limits. The cities of Worms, Mainz, Bingen and Kreuznach mark its corners.

Nierstein is the wine capital of Rheinhessen, its streets lined with the dignified houses of long-established wine merchants. Wines produced from the narrow strip of Niersteiner vineyards that front the river are relatively rare, but the town name is borrowed by the Großlage Gutes Domtal that stretches back from the outskirts of the town into the heart of the region, and by the even larger Bereich Nierstein.

Indeed, Rheinhessen is divided into only three Bereiche: Nierstein for the eastern and south-central part, Bingen for the western and north-central, and Wonnegau for the so-called "happy-land" around Worms.

September; in Ingelheim, a "Wein-Kolleg". Details from the state's tourist board (Postfach 1420, D-5400 Koblenz). Vineyard trails in Bingen, Flonheim, Alsheim and elsewhere.

Wine festivals
Gau-Odernheim (last w/e in May), Alsheim (2nd w/e in June), Nackenheim (last w/e in July or 1st in Aug), Nierstein (1st w/e in Aug), Oppenheim (2nd w/e in Aug), Guntersblum (2nd to last w/e in Aug), Worms fried fish festival (last w/e in Aug), Bingen (1st to 2nd w/e in Sept), Alzey (3rd w/e in Sept), Ingelheim red wine festival (last w/e in Sept and 1st in Oct).

Food and drink
The Rheinhessen has plenty of small restaurants and inns, serving country specialities such as potato soup and dumplings, asparagus, ham – and plenty of wine. One local dish is simply described in dialect: "Weck, Worscht, Woi" – bread roll, sausage and wine. There are also excellent hotels and restaurants, particularly in Worms and Mainz.

Regional Wine Information Office
Rheinhessenwein e.V.
An der Brunnenstube 33–35
6500 Mainz
Tel: 06131-681057/58

▶ The heraldic carving of massive oak barrel-heads is still a living art-form. German barrels, unlike those of Bordeaux and Burgundy, are permanent fixtures in the cellar.

Traditional regional divisions are more specific. They distinguish the Bingen area from that of Ingelheim to the west, known traditionally for light red Spätburgunder. It was at Ingelheim that Charlemagne had a manor, from which legend says he looked north across the Rhine in winter and noticed how the snow thawed first on the slope he caused to be planted as the Johannisberg. The western villages neighbouring the Nahe, close to Bad Kreuznach, are locally known as the Rheinhessen Switzerland: a hilly corner producing fruity light wines. The river-villages north and south of Nierstein are the Rheinterrasse: the aristocrats of the Rheinhessen. The important central district round Alzey is called the Hügelland, the hill country: cooperatives here make some very pleasant fresh and balanced wines. The Wonnegau and the region of Worms in the south produce wines that are generally weightier than those from the rest of the region.

Throughout Rheinhessen the units of small-holding are very small, and most of the wine is made by cooperatives, some of which have made international reputations.

LIEBFRAUMILCH

The official definition of a Liebfraumilch is a wine "of pleasant character" and medium sweetness (technically more than 18 grams per litre of sugar, the upper limit of "halbtrocken" wines). It must be made predominantly from Riesling, Müller-Thurgau, Silvaner and/or Kerner and must have the essential fruit flavour of one or more of these grapes (although it may not bear a grape name). It must be white, of QbA quality, and be grown in the Rheinhessen, the Rheinpfalz, the Nahe or the Rheingau. It is Germany's most widely exported wine.

Originally, "Liebfraumilch" – also spelt Liebfrauenmilch, "milk of Our Lady" – was the name given to the wine produced from the vineyard adjacent to the Liebfrauenkirche, the Church of Our Lady, in the city of Worms. Admired by many, the area of production slowly increased, so that supply and demand have remained in balance.

Liebfraumilch is the wine for all occasions. As such it is expected to be agreeable and refreshing, and for these qualities it is welcomed everywhere, particularly in the United States and Great Britain where it enjoys great popularity.

VINEYARDS

50

BEREICH BINGEN

GROSSLAGE SANKT ROCHUSKAPELLE

Bingen Ortsteil Kempten
Schloßberg-
   Schwätzerchen 1 P
Kirchberg 2
Kapellenberg 3
Pfarrgarten 4 P

– Ortsteil Gaulsheim
Pfarrgarten 4 P

– Ortsteil Büdesheim
Schloßberg-
   Schwärtzerchen
   1 P
Bubenstück 5
Osterberg 6
Rosengarten 7
Scharlachberg 8
Schelmenstück 9 P
Schwarzenberg 10

– Ortsteil Dietersheim
Schelmenstück 9 P

– Ortsteil Sponsheim
Palmenstein 11

Grolsheim
Ölberg 12

Gensingen
Goldberg 13

Horrweiler
Goldberg 13 a
Gewürzgärtchen 14

Welgesheim
Kirchgärtchen 15

Biebelsheim
Honigberg 16
Kieselberg 17

Pfaffen-Schwabenheim
Hölle 18
Mandelbaum 19
Sonnenberg 20

Zotzenheim
Johannisberg 21
Klostergarten 22

Badenheim
Galgenberg 23
Römerberg 24

Aspisheim
Johannisberg 25
Sonnenberg 26

Bingen Ortsteil Dromersheim
Honigberg 27
Klosterweg 29
Mainzerweg 30

Ockenheim
Laberstall 31
Hockenmühle 32
St. Jakobsberg 33
Klosterweg 34
Kreuz 35
Schönhölle 36

GROSSLAGE ABTEY

Gau-Algesheim
Steinert 37
Johannisberg 38
Goldberg 39
Rothenberg 40

– Ortsteil Laurenziberg
St. Laurenzikapelle 41

Appenheim
Daubhaus 42
Hundertgulden 43
Eselspfad 44
Drosselborn 45

Nieder-Hilbersheim
Honigberg 46
Steinacker 47
Mönchspforte 48 P

Ober-Hilbersheim
Mönchspforte 48 P

Sprendlingen
Klostergarten 49
Honigberg 50
Hölle 51
Sonnenberg 52
Wißberg 53

Sankt Johann
Klostergarten 54
Steinberg 55
Geyersberg 56

Wolfsheim
Götzenborn 57
Osterberg 58
Sankt Kathrin 59

Partenheim
Sankt Georgen 60
Steinberg 61

GROSSLAGE RHEINGRAFEN-STEIN

Pleitersheim
Sternberg 62

Volxheim
Mönchberg 63
Alte Römerstraße 64 P
Liebfrau 65

Hackenheim
Klostergarten 66
Sonnenberg 67
Galgenberg 68
Gewürzgarten 69
Kirchberg 70

Freilaubersheim
Alte Römerstraße 64 P
Kirchberg 70 a
Fels 71
Rheingrafenberg 72
Reichskeller 73

Tiefenthal
Graukatz 74

Fürfeld
Kapellenberg 75
Eichelberg 76
Steige 77

Stein-Bockenheim
Sonnenberg 78

Wonsheim
Sonnenberg 78 a
Hölle 79
Martinsberg 85 P

Neu-Bamberg
Eichelberg 76 a
Kletterberg 80
Kirschwingert 81
Heerkretz 82

Siefersheim
Heerkretz 82 a
Goldenes Horn 83
Höllberg 84
Martinsberg 85 P

Wöllstein
Haarberg-
   Katzensteg 86
Ölberg 87
Äffchen 88
Hölle 89

Eckelsheim
Kirchberg 90
Eselstreiber 91
Sonnenköpfchen 92

GROSSLAGE ADELBERG

Nieder-Wiesen
Wingertsberg 93

Nack
Ahrenberg 94

Wendelsheim
Heiligenpfad 95
Steigerberg 96

Flonheim
Bingerberg 98 P
Rotenpfad 100
Klostergarten 101
Geisterberg 102 P

– Ortsteil Uffhofen
Pfaffenberg 97
Bingerberg 98 P
La Roche 99
Geisterberg 102 P

Erbes-Büdesheim
Bingerberg 98 P
Geisterberg 102 P
Vogelsang 103

Bornheim
Hähnchen 104
Hütte-Terrassen 105
Kirchenstück 106
Schönberg 107 P

Lonsheim
Schönberg 107 P
Mandelberg 108

Bermersheim v. d. H.
Klostergarten 109
Hildegardisberg 110

Armsheim
Goldstückchen 111
Geiersberg 112

– Ortsteil Schimsheim
Leckerberg 113

Ensheim
Kachelberg 114 a

Wörrstadt
Rheingrafenberg 115

– Ortsteil Rommersheim
Kachelberg 114

Sulzheim
Greifenberg 116
Honigberg 117
Schildberg 118

GROSSLAGE KURFÜRSTEN-STÜCK

Gumbsheim
Schloßhölle 119 P

Gau-Bickelheim
Bockshaut 120 P
Saukopf 121
Kapelle 122

Wallertheim
Vogelsang 123
Heil 124

Wöllstein
Schloßhölle 119 P
Bockshaut 120 P

Gau-Weinheim
Wißberg 125
Kaisergarten 126
Geyersberg 127

Vendersheim
Sonnenberg 128
Goldberg 129

GROSSLAGE KAISERPFALZ

Jugenheim
St. Georgenberg 130
Goldberg 131
Hasensprung 132
Heiligenhäuschen 133

Engelstadt
Adelpfad 134
Römerberg 135

Bubenheim
Kallenberg 136
Honigberg 137

Schwabenheim
Sonnenberg 138
Schloßberg 139 a
Klostergarten 140

Ingelheim
Schloß Westerhaus 144 P

– Ortsteil Groß-Winternheim
Schloßberg 139
Klosterbruder 141
Bockstein 142
Heilighäuschen 143
Schloß Westerhaus 144 P
Sonnenhang 145
Rheinhöhe 146
Sonnenberg 147
Burgberg 148
Kirchenstück 149

(Map labels, right side:)
Büdesheim
Dietersheim
Sponsheim
Großlage
Grolsheim
St. Rochuskapelle
Gensing
Bad Kreuznach
67
68
Hackenheim
69
70
71
72
Frei-Laubersheim
Großlage Rheingrafenstein
Nie-Bamberg
77
76 a
73
Fürfeld 75
75
74
Tiefenthal

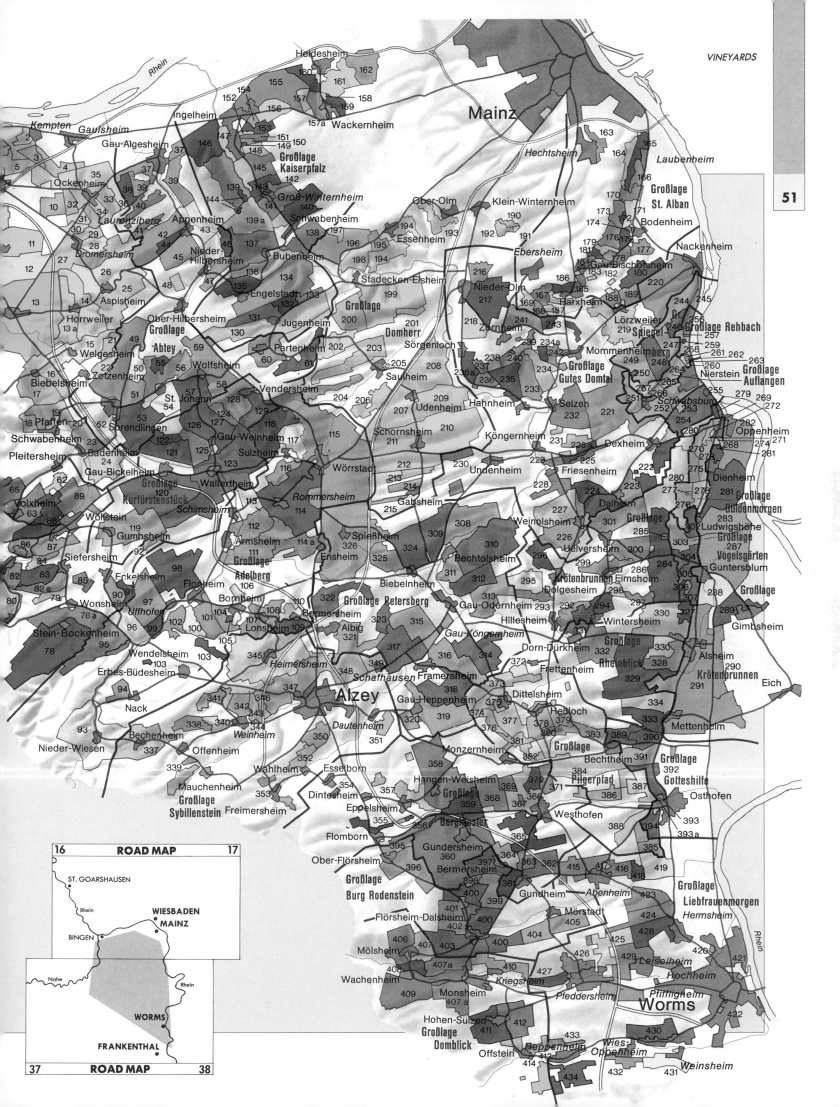

Rhein

Kempten *Gaulsheim* Heidesheim
2 Ingelheim 162
Gau-Algesheim 160 161
152 154 155 157 158
153 156 157a Wackernheim 159
Mainz
5 35 146 147 148 150 149 151
Ockenheim 37 145 **Großlage**
10 32 39 **Kaiserpfalz** 163
31 34 36 139 143 142 Hechtsheim 164 165
30 29 41 40 144 141 *Groß-Winternheim* Laubenheim
11 28 42 43 139 a 140 197 **Großlage**
27 44 45 137 138 Schwabenheim 166 **St. Alban**
Dromersheim 46 Bubenheim 194 Ober-Olm Klein-Winternheim 170 171
12 26 25 47 136 134 196 195 193 190 173 174 172 Bodenheim
13 14 48 135 Engelstadt 133 199 Stadecken-Elsheim 198 194 192 191 179 181 176 177 Nackenheim
Aspisheim 132 216 Nieder-Olm 186 183 182 180 220
13 a 131 Jugenheim 200 201 217 169 167 185 188 189 244 245
Horrweiler 130 Domherr Sörgenloch 218 241 168 187 Lörzweiler 256
15 21 49 **Großlage** 202 203 Zornheim 239 234a 243 219 Spiegel 246 **Großlage Rehbach**
Welgesheim 55 59 60 **Abtey** 205 208 238 237 242 250 249 248 247 257 259
16 50 56 Wolfsheim 61 Sauheim 236a 240 234 Mommenheim 261 262
Biebelsheim Zotzenheim 57 58 204 206 207 209 Hahnheim 235 233 251 267 266 265 263 Nierstein **Großlage**
17 54 St. Johann 128 Udenheim 236 Selzen 252 253 255 Auflangen
18 Pfaffen- 20 52 53 127 124 129 118 117 Schornsheim 210 232 221 254 Schwabsburg 279 269 272
Schwabenheim 23 Sprendlingen 126 125 123 115 211 Königernheim 231 225a 280 282
Pleitersheim 24 Badenheim 122 121 116 Wörrstadt 212 230 Friesenheim 225 270 Oppenheim 271
Gau-Bickelheim 120 113 213 228 222 277 279 274 281
65 62 89 **Großlage** Wallertheim 214 Undenheim 229 224 223 275 Dienheim
Volxheim 63 88 **Kurfürstenstück** Rommersheim 215 Gabsheim 227 301 276 278 281 **Großlage**
86 87 119 *Schimsheim* 114 308 Weinolsheim 226 **Großlage** 285 Güldenmorgen
84 Wöllstein Gumbsheim 112 Spießheim 309 310 296 299 286 284 302 Ludwigshöhe
82 83 85 98 **Großlage** 326 324 Bechtolsheim 295 Krötenbrunnen Eimsheim 300 303 **Großlage**
82 a Siefersheim Eckelsheim **Adelberg** 325 311 Uelversheim 298 297 287 304 Vogelsgärten
80 79 90 91 97 Flonheim 106 Biebelnheim 312 Dolgesheim 292 294 330 305 Guntersblum
Wonsheim 78 a *Uffhofen* 104 107 108 110 322 **Großlage** 313 293 306 **Großlage**
96 99 102 100 Bornheim Bermersheim **Petersberg** 323 315 Gau-Odernheim Hillesheim 327 288 289
Stein-Bockenheim 95 105 Lonsheim 109 Albib 321 316 Gau-Köngernheim Wintersheim 307 Gimbsheim
78 Wendelsheim 103 345 317 318 Dorn-Dürkheim 332 **Großlage** 328 Alsheim
Erbes-Büdesheim 103 Heimersheim 348 349 Framersheim 373 Frettenheim 372 331 **Rheinblick** 329 290 Krötenbrunnen
94 347 *Schafhausen* 375 Dittelsheim 330 291 Eich
Nack 341 346 Alzey Gau-Heppenheim 374 Heßloch 334
93 342 343 320 319 376 377 378 379 333 Mettenheim
Bechenheim 338 340 344 *Dautenheim* 351 381 380 383 389 390
Nieder-Wiesen 337 *Weinheim* 350 Monzernheim 382 **Großlage** Bechtheim 391 **Großlage**
339 Offenheim 358 370 371 **Pilgerpfad** 384 386 387 392 **Gottesheim**
Großlage Mauchenheim 353 Wahlheim Esselborn Hangen-Weisheim 369 366 367 Osthofen
Sybillenstein Freimersheim Dinteheim 357 359 368 Westhofen 388 393
Eppelsheim 355 356 Bergkloster 365 394 393a
Flomborn 395 Gundersheim 360 364 363 362 415 417 416 419 385
Ober-Flörsheim 396 Bermersheim 397 398 361 Abenheim 418 423 **Großlage**
Großlage 400 399 Gundheim 405 424 **Liebfrauenmorgen**
Burg Rodenstein 401 400 Mörstadt 404 428 *Herrnsheim*
Flörsheim-Dalsheim 402 400 426 425 429 420
406 407 403 Mölsheim 407a 410 427 *Leiselheim* 421 **Hochheim**
Wachenheim 408 409 Monsheim 407 a Kriegsheim Pfeddersheim *Pfifflilgheim* **Worms**
Hohen-Sülzen 412 433 430
Großlage 411 Heppenheim Wies- 432 422
Domblick Offstein 414 Oppenheim Weinsheim 431 434

51

16 **ROAD MAP** 17

ST. GOARSHAUSEN

Rhein **WIESBADEN**
MAINZ
BINGEN

Nahe
Rhein

WORMS

FRANKENTHAL

37 **ROAD MAP** 38

Täuscherspfad 150
Horn 151
Pares 152
Steinacker 153
Höllenweg 154
Rotes Kreuz 155
Lottenstück 156
Rabenkopf 157

Wackernheim
Rabenkopf 157 a
Schwalben 158
Steinberg 159

Heidesheim
Geißberg 160
Steinacker 161
Höllenberg 162

BEREICH NIERSTEIN

GROSSLAGE SANKT ALBAN

**Mainz
Ortsteil
Hechtsheim**
Kirchenstück 163

**– Ortsteil
Laubenheim**
Johannisberg 164
Edelmann 165
Klosterberg 166

– Ortsteil Ebersheim
Sand 167
Hüttberg 168
Weinkeller 169

Bodenheim
Mönchspfad 170
Burgweg 171
Ebersberg 172
Heitersbrünnchen 173
Reichsritterstift 174
Westrum 175
Hoch 176
Kapelle 177
Leidhecke 178
Silberberg 179
Kreuzberg 180

Gau-Bischofsheim
Glockenberg 181
Pfaffenweg 182
Kellersberg 183
Herrnberg 184

Harxheim
Börnchen 185
Schloßberg 186
Lieth 187

Lörzweiler
Ölgild 188
Hohberg 189

GROSSLAGE DOMHERR

Klein-Winternheim
Geiershöll 190
Villenkeller 191
Herrgottshaus 192

Ober-Olm
Kapellenberg 193

Essenheim
Teufelspfad 194
Römerberg 195

**Stadecken-Elsheim
Ortsteil Elsheim**
Bockstein 196
Tempelchen 197
Blume 198

– Ortsteil Stadecken
Lenchen 199
Spitzberg 200

Saulheim
Probstey 201
Schloßberg 202
Hölle 203
Haubenberg 204
Pfaffengarten 205
Heiligenhaus 206

Udenheim
Goldberg 207
Sonnenberg 208
Kirchberg 209

Schornsheim
Mönchspfad 210
Ritterberg 211
Sonnenhang 212

Gabsheim
Dornpfad 213
Kirchberg 214
Rosengarten 215

Also vineyards not registered as Einz. in the parishes of Budenheim, Mainz-Finthen and Mainz-Drais

GROSSLAGE GUTES DOMTAL

Nieder-Olm
Klosterberg 216
Sonnenberg 217
Goldberg 218

Lörzweiler
Königstuhl 219

Nackenheim
Schmittskapellchen 220

**Nierstein
Ortsteil Schwabsburg**
Pfaffenkappe 221

Dexheim
Doktor 222

Dalheim
Steinberg 223
Kranzberg 224
Altdörr 225

Weinolsheim
Hohberg 226
Kehr 227

Friesenheim
Altdörr 225 a
Bergpfad 228
Knopf 229

Undenheim
Goldberg 230

Köngernheim
Goldgrube 231

Selzen
Rheinpforte 232
Gottesgarten 233
Osterberg 234

Hahnheim
Knopf 235
Moosberg 236

Sörgenloch
Moosberg 236 a

Zornheim
Vogelsang 237
Guldenmorgen 238
Mönchbäumchen 239
Dachgewann 240
Pilgerweg 241

Mommenheim
Osterberg 234 a
Silbergrube 242
Kloppenberg 243

GROSSLAGE SPIEGELBERG

Nackenheim
Engelsberg 244
Rothenberg 245

Nierstein
Rosenberg 246
Klostergarten 247
Findling 248
Kirchplatte 249
Schloß Hohenrechen 250
Ebersberg 251 P
Bildstock 252
Brückchen 253
Paterberg 254
Hölle 255

**– Ortsteil
Schwabsburg**
Ebersberg 251 P

GROSSLAGE REHBACH

Nierstein
Pettenthal 256
Brudersberg 257
Hipping 258
Goldene Luft 259

GROSSLAGE AUFLANGEN

Nierstein
Kranzberg 260
Zehnmorgen 261
Bergkirche 262
Glöck 263
Ölberg 264
Heiligenbaum 265
Orbel 266
Schloß Schwabsburg 267 P

**– Ortsteil
Schwabsburg**
Schloß Schwabsburg 267 P

GROSSLAGE GÜLDENMORGEN

Oppenheim
Daubhaus 268
Zuckerberg 269
Herrenberg 270 P
Sackträger 271
Schützenhütte 272
Kreuz 273 P
Gutleuthaus 274

Dienheim
Herrenberg 270 P
Kreuz 273 P
Falkenberg 275
Siliusbrunnen 276
Höhlchen 277
Tafelstein 278 P

Uelversheim
Tafelstein 278 P

GROSSLAGE KRÖTEN-BRUNNEN

Oppenheim
Schloßberg 279
Schloß 280 P
Paterhof 281 P
Herrengarten 282 P

Dienheim
Schloß 280 P
Paterhof 281 P
Herrengarten 282 P

Ludwigshöhe
Honigberg 283

Guntersblum
Steinberg 284
Sonnenhang 285
Sonnenberg 286
Eiserne Hand 287
Sankt Julianen-brunnen 288

Gimbsheim
Sonnenweg 289
Liebfrauenthal 290

Alsheim
Goldberg 291 P

Eich
Goldberg 291 P

Mettenheim
Goldberg 291 P

Hillesheim
Altenberg 292
Sonnheil 293

Wintersheim
Frauengarten 294

Dolgesheim
Kreuzberg 295
Schützenhütte 296

Eimsheim
Hexelberg 297
Sonnenhang 298
Römerschanze 299

Uelversheim
Aulenberg 300
Schloß 301

GROSSLAGE VOGELSGÄRTEN

Ludwigshöhe
Teufelskopf 302

Guntersblum
Kreuzkapelle 303
Steig-Terrassen 304
Bornpfad 305
Authental 306
Himmelthal 307

GROSSLAGE PETERSBERG

Bechtolsheim
Wingertstor 308
Sonnenberg 309
Homberg 310
Klosterberg 311

Gau-Odernheim
Herrgottspfad 312
Ölberg 313
Fuchsloch 314

Vogelsang 315

Framersheim
Zechberg 316
Kreuzweg 317
Hornberg 318

Gau-Heppenheim
Schloßberg 319
Pfarrgarten 320

Albig
Schloß Hammerstein 321 P
Hundskopf 322
Homberg 323

Alzey
Schloß Hammerstein 321 P

Biebelnheim
Pilgerstein 324
Rosenberg 325

Spiesheim
Osterberg 326

GROSSLAGE RHEINBLICK

Alsheim
Fischerpfad 327
Frühmesse 328
Römerberg 329
Sonnenberg 330

Dorn-Dürkheim
Hasensprung 331
Römerberg 332

Mettenheim
Michelsberg 333
Schloßberg 334

BEREICH WONNEGAU

GROSSLAGE SYBILLENSTEIN

Bechenheim
Fröhlich 337

Offenheim
Mandelberg 338

Mauchenheim
Sioner Klosterberg 339

Weinheim
(Ortsteil of Alzey)
Mandelberg 340
Hölle 341
Kirchenstück 342
Kapellenberg 343 P
Heiliger Blutberg 344

Heimersheim
(Ortsteil of Alzey)
Sonnenberg 345
Rotenfels 347 P

Alzey
Kapellenberg 343 P
Rotenfels 347 P
Römerberg 348
Wartberg 350

**– Ortsteil
Schafhausen**
Pfaffenhalde 349

Dautenheim
(Ortsteil of Alzey)
Himmelacker 351

Wahlheim
Schelmen 352

Freimersheim
Frankenstein 353

**GROSSLAGE
BERGKLOSTER**

Esselborn
Goldberg 354

Flomborn
Feuerberg 355
Goldberg 356

Eppelsheim
Felsen 357

Hangen-Weisheim
Sommerwende 358

Gundersheim
Höllenbrand 359
Königstuhl 360

Gundheim
Sonnenberg 361
Mandelbrunnen 362
Hungerbiene 363

Bermersheim
Hasenlauf 364

Westhofen
Rotenstein 365
Steingrube 366
Benn 367
Morstein 368
Brunnenhäuschen 369
Kirchspiel 370
Aulerde 371

**GROSSLAGE
PILGERPFAD**

Frettenheim
Heil 372

**Dittelsheim-Heßloch
Ortsteil Dittelsheim**
Leckerberg 373
Pfaffenmütze 374
Mönchhube 375
Kloppberg 376
Geiersberg 377

– Ortsteil Heßloch
Liebfrauenberg 378
Edle Weingärten
379
Mondschein 380

Monzernheim
Goldberg 381
Steinhöhl 382

Bechtheim
Hasensprung 383
Heiligkreuz 384

Osthofen
Rheinberg 385
Klosterberg 386
Liebenberg 387
Kirchberg 388

**GROSSLAGE
GOTTESHILFE**

Bechtheim
Rosengarten 389
Geyersberg 390
Stein 391

Osthofen
Hasenbiß 392
Neuberg 393
Leckzapfen 393 a
Goldberg 394

**GROSSLAGE
BURG
RODENSTEIN**

Ober-Flörsheim
Blücherpfad 395
Deutschherrenberg
396

Bermersheim
Seilgarten 397

**Flörsheim-Dalsheim
Ortsteil Dalsheim**
Hubacker 398
Sauloch 399
Steig 400 P
Bürgel 401

**– Ortsteil
Niederflörsheim**
Steig 400 P
Goldberg 402
Frauenberg 403

Mörstadt
Nonnengarten 404
Katzenbuckel 405

**GROSSLAGE
DOMBLICK**

Mölsheim
Zellerweg am
schwarzen Herr-
gott 406
Silberberg 407

Wachenheim
Rotenberg 408
Horn 409

Monsheim
Silberberg 407 a

**– Ortsteil
Kriegsheim**
Rosengarten 410

Hohen-Sülzen
Sonnenberg 411
Kirchenstück 412

Offstein
Engelsberg 413
Schloßgarten 414

**GROSSLAGE
LIEBFRAUEN-
MORGEN**

Worms
St. Cyriakusstift 420
Liebfrauenstift-
Kirchenstück 421
Remeyerhof 422

– Ortsteil Abenheim
Goldapfel 415
Klausenberg 416
Kapellenstück 417
Bildstock 418

**– Ortsteil
Herrnsheim**
Rheinberg 419
Lerchelsberg 423
Sankt Annaberg 424
Hochberg 425 P
Römersteg 428

**– Ortsteil
Pfeddersheim**
Hochberg 425 P
St. Georgenberg
426
Kreuzblick 427
Nonnenwingert
429 P

**– Ortsteil Wies-
Oppenheim**
Am Heiligen
Häuschen 432

– Ortsteil Leiselheim
Nonnenwingert
429 P

– Ortsteil Hochheim
Nonnenwingert
429 P

**– Ortsteil
Pfifflligheim**
Nonnenwingert
429 P

– Ortsteil Horchheim
Goldberg 430

**– Ortsteil
Weinsheim**
Burgweg 431

**– Ortsteil
Heppenheim**
Affenberg 433
Schneckenberg 434

"AP" NUMBERS

Before being sold in bottle all quality wines (QbA and QmP), and quality sparkling wines (Sekt), must receive an official control number (Amtliche Prüfungsnummer or "AP" number), which must later appear on the bottle label. To obtain an AP number, the bottler sends three samples of the wine to the local control centre. There are nine of these centres, each dealing with an area. With the samples the bottler must send a chemical analysis issued by an officially recognized laboratory. This shows the amount of alcohol, sugar, extract, acid and sulphur dioxide in the wine. Other basic information such as the date and size of the bottling must also be given.

One sample is tasted by a panel of between three and five experts who are not given the name of the bottler or supplier but only that of the wine. The other samples are kept by the authorities for at least two years in case a query should arise about the wine. Marks are awarded on a scale of points for bouquet, taste and balance.

The AP number identifies the control centre, the village or town of the bottler, the bottler's reference number, the application number of the bottling and the year of application.

The immediate purpose of the system is to maintain the quality of German wine. It also generates useful statistics about the styles of wine being bottled.

DLG AWARDS

The Deutsche Landwirtschaft Gesellschaft (DLG), the German Agricultural Society, holds annual national wine tastings for bronze, silver and gold medals (the latter now called the Großer Preis). Only wines that have obtained their AP number and have succeeded in an official regional competition may be entered for the DLG's National Wine Award, or Bundesweinprämierung.

At the DLG tasting, 3.5 points give a bronze medal, 4 a silver and 4.5 a Großer Preis. Juries judge the wines by region, grape variety and quality category. Of the 150,000 individual batches of wine bottled each year, about 3,000 get DLG medals.

The society also awards three types of Deutsches Weinsiegel (wine seal): a yellow seal for dry wines, a green for medium-dry and a red for others that meet with its approval.

RHEINPFALZ

One of Germany's most fertile, sunniest and most productive wine regions takes its English name, the Palatinate, from the former Counts Palatine of the Holy Roman Empire. The wine district takes its bearings not from a river but from a range of forested hills. It stretches in a narrow 80-kilometre (50-mile) band along the eastern flank of the Haardt mountains, from the southern edge of Rheinhessen to the French frontier where the Haardt become the Vosges. At the border, in an extraordinary sudden switch, the wines change from the flowery sweetness and lively attack of Germany to the savoury vinosity of Alsace.

With 21,900 hectares of vines, Rheinpfalz is marginally second in vineyard area to Rheinhessen – though sometimes a bigger producer. The southern half of the region, from Neustadt south, known as the Bereich Südliche Weinstraße, is Germany's most up-to-date and intensive vineyard. The last two decades have seen remarkable progress – in vine varieties, reorganization of vineyards and cellar technology. Natural conditions are so favourable that the region's potential is formidable. Its wines at present offer some of the best value in Germany – indeed in Europe.

Although Müller-Thurgau is the most-planted grape, here as in Rheinhessen, it is outplanted both by the new vine varieties (totalling over 6,075 hectares against 5,300 hectares of Müller-Thurgau) and by the combined totals of Riesling and Silvaner. Of the new varieties Kerner with 1,900 hectares and Morio-Muskat with 1,800 hectares are the most popular, Scheurebe rather less so. Here, as in Baden, the noble old secondary variety, the Ruländer or Pinot Gris, makes a respectable showing. Portugieser and Spätburgunder are grown for red wines.

To characterize Rheinpfalz wines as a whole is much more difficult than, for example, the generally mild products of Rheinhessen or the widely homogeneous styles of the Rheingau or Mosel. The finest Rheinpfalz wines – frequently Riesling – add to the classic Riesling character a generosity of ripeness that marks them as wines from a sunnier climate. They vary in finesse, in lively acidity and honeyed depths. Yet many regularly approach the ideal of what well-ripened Riesling can achieve. The same can be said for each other variety: its character is distinctly articulated by the favourable conditions – in the case of some of the aromatic varieties, the aromas can become almost overwhelming.

The 1971 wine law divided the entire region into only two Bereiche: Südliche Weinstraße for the south and Mittelhaardt-Deutsche Weinstraße for the north, with the city of Neustadt effectively dividing them. The international prestige of the region is centred on the half-dozen villages at the heart of the northern half, the Mittelhaardt.

Bad Dürkheim is the main town of the Mittelhaardt and the biggest wine commune in Germany. It musters almost 800 hectares of vineyards and three Großlagen: Feuerberg, Hochmess and Schenkenböhl. North of Bad Dürkheim Grünstadt marks the start of the Rheinpfalz vineyards in earnest and the line of Haardt villages that reaches a climax at Forst and Deidesheim. Freinsheim, Kallstadt and Ungstein all have good sites. South of Bad Dürkheim, the village of Wachenheim begins the real kernel of the Mittelhaardt. The great quality of Wachenheim and its neighbours is the elegance and delicacy they deliver with their element of honeyed, velvet ripeness and sometimes astonishing concentration of flavours. The Jesuitengarten in Forst is probably the most famous Rheinpfalz vineyard, although its neighbours on

▲ The Südliche Weinstraße is a sea of vines for over 80 kilometres (50 miles). Maikammer, in Großlage Mandelhöhe, lies at its northern (and generally better) end.

the hill, Ungeheuer, Pechstein, Kirchenstück and Freundstück, share its qualities. The vineyards of Deidesheim lie in the Großlagen Mariengarten and Hofstück. Most of the best sites are in the Großlage Mariengarten, but a very considerable exception is Ruppertsberg in the (Deidesheimer) Hofstück, with magnificent sites such as Reiterpfad, Spieß, Nußbien, Hoheburg and Gaisböhl. Most Mittelhaardt wines are sold under the Einzellage or Großlage name. The Bereich name is rarely found on a label.

From Neustadt south to the Alsace border the flourishing vineyards of the Bereich Südliche Weinstraße spread out into the plain, with the city of Landau at their centre. The great majority of wines here are made and marketed by the large, efficient cooperatives that are making the district famous for steadily increasing quality and generally remarkable value. Großlage rather than Einzellage names are the rule. Among the most notable are Ordensgut (Edesheim), Bischofskreuz (Walsheim), Kloster Liebfrauenberg (Bad Bergzabern) and Guttenberg (Schweigen). Even more usual is a grape variety name and the simple appellation Bereich Südliche Weinstraße.

TRAVEL INFORMATION

The wine country of the Rheinpfalz is strung together by a wine road so special it is known as the *Deutsche Weinstraße* – the German Wine Road. In its succession of half-timbered villages, inns and vineyards it indeed epitomizes them all. Walking in the forests – the Pfälzerwald nature park covers the entire Haardt Mountains – and eating in the taverns are the other recreations, apart from wine.

Wine festivals

Bad Dürkheim's sausage fair in September leads a score or more festivals, including a radish fair in Schifferstadt each May. Wine festivals include: Wachenheim (July), Deidesheim (Aug), Speyer & Obermoschel (Sept), Bockenheim & Landau (Oct).

Wine tasting and trails

Every village has well-signposted tasting cellars, and vineyard trails are found in Deidesheim, Edenkoben, Großkarlbach, Schweigen-Rechtenbach, Wachenheim and Ungstein.

Food and drink

Pfalzer Saumagen, inadequately translated as Palatinate haggis, typifies local food: hearty foundations for local wine and plenty of it. A Pfalz recipe for a pork stew begins "take as large a pot as possible . . ."

All the wine towns have their taverns and hotels, and there are many fine restaurants and inns. Bad Dürkheim has a famous annual Wurstmarkt (sausage fair – see Wine festivals) and is also a spa. Deidesheim typifies the dignified Rheinpfalz architectural style.

▼ The Forster Kirchenstück vineyard changed hands four centuries ago, and the new owners erected a plaque to mark their purchase.

Regional Wine Information Office
Rheinpfalz-Weinpfalz e.V.
Robert-Stolz-Straße 18
6730 Neustadt/Weinstraße
Tel: 06321-7583

◀▼ The ancient city of Neustadt is the pivot of the Palatinate, between the Mittelhaardt and the Südliche Weinstraße. Its wine-school has been a great producer of new grape varieties.

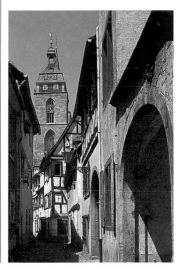

◀ Spätlese Riesling grapes are collected in the famous Gerümpel vineyard, with the little Mittelhaardt village of Wachenheim in the background. Late-picked wines from this region are some of Germany's most luscious.

VINEYARDS

BEREICH MITTELHAARDT/ DEUTSCHE WEINSTRAßE

GROSSLAGE SCHNEPFENFLUG VOM ZELLERTAL (ZELL)

Morschheim
Im Heubusch 1

Kirchheimbolanden
Schloßgarten 2

Bolanden
Schloßberg 3

Rittersheim
Am hohen Stein 4

Gauersheim
Goldloch 5

Stetten
Heilighäuschen 6

Albisheim
Heiligenborn 7

Einselthum
Klosterstück 8 P
Kreuzberg 9 P

Zell
(Ortsteil of Zellertal)
Klosterstück 8 P
Kreuzberg 9 P
Königsweg 10 P
Schwarzer
  Herrgott 11

Niefernheim
(Ortsteil of Zellertal)
Kreuzberg 9 P
Königsweg 10 P

Harxheim
(Ortsteil of Zellertal)
Herrgottsblick 12

Bubenheim
Hahnenkamm 13

Immersheim
Sonnenstück 14

Ottersheim/Zellertal
Bräunersberg 15

Rüssingen
Breinsberg 16

Kerzenheim
Esper 17

Other vineyards not registered as Einz. in Bischheim and Marnheim

GROSSLAGE GRAFENSTÜCK (BOCKENHEIM)

Bockenheim an der Weinstraße
Schloßberg 18
Vogelsang 19 P
Haßmannsberg 20
Burggarten 21
Klosterschaffnerei 22
Sonnenberg 23 P
Goldgrube 24
Heiligenkirche 25

Kindenheim
Vogelsang 19 P
Sonnenberg 23 P
Katzenstein 26
Burgweg 27

Mühlheim
(Ortsteil of Obrigheim)
Benn 28
Hochgericht 29

Obrigheim
Rosengarten 30
Mandelpfad 31

Colgenstein
(Ortsteil of Obrigheim)
Schloß 32

Former place-names may be used, such as Albsheimer Grafenstück (Großlage), Benn 28); Heidesheimer Grafenstück (Großlage), Schloß (32)

GROSSLAGE HÖLLENPFAD (GRÜNSTADT)

Mertesheim
St. Martinskreuz 33

Grünstadt
Bergel 37
Röth 38

– Ortsteil Asselheim
Goldberg 34
St. Stephan 35
Schloß 36

– Ortsteil Sausenheim
Hütt 39

Honigsack 40
Klostergarten 41

Neuleiningen
Feuermännchen 42
Sonnenberg 43
Schloßberg 44

Kleinkarlbach
Herrgottsacker 45
Herrenberg 46
Senn 47
Frauenländchen 48
Keiselberg 49

Battenberg
Schloßberg 50

GROSSLAGE SCHWARZERDE (KIRCHHEIM)

Kleinniedesheim
Schloßgarten 51
Vorderberg 52

Großniedesheim
Schaftberg 53

Heuchelheim bei Frankenthal
(Ortsteil of Grünstadt Land)
Steinkopf 54

Dirmstein
Herrgottsacker 55
Jesuitenhofgarten 56
Mandelpfad 57

Obersülzen
Schnepp 58

Heßheim
Lange Els 59

Gerolsheim
Lerchenspiel 60
Klosterweg 61

Laumersheim
Kapellberg 62
Mandelberg 63
Kirschgarten 64

Großkarlbach
Burgweg 65
Osterberg 66

Bissersheim
Held 67
Steig 68
Orlenberg 69
Goldbergh 70

Kirchheim an der Weinstraße
Kreuz 71
Römerstraße 72
Steinacker 73

Geißkopf 74

GROSSLAGE ROSENBÜHL (FREINSHEIM)

Lambsheim
Burgweg 75 P

Weisenheim am Sand
Burgweg 75 P
Hahnen 76
Hasenzeile 77
Halde 78
Altenberg 79
Goldberg 80 P

Freinsheim
Goldberg 80 P

Erpolzheim
Goldberg 80 P
Kieselberg 81

GROSSLAGE KOBNERT (KALLSTADT)

Dackenheim
Mandelröth 83
Kapellengarten 84
Liebesbrunnen 85

Weisenheim am Berg
Mandelgarten 86
Sonnenberg 87

Herxheim am Berg
Kirchenstück 88
Himmelreich 89
Honigsack 90

Friensheim
Musikantenbuckel 91
Oschelskopf 92
Schwarzes Kreuz 93

Erpolzheim
Kirschgarten 94

Ungstein
(Ortsteil of Bad Dürkheim)
Osterberg 95
Bettelhaus 96

Kallstadt
Kronenberg 97
Steinacker 98
Saumagen 98 a

Leistadt
(Ortsteil of Bad Dürkheim)
Kalkofen 99
Kirchenstück 100
Herzfeld 101

GROSSLAGE FEUERBERG (BAD DÜRKHEIM)

Bobenheim am Berg
Ohligpfad 102
Kieselberg 103

Weisenheim am Berg
Vogelsang 104

Kallstadt
Annaberg 105
Kreidkeller 106

Leistadt
(Ortsteil of Bad Dürkheim)
Herrenmorgen 107

Bad Dürkheim
Steinberg 108
Nonnengarten 109

Ellerstadt
Sonnenberg 110
Dickkopp 111
Bubeneck 112

Gönnheim
Martinshöhe 113

GROSSLAGE HONIGSÄCKEL (UNGSTEIN)

Ungstein
(Ortsteil of Bad Dürkheim)
Weilberg 117
Herrenberg 118
Nußriegel 119

GROSSLAGE HOCHMESS (BAD DÜRKHEIM)

Ungstein
(Ortsteil of Bad Dürkheim)
Michelsberg 120 P

Bad Dürkheim
Michelsberg 120 P
Spielberg 121
Rittergarten 122
Hochbenn 123

GROSSLAGE SCHENKENBÖHL (WACHENHEIM)

Bad Dürkheim
Abtsfronhof 124
Fronhof 125
Fuchsmantel 126 P

Wachenheim
Fuchsmantel 126 P
Königswingert 127
Mandelgarten 128
Odinstal 129
Schloßberg 130

GROSSLAGE SCHNEPFENFLUG AN DER WEINSTRASSE (FORST AN DER WEINSTRASSE)

Friedelsheim
Kreuz 131
Schloßgarten 132
Bischofsgarten 133 P

Wachenheim
Bischofsgarten 133 P
Luginsland 134

Forst an der Weinstraße
Bischofsgarten 133 P
Süßkopf 135
Stift 136

Deidesheim
Letten 137

GROSSLAGE MARIENGARTEN (FORST AN DER WEINSTRASSE)

Wachenheim
Böhlig 138
Belz 139
Rechbächel 140
Goldbächel 141
Gerümpel 142
Altenburg 143

Forst an der Weinstraße
Musenhang 144
Pechstein 145
Jesuitengarten 146
Kirchenstück 147
Freundstück 148
Ungeheuer 149
Elster 150

Deidesheim
Herrgottsacker 151
Mäushöhle 152
Kieselberg 153
Kalkofen 154
Grainhübel 155
Hohenmorgen 156
Leinhöhle 157
Langenmorgen 158
Paradiesgarten 159

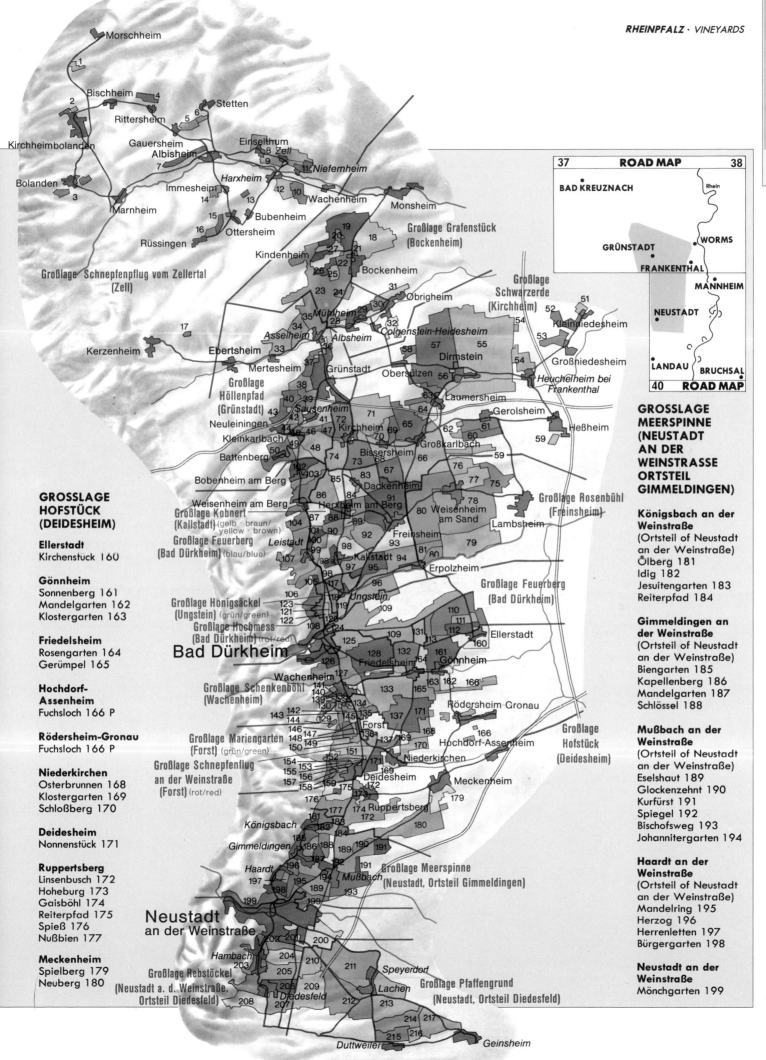

Morschheim

Bischheim

Rittersheim

Stetten

Gauersheim
Albisheim

Einselthum
Zell

Kirchheimbolanden

Niefernheim

Bolanden

Harxheim

Immesheim

Wachenheim

Monsheim

Marnheim

Bubenheim

**Großlage Grafenstück
(Bockenheim)**

Ottersheim

Rüssingen

Kindenheim

**Großlage
Schwarzerde
(Kirchheim)**

Kleinniedesheim

**Großlage Schnepfenpflug vom Zellertal
(Zell)**

Bockenheim

Öbrigheim

Großniedesheim

Kerzenheim

Mühlheim

Colgenstein-Heidesheim

*Heuchelheim bei
Frankenthal*

Ebertsheim

Asselheim

Albsheim

Dirmstein

Mertesheim

Grünstadt

Obersülzen

**Großlage
Höllenpfad
(Grünstadt)**

Laumersheim

Gerolsheim

Heßheim

Neuleiningen

Sausenheim

Kirchheim

**GROSSLAGE
MEERSPINNE
(NEUSTADT
AN DER
WEINSTRASSE
ORTSTEIL
GIMMELDINGEN)**

Kleinkarlbach

Großkarlbach

**Königsbach an der
Weinstraße**
(Ortsteil of Neustadt
an der Weinstraße)
Ölberg 181
Idig 182
Jesuitengarten 183
Reiterpfad 184

Battenberg

Bissersheim

**Großlage Rosenbühl
(Freinsheim)**

Bobenheim am Berg

Dackenheim

**GROSSLAGE
HOFSTÜCK
(DEIDESHEIM)**

Weisenheim am Berg

Herxheim am Berg

**Gimmeldingen an
der Weinstraße**
(Ortsteil of Neustadt
an der Weinstraße)
Biengarten 185
Kapellenberg 186
Mandelgarten 187
Schlössel 188

Ellerstadt
Kirchenstück 160

Gönnheim
Sonnenberg 161
Mandelgarten 162
Klostergarten 163

**Großlage Kobnert
(Kallstadt)** (gelb - braun/
yellow - brown)

**Großlage Feuerberg
(Bad Dürkheim)** (blau/blue)

Leistadt

Weisenheim
am Sand

Lambsheim

Freinsheim

Friedelsheim
Rosengarten 164
Gerümpel 165

**Großlage Honigsäckel
(Ungstein)** (grün/green)

Kallstadt

Erpolzheim

**Großlage Feuerberg
(Bad Dürkheim)**

**Mußbach an der
Weinstraße**
(Ortsteil of Neustadt
an der Weinstraße)
Eselshaut 189
Glockenzehnt 190
Kurfürst 191
Spiegel 192
Bischofsweg 193
Johannitergarten 194

**Hochdorf-
Assenheim**
Fuchsloch 166 P

**Großlage Hochmess
(Bad Dürkheim)** (rot/red)

Ungstein

Bad Dürkheim

Ellerstadt

**Rödersheim-
Gronau**
Fuchsloch 166 P

Wachenheim

Friedelsheim

Gönnheim

Niederkirchen
Osterbrunnen 168
Klostergarten 169
Schloßberg 170

**Großlage Schenkenböhl
(Wachenheim)**

Rödersheim-Gronau

**Haardt an der
Weinstraße**
(Ortsteil of Neustadt
an der Weinstraße)
Mandelring 195
Herzog 196
Herrenletten 197
Bürgergarten 198

Deidesheim
Nonnenstück 171

**Großlage Mariengarten
(Forst)** (grün/green)

Forst

Hochdorf-Assenheim

**Großlage
Hofstück
(Deidesheim)**

Ruppertsberg
Linsenbusch 172
Hoheburg 173
Gaisböhl 174
Reiterpfad 175
Spieß 176
Nußbien 177

**Großlage Schnepfenflug
an der Weinstraße
(Forst)** (rot/red)

Deidesheim

Niederkirchen

Meckenheim

**Neustadt an der
Weinstraße**
Mönchgarten 199

Meckenheim
Spielberg 179
Neuberg 180

Königsbach

Ruppertsberg

Gimmeldingen

**Großlage Meerspinne
(Neustadt, Ortsteil Gimmeldingen)**

Haardt

Mußbach

**Neustadt
an der Weinstraße**

Hambach

**Großlage Rebstöckel
(Neustadt a. d. Weinstraße,
Ortsteil Diedesfeld)**

Speyerdorf

Lachen

**Großlage Pfaffengrund
(Neustadt, Ortsteil Diedesfeld)**

Diedesfeld

Duttweiler

Geinsheim

37 **ROAD MAP** 38

BAD KREUZNACH

Rhein

GRÜNSTADT

WORMS

FRANKENTHAL

MANNHEIM

NEUSTADT

LANDAU

BRUCHSAL

40 **ROAD MAP**

**GROSSLAGE
REBSTÖCKEL
(NEUSTADT
AN DER
WEINSTRASSE
ORTSTEIL
DIEDESFELD)**

**Neustadt an der
Weinstraße**
Grain 200
Erkenbrecht 201

**Hambach an der
Weinstraße**
(Ortsteil of Neustadt
an der Weinstraße)
Kaiserstuhl 202
Kirchberg 203
Feuer 204
Schloßberg 205

**Diedesfeld an der
Weinstraße**
(Ortsteil of Neustadt
an der Weinstraße)
Ölgässel 206
Johanniskirchel 207
Paradies 208

**GROSSLAGE
PFAFFENGRUND
(NEUSTADT
AN DER
WEINSTRASSE,
ORTSTEIL
DIEDESFELD)**

Diedesfeld
(Ortsteil of Neustadt
an der Weinstraße)
Berg 209

Hambach/Weinstraße
(Ortsteil of Neustadt)
Römerbrunnen 210

Lachen-Speyerdorf
(Ortsteil of Neustadt
an der Weinstraße)
Langenstein 211
Lerchenböhl 212
Kroatenpfad 213

Duttweiler
(Ortsteil of Neustadt
an der Weinstraße)
Kreuzberg 214
Mandelberg 215
Kalkberg 216

Geinsheim
(Ortsteil of Neustadt
an der Weinstraße)
Gässel 217

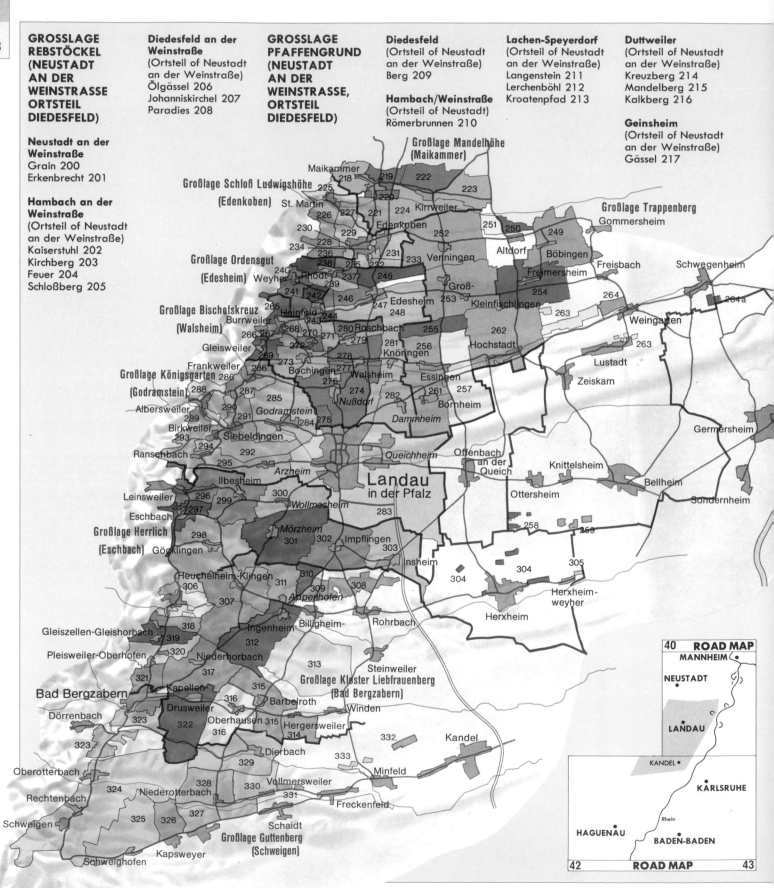

BEREICH SÜDLICHE WEINSTRASSE

GROSSLAGE MANDELHÖHE (MAIKAMMER)

Maikammer
Alsterweiler
   Kapellenberg 218
Kirchenstück 219
Immengarten 220
Heiligenberg 221

Kirrweiler
Römerweg 222
Mandelberg 223
Oberschloß 224

GROSSLAGE SCHLOSS LUDWIGSHÖHE (EDENKOBEN)

St. Martin
Kirchberg 225
Baron 226
Zitadelle 227

Edenkoben
Bergel 228
Heilig Kreuz 229
Klostergarten 230
Heidegarten 231
Kirchberg 232
Blücherhöhe 233
Mühlberg 234
Schwarzer Letten
   235
Kastaniengarten 236

GROSSLAGE ORDENSGUT (EDESHEIM)

Rhodt unter Rietburg
Klosterpfad 237
Schloßberg 238
Rosengarten 239

Weyher in der Pfalz
Michelsberg 240
Heide 241

Hainfeld
Letten 242
Kapelle 243
Kirchenstück 244

Edesheim
Forst 245
Mandelhang 246
Schloß 247
Rosengarten 248

GROSSLAGE TRAPPENBERG (HOCHSTADT)

Böbingen
Ortelberg 249

Altdorf
Gottesacker 250
Hochgericht 251

Venningen
Doktor 252

Groß- und Kleinfischlingen
Kirchberg 253

Freimersheim
Bildberg 254

Essingen
Roßberg 255
Sonnenberg 256
Osterberg 257

Ottersheim
Kahlenberg 258

Knittelsheim
Gollenberg 259 P

Bellheim
Gollenberg 259 P

Bornheim
Neuberg 261

Hochstadt
Roter Berg 262

Zeiskam
Klostergarten 263 P

Lustadt
Klostergarten 263 P

Weingarten
Schloßberg 264

Schwegenheim
Bründelsberg 264 a

Römerberg (bei Speyer)
Ortsteil Mechtersheim
Schlittberg 264 b
Alter Berg 264 c P

– Ortsteil Heiligenstein
Alter Berg 264 c P
Narrenberg 264 d P

– Ortsteil Berghausen
Narrenberg 264 d P

Also vineyards without site-names in the parishes of Gommersheim (22ha) and Offenbach (0.6ha).

GROSSLAGE BISCHOFSKREUZ (WALSHEIM)

Burrweiler
Altenforst 265
St. Annaberg 266
Schäwer 267
Schloßgarten 268

Gleisweiler
Hölle 269

Flemlingen
Herrenbuckel 270
Vogelsprung 271
Zechpeter 272

Böchingen
Rosenkranz 273

Nußdorf
(Ortsteil of Landau in der Pfalz)
Herrenberg 274
Kaiserberg 275
Kirchenstück 276

Walsheim
Forstweg 277
Silberberg 278

Roschbach
Simonsgarten 279
Rosenkränzel 280

Knöringen
Hohenrain 281

Dammheim
(Ortsteil of Landau in der Pfalz)
Höhe 282

GROSSLAGE KÖNIGSGARTEN (GODRAMSTEIN)

Landau in der Pfalz
incl. Queichheim and Mörlheim
Altes Löhl 283

Godramstein
(Ortsteil of Landau in der Pfalz)
Klostergarten 284
Münzberg 285

Frankweiler
Kalkgrube 286
Biengarten 287

Albersweiler
Latt 288
   (St. Johann)
Kirchberg 289

Siebeldingen
Mönchspfad 290
Im Sonnenschein 291
Rosenberg 292 P

Birkweiler
Rosenberg 292 P
Kastanienbusch 293
Mandelberg 294

Ranschbach
Seligmacher 295 P

Arzheim
(Ortsteil of Landau in der Pfalz)
Rosenberg 292 P
Seligmacher 295 P

Vineyard (6ha) not registered as Einz. in the parish of Gräfenhausen.

GROSSLAGE HERRLICH (ESCHBACH)

Leinsweiler
Sonnenberg 296 P

Eschbach
Hasen 297

Göcklingen
Kaiserberg 298

Ilbesheim
Sonnenberg 296 P
Rittersberg 299

Wollmesheim
(Ortsteil of Landau in der Pfalz)
Mütterie 300

Mörzheim
(Ortsteil of Landau in der Pfalz)
Pfaffenberg 301

Impflingen
Abtsberg 302

Insheim
Schäfergarten 303 P

Rohrbach
Schäfergarten 303 P

Herxheim bei Landau in der Pfalz
Engelsberg 304

Herxheimweyher
Am Gaisberg 305

GROSSLAGE KLOSTER LIEBFRAUENBERG (BAD BERGZABERN)

Klingenmünster
Maria Magdalena 306

Göcklingen
Herrenpfad 307 P

Heuchelheim-Klingen
Herrenpfad 307 P

Rohrbach
Mandelpfad 308 P

Billigheim-Ingenheim
Mandelpfad 308 P
   (Billigheim)
Venusbuckel 309
   (Billigheim)
Sauschwänzel 310
   (Billigheim)
Steingebiß 311
   (Appenhofen)
Pfaffenberg 312
   (Ingenheim)
Rosenberg 313 P
   (Mühlhofen and Billigheim)

Steinweiler
Rosenberg 313 P

Winden
Narrenberg 314 P

Hergersweiler
Narrenberg 314 P

Barbelroth
Kirchberg 315

Oberhausen
Frohnwingert 316

Niederhorbach
Silberberg 317

Gleiszellen-Gleishorbach
Kirchberg 318
Frühmess 319

Pleisweiler-Oberhofen
Schloßberg 320

Bad Bergzabern
Altenberg 321

Kapellen-Drusweiler
Rosengartan 322

GROSSLAGE GUTTENBERG (SCHWEIGEN)

Bad Bergzabern
Wonneberg 323 P

Dörrenbach
Wonneberg 323 P

Oberotterbach
Sonnenberg 324 P

Schweigen-Rechtenbach
Sonnenberg 324 P

Schweighofen
Sonnenberg 324 P
Wolfsberg 325

Kapsweyer
Lerchenberg 326

Steinfeld
Herrenwingert 327

Niederotterbach
Eselsbuckel 328

Dierbach
Kirchhöh 329

Vollmersweiler
Krapfenberg 330

Freckenfeld
Gräfenberg 331

Kandel
Galgenberg 332

Minfeld
Herrenberg 333

HESSISCHE BERGSTRASSE

Germany's smallest separate wine region lies across the Rhine from Worms, in steep – even terraced – hills north of Heidelberg with a westerly outlook over the Rhine valley. The topography is similar to that of northern Baden, and geographically, if not officially, the region is a continuation of Baden. The Baden vineyards begin at Heidelberg, only 30km (18 miles) to the south. The vineyards are protected by the Odenwald hills to the east, and the southwest-facing slopes provide good exposure. Average temperatures are high, on a par with Baden.

The region is divided into two Bereiche: Umstadt, a remote forested area, away from the Rhine east of Darmstadt, and Starkenburg, a north–south hillside 16km (10 miles) long, containing Bensheim, Heppenheim and five other villages with three Großlagen and 18 Einzellagen. A couple of vineyards at Seeheim and Alsbach form a northerly continuation of the Starkenburg.

With light sandy loam on its west slopes, Starkenburg is warm enough to ripen the Riesling which dominates its vineyards, and Müller-Thurgau, Ruländer, Silvaner, Gewürztraminer, Spätburgunder, Kerner, Ehrenfelser, Scheurebe and Weißburgunder are also grown. From Zwingenberg to Bensheim the soil is decomposed granite, with yellow sandstone and loess in the Heppenheim vineyards. Late-harvest Ruländers in Heppenheim can have great character and have reached Trockenbeerenauslese in sweetness. The town of Bensheim, the centre of the Bereich, also has a small estate (in the Großlage Wolfsmagen) with an important yield of Rotberger, made into rosé. The five small vineyards that make up the isolated Umstadt Bereich grow Müller-Thurgau, Silvaner, Ruländer and Riesling. The total area under vine is 380 hectares.

There are over 1,000 growers, many part-time, and most of the wine is made in the two cooperatives, the Bergsträßer at Heppenheim and the Odenwälder at Groß Umstadt. Both have Weinstuben, as do a score of small growers and the State Domain. The holdings are small and the vineyards often steep, making mechanization difficult. Most Hessiche Bergstraße wine is drunk locally, either in cafés and restaurants or in Weinstuben and Straußwirtschaften – growers' taverns.

▼ A steep vineyard in the Hessische Bergstraße still has its share of fruit trees in almost Italian-style "promiscuous cultivation". Modern monoculture is miles away.

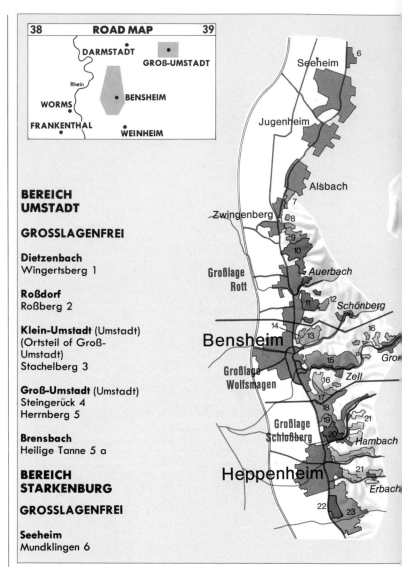

ROAD MAP 38 39

DARMSTADT
GROSS-UMSTADT
Rhein
BENSHEIM
WORMS
FRANKENTHAL
WEINHEIM

BEREICH UMSTADT

GROSSLAGENFREI

Dietzenbach
Wingertsberg 1

Roßdorf
Roßberg 2

Klein-Umstadt (Umstadt)
(Ortsteil of Groß-Umstadt)
Stachelberg 3

Groß-Umstadt (Umstadt)
Steingerück 4
Herrnberg 5

Brensbach
Heilige Tanne 5 a

BEREICH STARKENBURG

GROSSLAGENFREI

Seeheim
Mundklingen 6

TRAVEL INFORMATION

This small but attractive region is much visited by townspeople from nearby Darmstadt and Frankfurt. It is a land of orchards as well as vines: it is known as the "Spring Garden" from its profusion of blossoms. Much of the wine made there is drunk by the visitors. The taverns and winegrowers' Stuben apart, the main attractions are the little towns which line the edge of the Rhine valley. Heppenheim with its ancient marketplace, town hall and nearby Starkenburg castle, is especially worth a visit. The Staatspark, near Bensheim, is a botanical garden which takes full advantage of the Bergstraße's benign climate.

The forest country to the east is a nature park, with a spa at Grasellenbach. Signposted tourist roads recalling German legends run through the region: the *Siegfriedstraße* and the *Nibelungenstraße* run from west to east. The Bergstraße itself, which offers castles and vineyards, follows the line of the hills from north to south. Heidelberg (*see* Baden) is not far to the south.

Regional Wine Information Office
Weinbauverband Bergstraße
Königsberger Straße 4
6148 Heppenheim/Bergstraße
Tel: 06252-77101

GROSSLAGE WOLFSMAGEN

Bensheim
Kalkgasse 13
Kirchberg 14
Streichling 15 P
Hemsberg 16 P
Paulus 17

Zell
(Ortsteil of Bensheim)
Streichling 15 P
Hemsberg 16 P

Gronau
(Ortsteil of Bensheim)
Hemsberg 16 P

GROSSLAGE SCHLOSSBERG

Heppenheim
Stemmler 18 P
Centgericht 19
Steinkopf 20 P
Maiberg 21 P
Guldenzoll 22
Eckweg 23

Hambach
(Ortsteil of Heppenheim)
Stemmler 18 P
Steinkopf 20 P
Maiberg 21 P

Erbach
(Ortsteil of Heppenheim)
Maiberg 21 P

GROSSLAGE ROTT

Alsbach
Schöntal 7

Zwingenberg
Steingeröll 8
Alte Burg 9

Auerbach
(Ortsteil of Bensheim)
Höllberg 10
Fürstenlager 11

Schönberg
(Ortsteil of Bensheim)
Herrnwingert 12

SUMMARY OF RECENT VINTAGES IN THE FIVE MAIN EXPORTING REGIONS

		MOSEL-SAAR-RUWER	NAHE	RHEIN-GAU	RHEIN-HESSEN	RHEIN-PFALZ
TOTAL QUANTITY OF WINE DECLARED AT HARVEST, IN HECTOLITRES						
1985		1,195,000	263,000	180,000	1,082,000	1,388,000
1984		1,106,000	312,000	163,000	1,855,000	2,311,000
1983		1,829,000	612,000	298,825	3,400,000	3,252,000
1982		2,365,000	716,700	485,000	3,773,000	3,847,000
1981		1,113,500	249,900	171,500	1,724,500	2,166,700
1980		571,500	132,600	101,500	1,145,000	1,593,900
1979		1,090,000	265,000	280,000	1,480,000	2,550,000
1976		1,040,000	366,000	228,000	1,960,000	2,310,000
PERCENTAGE OF QUALITY WINE, BY CATEGORY						
1985	QbA	63	57	40	38	47
	Kabinett	27	27	53	28	32
	Spätlese	8	13	6	29	17
	Auslese	2	3	1	5	4
1984	QbA	79	82	73	78	75
	Kabinett	1	1	1	6	7
	Spätlese	—	—	—	1	2
	Auslese	—	—	—	—	—
1983	QbA	43	48	30	46	52
	Kabinett	12	15	50	19	23
	Spätlese	31	25	19	25	16
	Auslese	9	8	0	2	3
1982	QbA	61	67	74	73	72
	Kabinett	30	24	25	18	12
	Spätlese	4	5	0	7	4
	Auslese	2	1	0	0	0
1981	QbA	63	54	71	54	54
	Kabinett	28	35	25	35	33
	Spätlese	9	10	2	10	11
	Auslese	0	1	0	1	2
1980	QbA	75	60	83	57	62
	Kabinett	15	24	15	23	20
	Spätlese	2	9	0	17	12
	Auslese	0	1	0	3	2
1979	QbA	37	16	59	16	46
	Kabinett	14	25	32	21	28
	Spätlese	38	48	7	58	17
	Auslese	11	11	0	5	3
1976	QbA	8	11	11	6	20
	Kabinett	10	26	22	8	30
	Spätlese	34	38	46	64	33
	Auslese	46	25	20	22	15
	Beeren-auslese	2	1	1	2	2

EASTERN ZONE

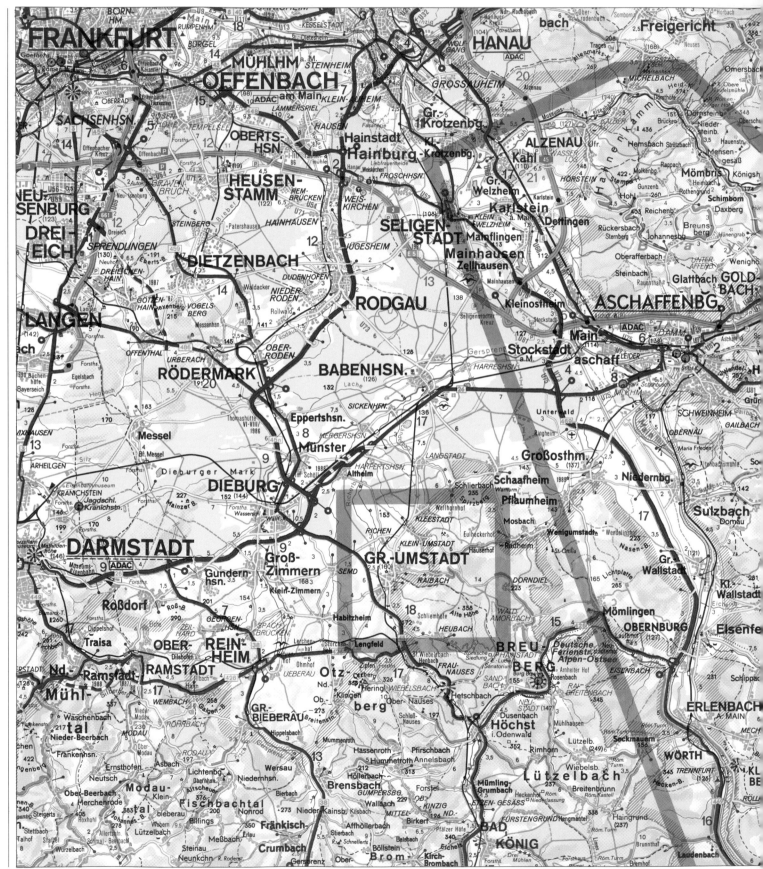

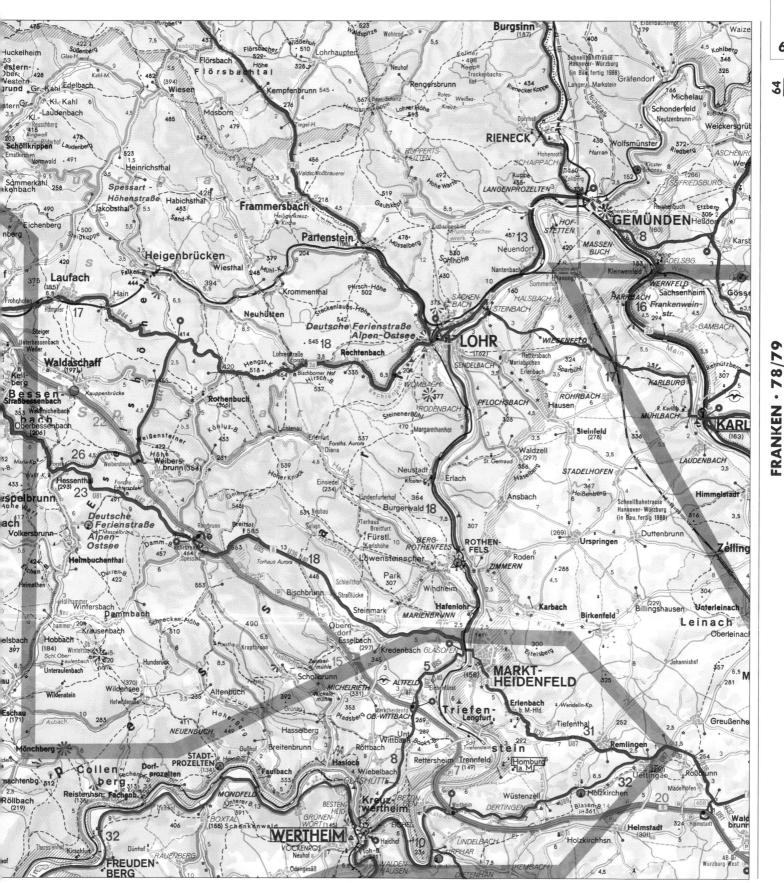

64

63

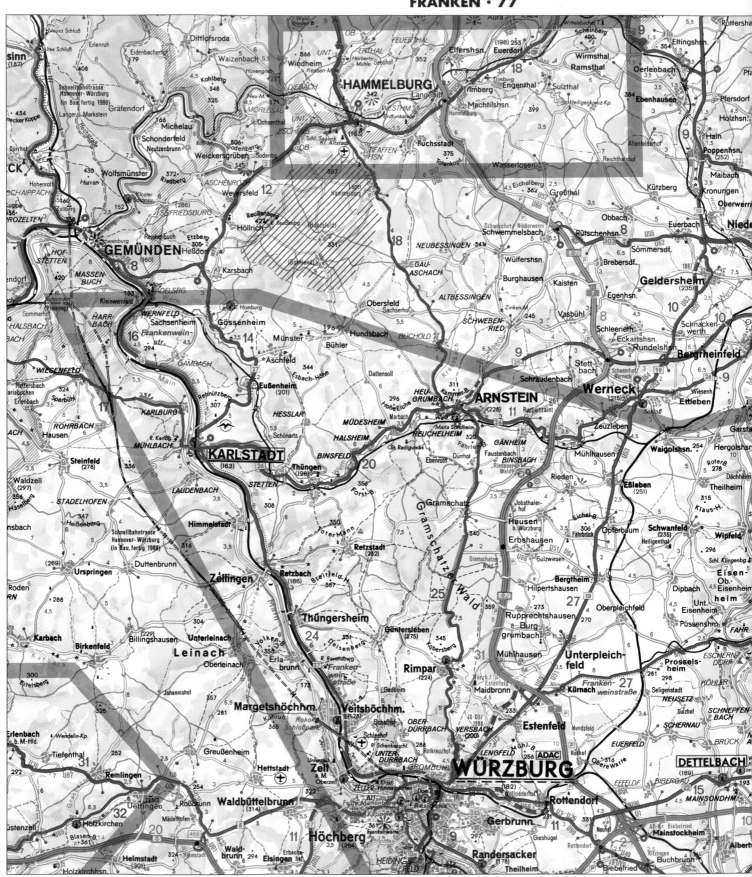

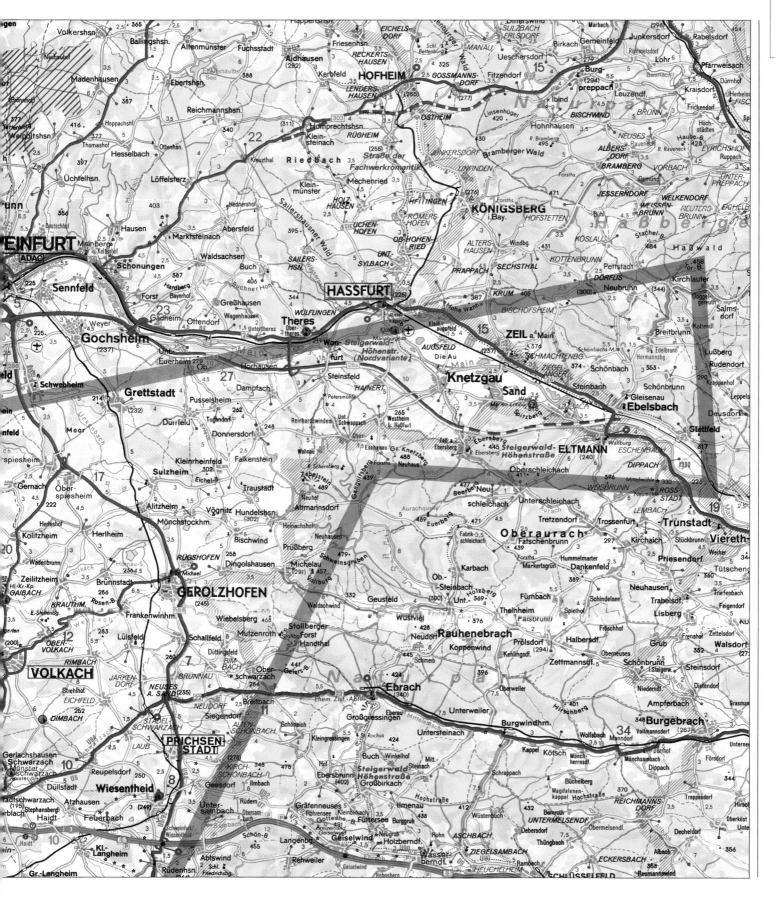

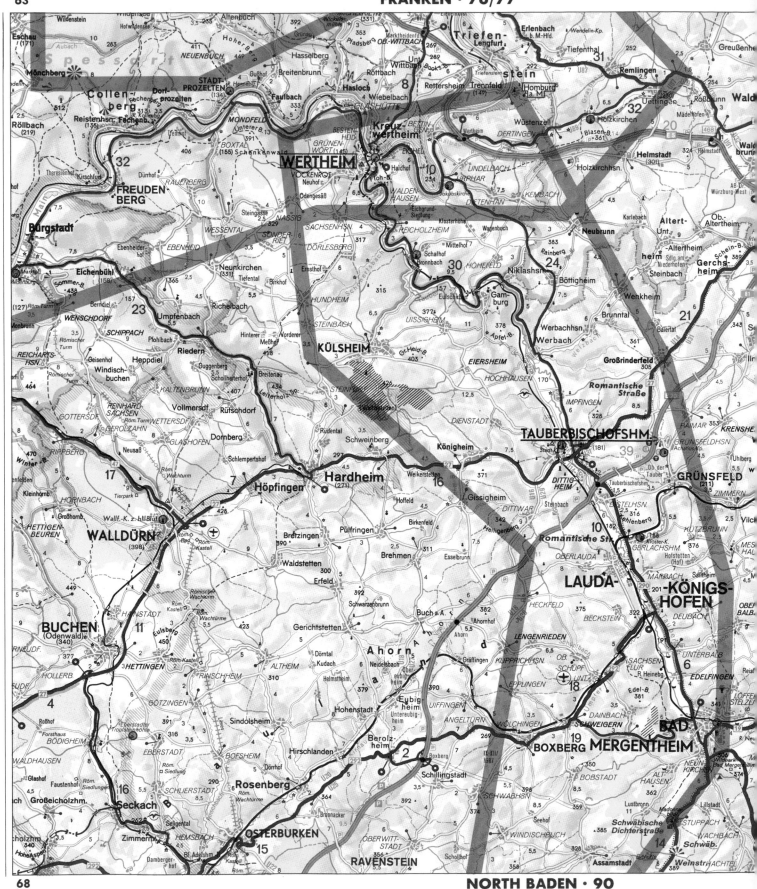

67

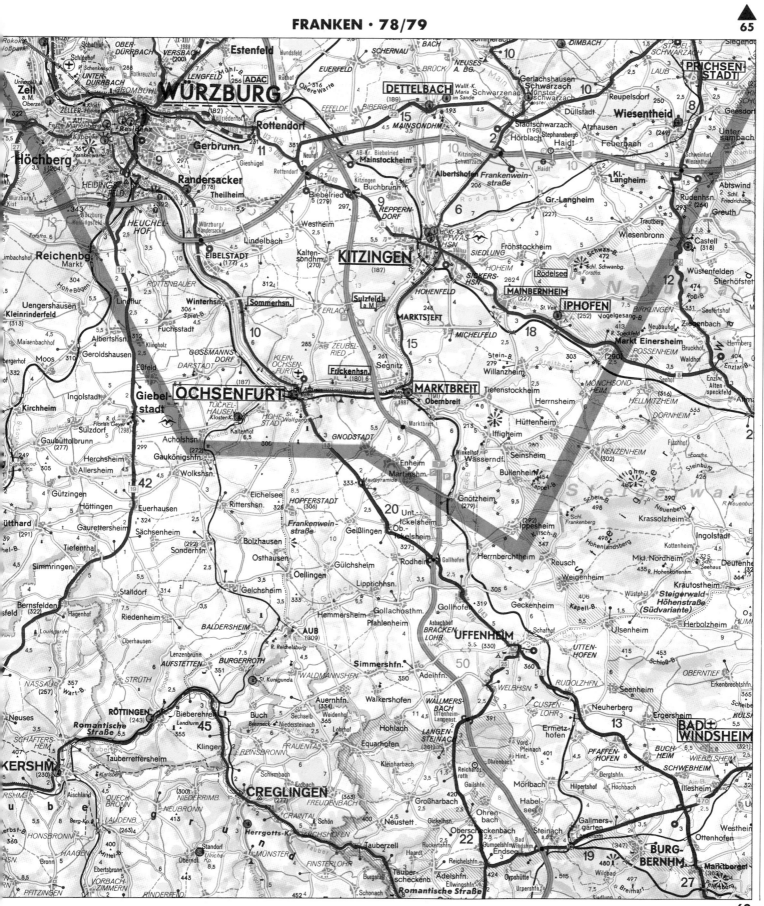

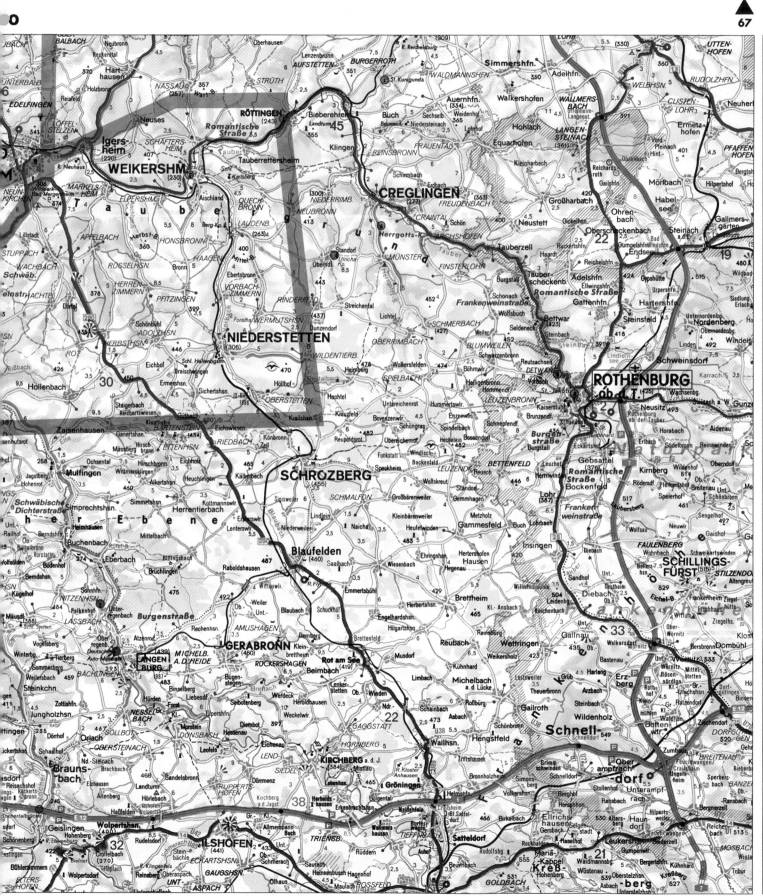

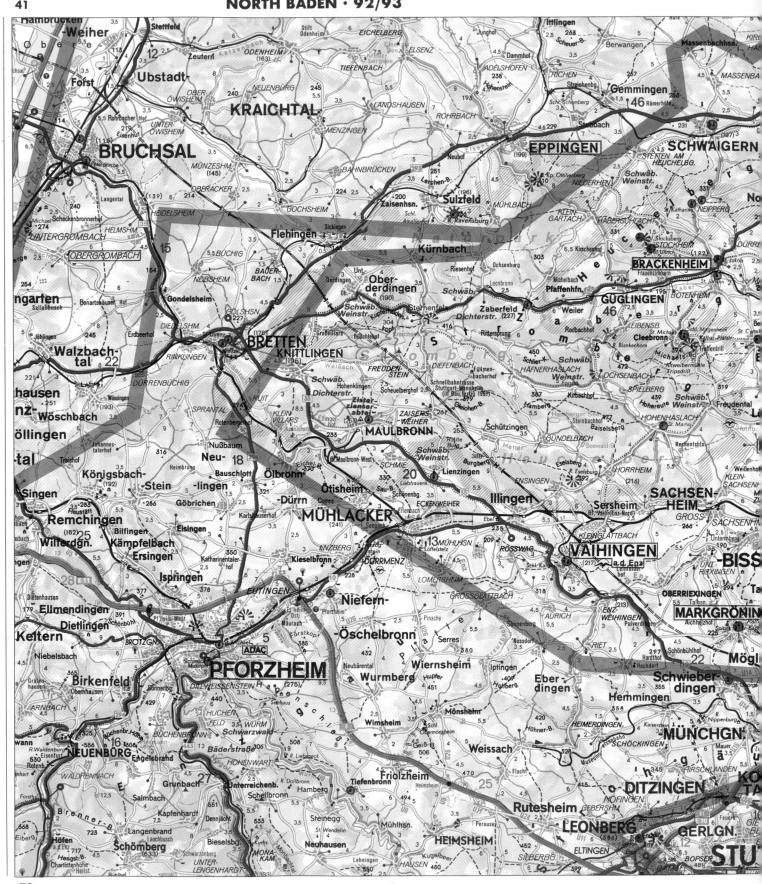

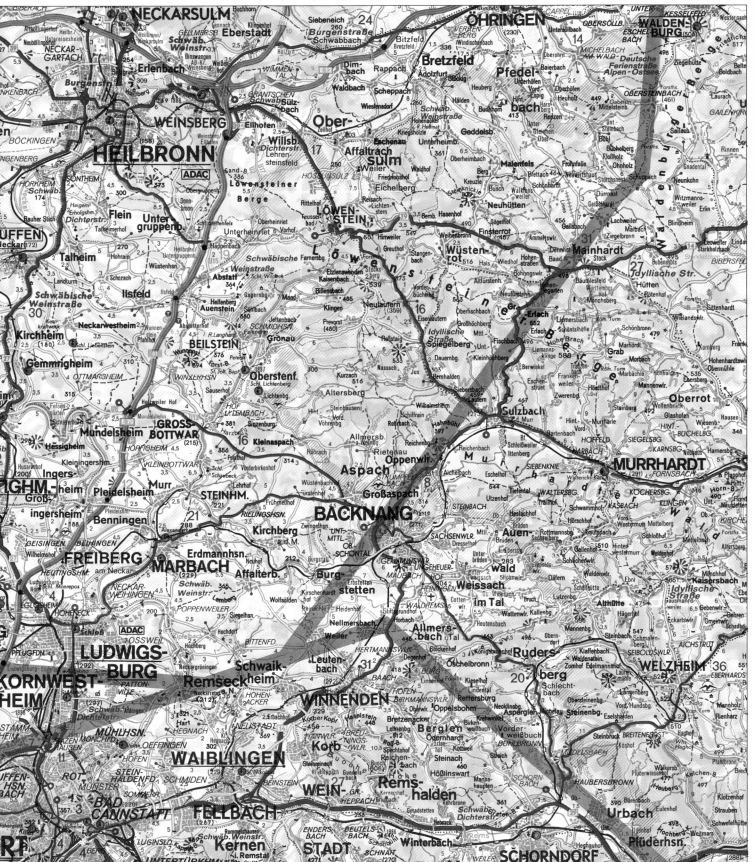

70

72

97

Oberlen
genhardt
Buhlhof
(581)
UNTER-
LENGENHARDT
KAM
HAUSEN 480
MALMSHEIM
RENNINGEN
12
STUTTGART
BAD LIEBENZELL
(333)
MÜNKLINGEN 3
MERKLINGEN
Schwäb.
WARMBRONN
15
MAISEN-
BACH
BEINBERG
721 7,5
Calmbach
Zainen
Thermalb.
UNTERHAUGSTETT
Georgenau
MÖTTINGEN
Freundschafts-
straße
Kindelbg.
Dichterstraße Warmbr. K.
Magstadt
Freundschafts-
straße Igelsloch
296 Siedhichtür
675
Oberkollbach
Obr.
 ALZEN-
BG.
Simmozhm.
Büchelbronn
WEIL
DER STADT
(405)
17
ZAVELSTN.
CALW
(347)
Althengstett Ostelshm.
Grafenau
Döffingen
SINDELFINGEN
(446)
BAD
TEINACH-
Gechingen
551
Aidlingen
BÖBLINGEN
WILDBERG
Ehningen
15
Holz-
gerlingen
Schönaich
HERRENBERG
NAGOLD
(411)
TÜBINGEN
(341)
Rottenburg
(349)
ROTTENBURG
REUTLINGEN
HORB
a.N.
MÖSSINGEN

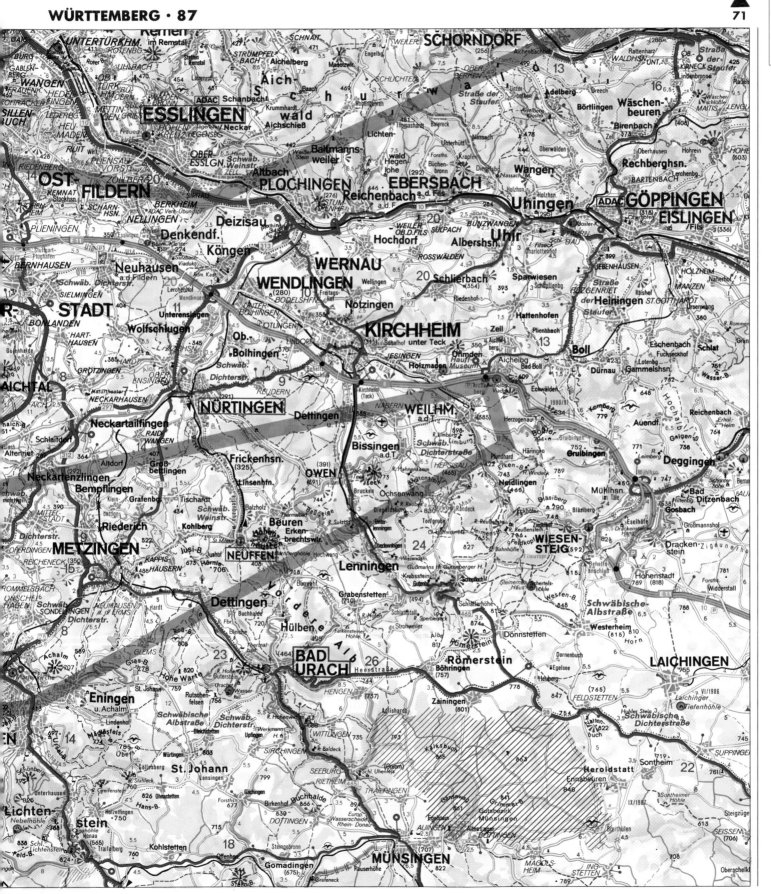

FRANKEN

Eighty kilometres (50 miles) east of the Rheingau, beyond the city of Frankfurt, the river Main, flowing to join the Rhine at Mainz, scribbles a huge drunken W through the irregular limestone and red marl hills of Franken (Franconia), the northern extremity of Bavaria.

The centre of the region is the baroque city of Würzburg. Its most famous vineyard, sloping down to the Main within the city itself, is Würzburger Stein. The name Stein has been traditionally borrowed by foreigners to describe Franconian wine generically (as the English shortened Hochheim to "hock" for all Rhine wines). "Steinwein" comes in fat flagons called Bocksbeutels, thus distinguishing itself from almost all other German wines.

This is probably the extent of popular knowledge. Frankenwein is a somewhat specialized subject, not least because a severe, "continental" climate often results in a small harvest, and most of the wine is drunk in Bavaria, particularly in Munich, or in the wealthy cities of northern Germany. The area is exceptionally diffuse and far less easy to comprehend than regions such as the Rheingau or Mosel-Saar-Ruwer. But effort has its reward and the wines of Franken are well worth getting to know.

Traditionally, Franken has made its best wine with the Silvaner, and here (and in certain exceptional sites elsewhere, such as the Nierstein Rheinterrasse and parts of the Kaiserstuhl), it can reach considerable heights. The wine is full-bodied with a noble breadth and substance; dense, even sticky in its intensity. It is regularly compared with white burgundy, not for its flavour but for sheer vinosity and ability to match rich food at table.

Although Müller-Thurgau, the most widely grown wine in the region – it covers 50 per cent of the vineyard area – cannot quite match Silvaner for depth and seriousness, it can produce excellent *spritzig* wine in Franken, quite above its theoretical station. Scheurebe and the new Perle can do better still. Bacchus tends to be rather aromatic here and less characteristic of the region. Kerner is also aromatic. Rieslaner, in a ripe year, can make excellent Auslesen with the breadth of a Silvaner and the depth of a Riesling. The 1976 vintage in the Steigerwald produced some extraordinary wines with a bouquet like salty honey.

Auslesen, however, are rarer in Franken than elsewhere in Germany, and Beeren- and Trockenbeerenauslesen very rare indeed. Although one of the most famous wines of all time, a Würzburger Stein of the (almost literally) immortal vintage of 1546, was certainly as sweet as a Beerenauslese when it started on its long career (it was drunk, with awe, at the age of 420), the Franken style generally finds its best expression in Kabinett and Spätlesen – and sometimes in well-balanced QbA wines.

This rambling region is divided into three Bereiche: Mainviereck for its lower reaches towards Frankfurt; Maindreieck for its heart, the district of Würzburg; and Steigerwald for its eastern extremities, with the sternest climate of all. The river Main is the unifying factor of the two western Bereiche. Further east the pattern becomes less clear.

The Bereich Mainviereck extends across the famous Spessart forest from Aschaffenburg in the northwest down to Kreuzwertheim in the first trough of the W described by the Main. The very limited vineyard area is all close to the river with the exception of Rück, a little eastern side-valley.

The eastern trough of the W, in the Bereich Maindreieck, is the centre of Franken wine production, with Würzburg at its heart. The main concentrations of vines are in the villages north and

▲ Miltenberg, on the Main, is typical of the scattered Franken wine districts in having only one vineyard site: the south-facing lower slopes of the Burgstadt, the forest-crowned hill that looms over the town.

south of Würzburg along the river, all on limestone, down to Frickenhausen, the foot of the eastern trough, and north again in bends in the river higher up around Escherndorf and Nordheim, still on limestone but here with an overlay of marly clay. The famous hill of Escherndorfer Lump makes great Silvaners from this soil structure. The wines of all the principal vineyards can be tasted and compared at the big, bustling Weinstuben of the three great Würzburg estates, the Juliusspital, the Bürgerspital and the Staatliche Hofkeller (see Travel Information).

Bereich Steigerwald consists of a collection of scattered vineyards in a hundred warm corners, with no helpful river valley to string them together. Iphofen, Rödelsee and Castell are the best-known wine communities, all on heavier marly clay soil which demands a fine summer but can produce both full-bodied and nicely nuanced wines.

The Bereich names are frequently used for Franken wine, partly because a great number of the far-flung vineyards are included in no Großlage. The majority of the wine, as in Rheinhessen and Baden, is made by cooperatives.

TRAVEL INFORMATION

The sprawling wine region of Franken follows the river Main as it meanders through the forests of central Germany. The Rhine, with its lighthearted atmosphere, is left behind as the traveller enters the heart of Central Europe, a land of forests, ancient cities and baroque masterpieces.

Places to visit

Würzburg: the capital of Franken and an architectural masterpiece, the epicentre of the German Baroque. It is also the home of the greatest Franken wine estates. These manage to combine art and wine in happy sympathy. The Bavarian State Cellars, for instance, houses its casks in the vaults beneath the great Residenz of the former prince-bishops of this most Catholic of cities. The cellars are grand enough, but the Residenz itself, with its Tiepolo ceilings and other decorations, is magnificent.

The Residenz was built in the mid-eighteenth century to the designs of Balthasar Neumann, the court architect. Tiepolo, the Venetian master of the fresco, was commissioned to depict two incidents in Barbarossa's life in the Kaisersaal or Imperial Hall. The Kaisersaal is now the venue for a Mozartfest during the second half of June, and the galleries host exhibitions.

Earlier in the city's history the ruling prince-bishops built the Marienberg fortress, which now houses the Mainfränkisches Museum. The greatest treasures here are the works of the late-Gothic sculptor Riemenschneider, the Master of Würzburg. He specialized in superbly detailed limewood altar-pieces and free-standing figures. The Romanesque St. Kilian Cathedral also houses works by Riemenschneider. The State Cellars apart, winelovers can imbibe culture as well as Franken wine at various ancient cellars such as that beneath the Juliusspital (Juliuspromenade, tel: 0931-54080), which belongs to a church charity, and the Bürgerspital (Theaterstraße, tel: 0931-13861),

a municipal one. The Juliusspital's cellar dates from 1699, the buildings of the Bürgerspital date from the Middle Ages. The charity, which is dedicated to the Holy Ghost, was founded in 1413 for the relief of Würzburg's aged citzens.

Other places to visit include Dettelbach: a small town on the Main east of Würzburg, noted for its 36 towers. Iphofen: an old town deep in the countryside east of the Main, on the edge of the Steigerwald.

Wine festivals

Würzburg has a festival in late September, Gambach in late October. Others include: Röttingen (late May), Dettelbach & Stammheim (early June), Rimbach (3rd w/e in June), Obereisenheim (early July), Aschaffenburg (2nd w/e in July), Castell (3rd w/e in July), Homburg (end July), Volkach (mid Aug), Escherndorf (2nd w/e in Sept and also in Oct), Fahr (mid-Oct).

Food and drink

Franken is known for beer as well as wine: many towns and villages have their own breweries. Plum and other fruit brandies are also made here. Nowhere else in Germany has quite Franken's profusion of inns, serving food such as pig's knuckle and Sauerkraut, grilled sausages and *Meerefischli* — small fish from the rivers.

Regional Wine Information Office

Frankenwein-Frankenland e.V.
Juliusspital-Weingut
Postfach 5848
8700 Würzburg
Tel: 0931-12093

BEREICH MAINVIERECK

GROSSLAGE REUSCHBERG

Hörstein
(Ortsteil of Alzenau)
Abtsberg 1
Other vineyards 2

GROSSLAGENFREI

Wasserlos
(Ortsteil of Alzenau)
Schloßberg 3
Luhmannchen 3 a

Michelbach
(Ortsteil of Alzenau)
Steinberg 4
Apostelgarten 5

Aschaffenburg
Pompejaner 6
Godelsberg 6 a

Obernau
(Ortsteil of Aschaffenburg)
Sanderberg 7

Rottenberg
(Ortsteil of Hösbach)
Gräfenstein 7 a

GROSSLAGE HEILIGENTHAL

Großostheim
Reischklingeberg 8
Harstell 9
Also vineyards in the parish of Wenigumstadt

GROSSLAGENFREI

Großwaltstadt
Lützeltalerberg 10

Rück
(Ortsteil of Elsenfeld)
Johannisberg 11
Schalk 11 a
Jesuitenberg 12

Erienbach am Main
Hochberg 13

Klingenberg am Main
Hochberg 14
Einsiedel 14 a
Schloßberg 15

Großheubach
Bischofsberg 16

ROAD MAP

62		63

OFFENBACH

ASCHAFFENBURG

Main

DARMSTADT

GROSS-
UMSTADT

BAD MERGENTHEIM

39	ROAD MAP	66

Engelsberg
(Ortsteil of
Großheubach)
Klostergarten 17

Miltenberg
Steingrübler 18

Bürgstadt
Mainhölle 19
Centgrafenberg 20

Dorfprozelten
Predigtstuhl 21

Kreuzwertheim
Kaffelstein 22

**BEREICH
MAINDREIECK**

GROSSLAGENFREI

Homburg am Main
(Ortsteil of
Triefenstein)
Kallmuth 23
Edelfrau 24

Lengfurt
(Ortsteil of
Triefenstein)
Alter Berg 25
Oberrot 26

**Erlenbach (bei
Marktheidenfeld)**
incl. Ortsteil
Tiefenthal
Krähenschnabel 27 P

Marktheidenfeld
Kreuzberg 27 a

Remlingen
Krähenschnabel 27 P
Sonnenhain 27 b

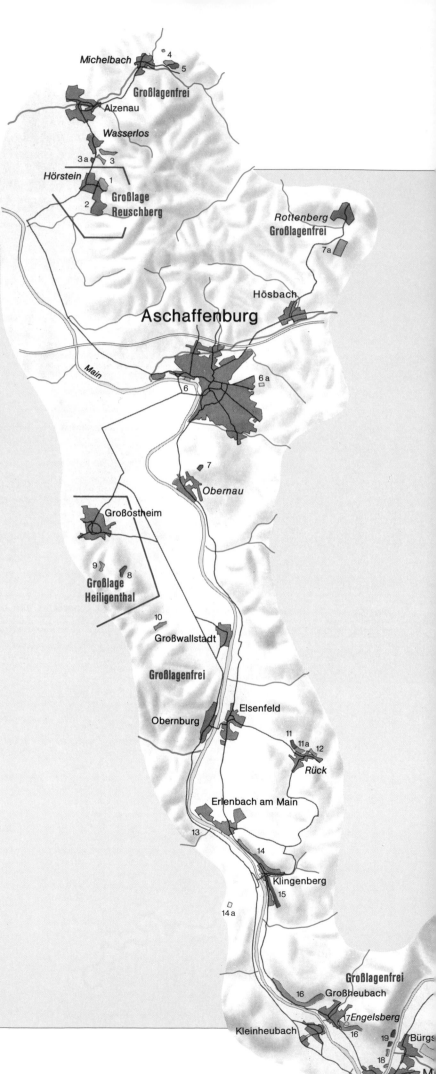

| 64 | **ROAD MAP** | 65 |

GROSSLAGE BURG (HAMMELBURG)

Saaleck
(Ortsteil of Hammelburg)
Schloßberg 28

Hammelburg
Heroldsberg 29
Trautlestal 30

Feuerthal
(Ortsteil of Hammelburg)
Kreuz 30 a

Westheim
(Ortsteil of Hammelburg)
Längberg 30 b

Trimberg
(Ortsteil of Elfershausen)
Schloßberg 30 c P

Engenthal
(Ortsteil of Elfershausen)
Schloßberg 30 c P

Machtilshausen
(Ortsteil of Elfershausen)
Sommerleite 30 d

Ramsthal
St. Klausen 31

Wirmsthal
(Ortsteil of Euerdorf)
Scheinberg 32

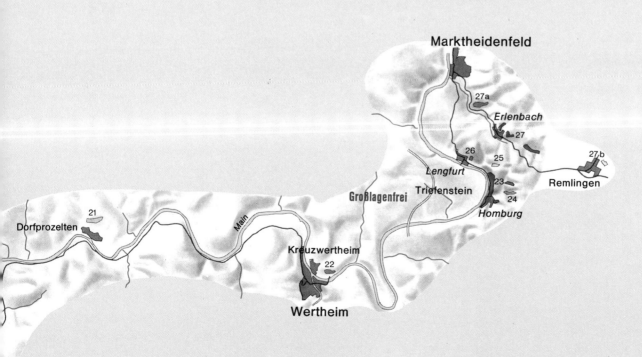

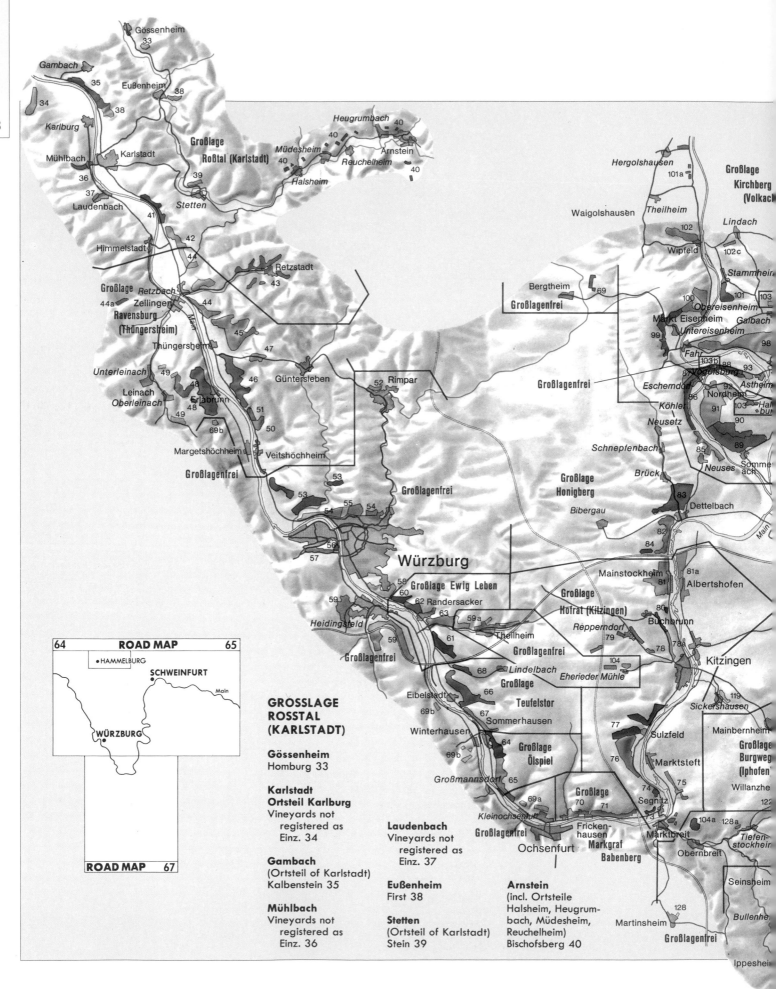

Gössenheim
33

Gambach

35
Eußenheim
38

34

38

Karlburg

Mühlbach
Karlstadt

36

**Großlage
Roßtal (Karlstadt)**

Müdesheim
40

Heugrumbach
40

40

Arnstein

Reuchelheim
40

Halsheim
40

37

Laudenbach
41
Stetten

39

Himmelstadt
42

44

Retzstadt

43

Großlage
Retzbach
44a
Zellingen

44

Hergolshausen

101a

**Großlage
Kirchberg
(Volkach)**

Waigolshausen
Theilheim

Lindach

102

Wipfeld

102c

**Ravensburg
(Thüngersheim)**

45

Bergtheim

69

Großlagenfrei

Stammheim

100

101

Ravensburg

47

99

Markt Eisenheim
Untereisenheim
Galbach

102c

Thüngersheim

Unterleinach
49

46

Günterstheim

52
Rimpar

Großlagenfrei

Fahr
103b

88

98

93

Leinach
48
Oberleinach
48

51

Eschendorf
86
Vogelsburg
92
87

103

Köhler
91

Nordheim
90

Astheim

49
69b

50

53

**Großlage
Honigberg**

Bibergau

Neusetz

85

89

*Somme-
bach*

Margetshöchheim
Veitshöchheim

Brück

83

Schnepfenbach

Neuses

Großlagenfrei

53

55
54

Großlagenfrei

Dettelbach

54

Mainstockheim
81a

82

84

56

57

Würzburg

58
60

Großlage Ewig Leben

62 Randersacker

81

Albertshofen

80

Buchbrunn

59

Heidingsfeld

63

59a

Theilheim

**Großlage
Hofrat (Kitzingen)**

Repperndorf
79

78

78a

Kitzingen

59

61

Großlagenfrei

104

Eherieder Mühle

119

Sickershausen

68
Lindelbach

**Großlage
Teufelstor**

77

Mainbernheim

**GROSSLAGE
ROSSTAL
(KARLSTADT)**

Eibelstadt

66

Sulzfeld

**Großlage
Burgweg
(Iphofen)**

Gössenheim
Homburg 33

69b

67
Sommerhausen

64

76

75

Marktsteft

Willanzhe

**Karlstadt
Ortsteil Karlburg**
Vineyards not
registered as
Einz. 34

Winterhausen

**Großlage
Ölspiel**

74

Segnitz

127

Gambach
(Ortsteil of Karlstadt)
Kalbenstein 35

Großmannsdorf
65

70
71

Laudenbach
Vineyards not
registered as
Einz. 37

Großlagenfrei

Kleinochsenfurt

**Großlage
Burgweg
(Iphofen)**

Seinsheim

Mühlbach
Vineyards not
registered as
Einz. 36

Eußenheim
First 38

Stetten
(Ortsteil of Karlstadt)
Stein 39

Frickenhausen

Ochsenfurt

**Markgraf
Babenberg**

Marktbreit

Obernbreit

104a

128a

*Tiefen-
stockhei*

128

Arnstein
(incl. Ortsteile
Halsheim, Heugrum-
bach, Müdesheim,
Reuchelheim)
Bischofsberg 40

Martinsheim

Bullenhe

Großlagenfrei

Ippeshei

64 **ROAD MAP** 65
• HAMMELBURG
SCHWEINFURT
Main
WÜRZBURG
ROAD MAP 67

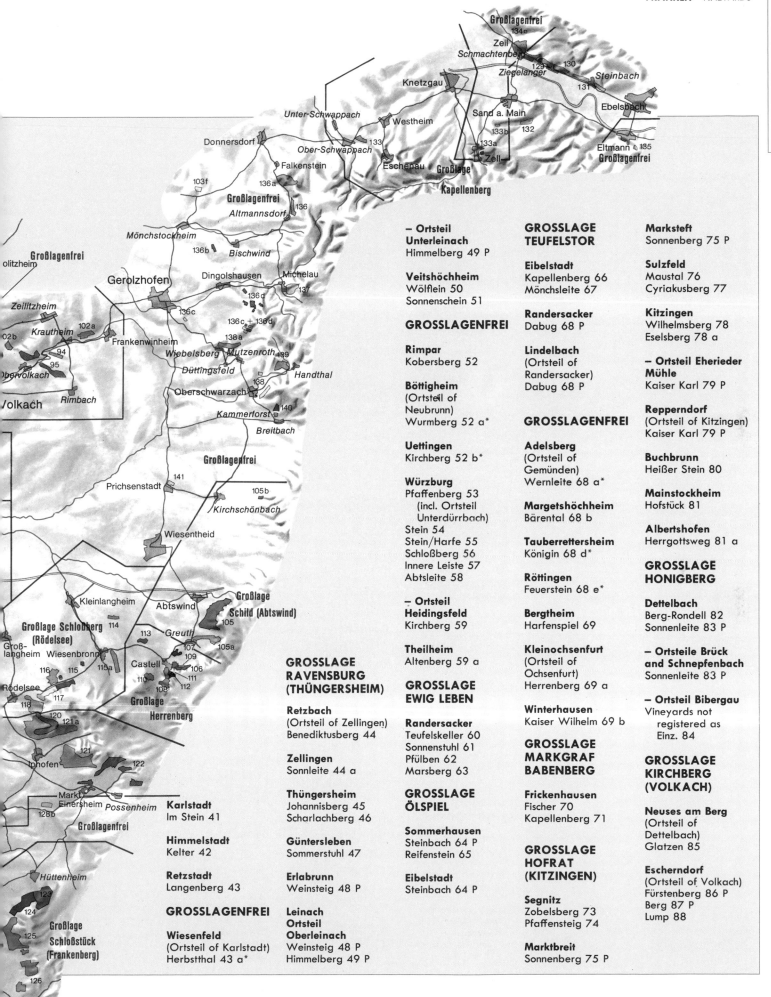

Großlagenfrei
134 a
Zeil
Schmachtenberg
Ziegelanger 129 130
131 *Steinbach*
Knetzgau
Ebelsbach
Unter-Schwappach
Westheim
Sand a. Main
Donnersdorf
Ober-Schwappach 133 133b 132
Falkenstein 133a
Eschenau *Zell* *Eltmann* 135
Großlage Großlagenfrei
Kapellenberg
103f 136a
Großlagenfrei
Altmannsdorf 136
Mönchstockheim
Großlagenfrei 136b *Bischwind*
olitzheim
Gerolzhofen Dingolshausen *Michelau*
Zeilitzheim 136d 137
102a 136c
Krautheim 136c + 136d
02b 94 Frankenwinheim 138a
95 *Wiebelsberg* *Mutzenroth* 139
Obervolkach *Düttingsfeld* *Handthal*
Oberschwarzach 138
Volkach *Rimbach* *Breitbach* 140
Kammerforst
Großlagenfrei
Prichsenstadt 141
Kirchschönbach 105b
Wiesentheid
Kleinlangheim Abtswind **Großlage**
Schild (Abtswind)
Großlage Schloßberg 114 105
(Rödelsee) 113 *Greuth*
Großlangheim Wiesenbronn 107 105a
109
Rödelsee Castell 106
118 110 111
117 108 112
120 **Großlage**
121a **Herrenberg**
121
phofen 122
Markt
Einersheim *Possenheim*
128b
Großlagenfrei
Hüttenheim
123
124
Großlage
125 **Schloßstück**
(Frankenberg)
126

– Ortsteil
Unterleinach
Himmelberg 49 P

Veitshöchheim
Wölflein 50
Sonnenschein 51

GROSSLAGENFREI

Rimpar
Kobersberg 52

Böttigheim
(Ortsteil of
Neubrunn)
Wurmberg 52 a*

Uettingen
Kirchberg 52 b*

Würzburg
Pfaffenberg 53
(incl. Ortsteil
Unterdürrbach)
Stein 54
Stein/Harfe 55
Schloßberg 56
Innere Leiste 57
Abtsleite 58

– Ortsteil
Heidingsfeld
Kirchberg 59

Theilheim
Altenberg 59 a

GROSSLAGE
RAVENSBURG
(THÜNGERSHEIM)

Retzbach
(Ortsteil of Zellingen)
Benediktusberg 44

Zellingen
Sonnleite 44 a

Thüngersheim
Johannisberg 45
Scharlachberg 46

Güntersleben
Sommerstuhl 47

Erlabrunn
Weinsteig 48 P

Leinach
**Ortsteil
Oberleinach**
Weinsteig 48 P
Himmelberg 49 P

GROSSLAGE
TEUFELSTOR

Eibelstadt
Kapellenberg 66
Mönchsleite 67

Randersacker
Dabug 68 P

Lindelbach
(Ortsteil of
Randersacker)
Dabug 68 P

GROSSLAGENFREI

Adelsberg
(Ortsteil of
Gemünden)
Wernleite 68 a*

Margetshöchheim
Bärental 68 b

Tauberrettersheim
Königin 68 d*

Röttingen
Feuerstein 68 e*

Bergtheim
Harfenspiel 69

Kleinochsenfurt
(Ortsteil of
Ochsenfurt)
Herrenberg 69 a

Winterhausen
Kaiser Wilhelm 69 b

GROSSLAGE
MARKGRAF
BABENBERG

Frickenhausen
Fischer 70
Kapellenberg 71

GROSSLAGE
HOFRAT
(KITZINGEN)

Segnitz
Zobelsberg 73
Pfaffensteig 74

Marktbreit
Sonnenberg 75 P

Marksteft
Sonnenberg 75 P

Sulzfeld
Maustal 76
Cyriakusberg 77

Kitzingen
Wilhelmsberg 78
Eselsberg 78 a

– Ortsteil Eherieder
Mühle
Kaiser Karl 79 P

Repperndorf
(Ortsteil of Kitzingen)
Kaiser Karl 79 P

Buchbrunn
Heißer Stein 80

Mainstockheim
Hofstück 81

Albertshofen
Herrgottsweg 81 a

GROSSLAGE
HONIGBERG

Dettelbach
Berg-Rondell 82
Sonnenleite 83 P

– Ortsteile Brück
and Schnepfenbach
Sonnenleite 83 P

– Ortsteil Bibergau
Vineyards not
registered as
Einz. 84

GROSSLAGE
KIRCHBERG
(VOLKACH)

Neuses am Berg
(Ortsteil of
Dettelbach)
Glatzen 85

Escherndorf
(Ortsteil of Volkach)
Fürstenberg 86 P
Berg 87 P
Lump 88

GROSSLAGE
EWIG LEBEN

Randersacker
Teufelskeller 60
Sonnenstuhl 61
Pfülben 62
Marsberg 63

GROSSLAGE
ÖLSPIEL

Sommerhausen
Steinbach 64 P
Reifenstein 65

Eibelstadt
Steinbach 64 P

GROSSLAGENFREI

Karlstadt
Im Stein 41

Himmelstadt
Kelter 42

Retzstadt
Langenberg 43

GROSSLAGENFREI

Wiesenfeld
(Ortsteil of Karlstadt)
Herbstthal 43 a*

Köhler
(Ortsteil of Volkach)
Fürstenberg 86 P

Neusetz
(Ortsteil of
Dettelbach)
Fürstenberg 86 P

Untereisenheim
(Ortsteil of Markt
Eisenheim)
Berg 87 P
Sonnenberg 99
Small parts of the
above vineyard
belong to No. 100

Sommerach
Katzenkopf 89
Rosenberg 90 P

Hallburg
(Ortsteil of Volkach)
Rosenberg 90 P
Kreuzberg 92 P

Nordheim
Vögelein 91
Kreuzberg 92 P

Astheim
(Ortsteil of Volkach)
Karthäuser 93

Krautheim
(Ortsteil of Volkach)
Sonnenleite 94

Obervolkach
(Ortsteil of Volkach)
Landsknecht 95 P

Rimbach
(Ortsteil of Volkach)
Landsknecht 95 P

Gaibach
(Ortsteil of Volkach)
Kapellenberg 97

Volkach
(incl. Ortsteil Fahr)
Ratsherr 98

Obereisenheim
(Ortsteil of Markt
Eisenheim)
Höll 100

Stammheim
(Ortsteil of
Kolitzheim)
Eselsberg 101

Theilheim
(Ortsteil of
Waigolshausen)
Mainleite 101 a P

Hergolshausen
(Ortsteil of
Waigolshausen)
Mainleite 101 a P

Wipfeld
Zehntgraf 102

Frankenwinheim
Rosenberg 102 a

Zeilitzheim
(Ortsteil of
Kolitzheim)
Heiligenberg 102 b

Lindach
(Ortsteil of
Kolitzheim)
Kreuzpfad 102 c

Also vineyards in the
parishes of Neusetz,
Köhler (Ortsteil of
Volkach), Fahr and
Schwarzenau
(Ortsteil of
Schwarzenach)

GROSSLAGENFREI

Hallburg
(Ortsteil of Volkach)
Schloßberg 103

Gaibach
(Ortsteil of Volkach)
Schloßpark 103 a

Vogelsburg
(Ortsteil of Volkach)
Pforte 103 b

Schweinfurt
Peterstirn 103 c*
Mainleite 103 d*

Mainberg
(Ortsteil of
Schonungen)
Schloß 103 e*

Mönchsteckheim
(Ortsteil of Sulzheim)
Mönchberg 103 f

Kitzingen
Ortsteil Eherieder
Mühle
Eherieder Berg 104

Obernbreit
Kanzel 104 a

Tauberzell
(Ortsteil of
Adelshofen)
Hasennestle 104 b*

**BEREICH
STEIGERWALD**

**GROSSLAGE
SCHILD
(ABTSWIND)**

Abtswind
Altenberg 105

Greuth
(Ortsteil of Castell)
Bastel 105 a

**Prichsenstadt
Ortsteil
Kirchschönbach**
Mariengarten 105 b

**GROSSLAGE
HERRENBERG**

The sites 106 and
108 also belong to
Großlage Schild

Castell
Bausch 106
Hohnart 107
Kirchberg 108
Feuerbach 109
Kugelspiel 110
Reitsteig 111
Schloßberg 112
Trautberg 113

**GROSSLAGE
SCHLOSSBERG
(RÖDELSEE)**

Parts of Einz. 120
also belong to this
Großlage

Kleinlangheim
Wutschenberg 114

Wiesenbronn
Wachhügel 115
Geißberg 115 a

Großlangheim
Kiliansberg 116

Rödelsee
Schwanleite 117
Küchenmeister 118

Sickershausen
(Ortsteil of Kitzingen)
Storchenbrünnle 119

Also vineyards in
the parishes of
Mainbernheim and
Hoheim (Ortsteil of
Kitzingen)

**GROSSLAGE
BURGWEG
(IPHOFEN)**

Iphofen
Julius-Echter-Berg
120
Kalb 121
Kronsberg 121 a

Possenheim
(Ortsteil of Iphofen)
Vogelsang 122 P

Markt Einersheim
Vogelsang 122 P

Willanzheim
Vineyards not
registered as Einz.

**GROSSLAGE
SCHLOSSSTÜCK
(FRANKENBERG)**

Hüttenheim
(Ortsteil of
Willanzheim)
Tannenberg 123

Seinsheim
Hohenbühl 124

Bullenheim
(Ortsteil of
Ippesheim)
Paradies 125

Ippesheim
Herrschaftsberg 126

Ergersheim
Altenberg 127*

Weimersheim
(Ortsteil of Ipsheim)
Roter Berg 127 a

Ingolstadt
(Ortsteil of
Sugenheim)
Rotenberg 127 a*

Weigenheim
Hohenlandsberg
127 b P*

Reusch
(Ortsteil of
Weigenheim)
Hohenlandsberg
127 b T*

Ipsheim
Burg Hoheneck 127 c P*

Kaubenheim
(Ortsteil of Ipsheim)
Burg Hoheneck 127 c P*

Walddachsbach
(Ortsteil of
Dietersheim)
Burg Hoheneck 127 c T*

Also vineyards in
Krassolzheim (Ortsteil
of Sugenheim),
Hump-
rechtsau, Rüdisbronn,
Külsheim, Ickelheim
(Orts. of Windsheim),
Walddachsbach and
Dottenheim (Orts. of
Dietersheim)

GROSSLAGENFREI

Martinsheim
Langenstein 128

Tiefenstockheim
(Ortsteil of
Seinsheim)
Stiefel 128 a

Iphofen
Domherr 128 b

Neundorf
(Ortsteil of
Sugenheim)
Hüßberg 128 c*
Mönchsbuck 128 d*
Sonneberg 128 e*
Wonne 128 f*

**Bad Windsheim
Ortsteil Oberntief**
Rosenberg 128 g*

**GROSSLAGE
KAPELLENBERG**

Schmachtenberg
(Ortsteil of Zeil am
Main)
Eulengrund 129

Ziegelanger
(Ortsteil of Zeil am
Main)
Ölschnabel 130

Steinbach
(Ortsteil of
Ebelsbach)
Nonnenberg 131

Sand am Main
Kronberg 132

Oberschwappach
(Ortsteil of Knetzgau)
Sommertal 133

GROSSLAGENFREI

Zell am Ebersberg
(Ortsteil of Knetzgau)
Schloßberg 133 a

Sand am Main
Himmelsbühl 133 b

Zeil am Main
Mönchshang 134

– Ortsteil Krum
Himmelreich 134 a

**Königsberg in
Bayern
Ortsteil Unfinden**
Kinnleitenberg 134 b

Eltmann
Schloßleite 135

Weiher
(Ortsteil of Viereth)
Weinberge 135 a*

Bamberg
Alter Graben 135 b*

Altmannsdorf
(Ortsteil of Michelau)
Sonnenwinkel 136

Donnersdorf
Falkenberg 136 a

Mönchstockheim
(Ortsteil of Sulzheim)
Köhler 136 b P

Dingolshausen
Köhler 136 b P

– Ortsteil Bischwind
Köhler 136 b P

Gerolzhofen
Köhler 136 b P
Arlesgarten 136 c

Michelau
Vollburg 137

Oberschwarzach
(incl. Ortsteile
Mutzenroth and
Düttingsfeld)
Herrenberg 138

**– Ortsteil
Wiebelsberg**
Dachs 138 a

Handthal
(Ortsteil of
Oberschwarzach)
Stollberg 139

Kammerforst
(Ortsteil of
Oberschwarzach)
Teufel 140

Prichsenstadt
Krone 141

WÜRTTEMBERG

The old principalities of Baden and Württemberg are united as a state, but remain separate as wine regions. Baden is much the bigger producer of the two, but a true Württemberger will argue that his wine is much the better – and, acting accordingly, consume his share and more. As a result it is rarely exported and the best bottles (which are expensive) almost never.

Growers therefore have the best of all possible motives to concentrate on quality: they, and their friends and acquaintances, are going to drink what they make themselves.

The landlocked regions of Germany only take on comprehensible shapes as they are encompassed and traversed by rivers. The river Neckar is almost a Mosel in Württemberg, ambling through the hills and fed by tributaries that provide the essential south slopes for vineyards. On the analogy of the Mosel picture, the huge car-factory city of Stuttgart is its Trier. Here and along the tributary Rems, flowing in from the east like the Ruwer to the Mosel, are the first and some of the best Württemberg vineyards, the Bereich Remstal-Stuttgart. Unlike the Mosel, however, the Neckar does not have the vines to itself. The side-valleys carry the vineyards west into the foothills of the Black Forest, east into Swabia, the rural heartland of southern Germany.

Württemberg, like the Mosel, concentrates on Riesling for its fine white wines. But its real speciality is red and rosé made of its own indigenous grape the Trollinger, and to a lesser extent the Schwarzriesling (the Pinot Meunier in French, with the German alias of Müllerrebe), the Portugieser, the Pinot Noir (Spätburgunder) and the Limberger, which may be a form of Burgundy's Gamay. Red plantings make up half the total; if the red is not fully red it is Weißherbst, rosé, as in Baden, or mixed with white grapes to make Schillerwein – a true local speciality.

TRAVEL INFORMATION

The winelands of the Neckar and its tributaries link classically romantic South German scenery and the rich modern city of Stuttgart. The locals are, statistics show, the leading wine drinkers in Germany and there are plenty of places to join them for a glass – so many that very little Württemberg wine leaves its homeland.

Places to visit
Stuttgart: shopping and conventions, ballet and museums are among attractions in this modern, prosperous city. Eßlingen: both the old and the new Rathaus, and indeed the entire core of this little town, are charming. Heilbronn: town on the Neckar with a wealth of old buildings. Ludwigsburg: the largest Baroque castle in Germany, with open-air theatre in summer. Other places of interest include: Weinstadt, Brackenheim, Bad Mergentheim.

Wine roads
The *Schwäbische Weinstraße* runs north from Metzingen along the river to Stuttgart, then loops through the wine country to end at Bad Mergentheim in the northeast. There are educational vineyard trails at Stuttgart, Gemmrigheim, Neckarsulm, Fellbach, Kernen, Remshalden, Vaihingen, Beilstein, Großbottwar, Bad Mergentheim and Ingelfingen.

Wine festivals
Stuttgart-Bad Cannstatt (end May), Bretzfeld-Schwabbach (mid-June), Heilbronn (3rd w/e in June), Beilstein (end July), Ingelfingen (mid-Aug), Remshalden (mid-Aug), Großbottwar (end Aug), Weinstadt (early Sept), Laudenbach (mid-Sept), Eßlingen (mid Sept), Metzingen (end Oct).

Wine museum
Stuttgart's wine museum is based in a cellar close to the Rotenberg vineyard. There is a library, and a wine education trail (with tasting facilities) starts from the museum.

Food and drink
Perhaps it is the riches of Stuttgart, perhaps culinary traditions. Whatever the cause, Württemberg has plenty of good restaurants and hotels, including castle hotels, to add to the ever-present inns and Weinstuben.

Regional Wine Information Office
Werbegemeinschaft Württembergischer Weingärtnergenossenschaften
Postfach 94
Heilbronner Straße 41
7000 Stuttgart 1
Tel: 0711-20401

◀ In many of the wine regions, radical reshaping of old vineyards has taken place. Flurbereinigung is the term for this totally revised landscape, with old terraces removed and easy access by road.

VINEYARDS

BEREICH KOCHER-JAGST-TAUBER

GROSSLAGE TAUBERBERG

Bad Mergentheim Ortsteil Markelsheim
Mönchsberg 1 P
Probstberg 2 P

Weikersheim
Hardt 3
Schmecker 4
Karlsberg 5

– Ortsteil Elpersheim
Mönchsberg 1 P
Probstberg 2 P

– Ortsteil Schäftersheim
Klosterberg 4 a

– Ortsteil Laudenbach
Schafsteige 6 P

– Ortsteil Haagen
Schafsteige 6 P

Niederstetten
Schafsteige 6 P

– Ortsteil Wermutshausen
Schafsteige 6 P

– Ortsteil Vorbachzimmern
Schafsteige 6 P

– Ortsteil Oberstetten
Schafsteige 6 P

GROSSLAGE KOCHERBERG

Dörzbach
Altenberg 7

Ingelfingen
Hoher Berg 8 P

– Ortsteil Criesbach
Hoher Berg 8 P
Burgstall 11 P

Künzelsau
Hoher Berg 8 P

– Ortsteil Belsenberg
Heiligkreuz 9

Niedernhall
Hoher Berg 8 P
Burgstall 11 P
Engweg 12 P
Altenberg 13 P

Weißbach
Engweg 12 P
Altenberg 13 P

Forchtenberg
Flatterberg 14 P

– Ortsteil Ernsbach
Flatterberg 14 P

Schöntal Ortsteil Bieringen
Schlüsselberg 15

Widdern
Hofberg 16 P

Neudenau Ortsteil Siglingen
Hofberg 16 P

Möckmühl
Hofberg 16 P
Ammerlanden 17

Hardthausen Ortsteil Kochersteinsfeld
Rosenberg 17 a

BEREICH WÜRTTEMBERGISCH UNTERLAND

(See map pages 146–147)

GROSSLAGE STAUFENBERG

Gundelsheim
Himmelreich 18

Bad Friedrichshall Ortsteil Duttenberg
Schön 19 P

– Ortsteil Offenau
Schön 19 P

Langenbrettach Ortsteil Brettach
Berg 20

Untereisesheim
Vogelsang 21

Oedheim
Kayberg 22 P

Erlenbach
Kayberg 22 P

Neckarsulm
Scheuerberg 23

Ellhofen
Ranzenberg 24 P

Weinsberg
Ranzenberg 24 P
Schemelsberg 25

– Ortsteil Gellmersbach
Dezberg 26 P

Eberstadt
Dezberg 26 P

Heilbronn
Stiftsberg 27 P
Wartberg 28
Stahlbühl 29

– Ortsteil Horkheim
Stiftsberg 27 P

Talheim
Stiftsberg 27 P

GROSSLAGE LINDELBERG

Neuenstein Ortsteil Kesselfeld
Schwobarjörgle 30 P

– Ortsteil Obersöllbach
Margarete 31 P

Öhringen Ortsteil Michelbach am Wald
Margarete 31 P
Dachsteiger 32 P

– Ortsteil Verrenberg
Goldberg 33 P
Verrenberg 35

Pfedelbach
Goldberg 33 P

– Ortsteil Untersteinbach
Dachsteiger 32 P

– Ortsteil Heuholz
Dachsteiger 32 P

– Ortsteil Harsberg
Dachsteiger 32 P

– Ortsteil Oberohrn
Dachsteiger 32 P

– Ortsteil Windischenbach
Goldberg 33 P

Wüstenrot Ortsteil Maienfels
Schneckenhof 36 P

Bretzfeld
Goldberg 33 P

– Ortsteil Geddelsbach
Schneckenhof 36 P

– Ortsteil Unterheimbach
Schneckenhof 36 P

– Ortsteil Adolzfurt
Schneckenhof 36 P

– Ortsteil Siebeneich
Himmelreich 37 P

– Ortsteil Schwabbach
Himmelreich 37 P

– Ortsteil Dimbach
Himmelreich 37 P

– Ortsteil Waldbach
Himmelreich 37 P

Langenbrettach Ortsteil Langenbeutingen
Himmelreich 37 P

GROSSLAGE SALZBERG

Eberstadt
Sommerhalde 39
Eberfürst 40

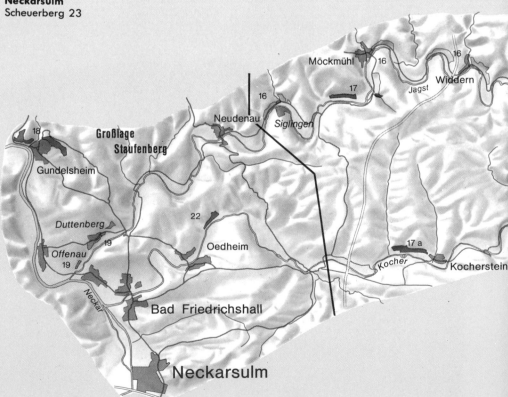

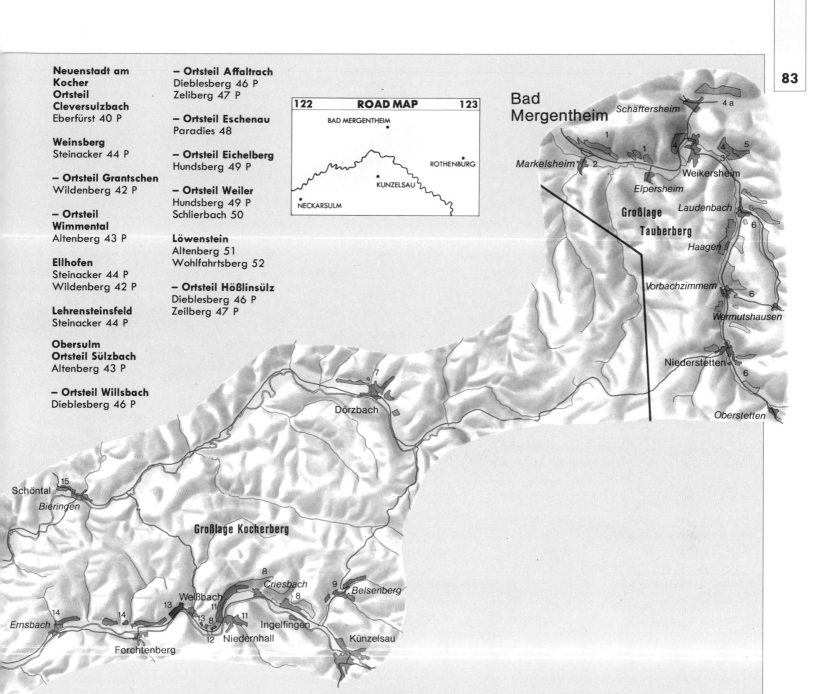

**Neuenstadt am
Kocher
Ortsteil
Cleversulzbach**
Eberfürst 40 P

Weinsberg
Steinacker 44 P

– Ortsteil Grantschen
Wildenberg 42 P

**– Ortsteil
Wimmental**
Altenberg 43 P

Ellhofen
Steinacker 44 P
Wildenberg 42 P

Lehrensteinsfeld
Steinacker 44 P

**Obersulm
Ortsteil Sülzbach**
Altenberg 43 P

– Ortsteil Willsbach
Dieblesberg 46 P

– Ortsteil Affaltrach
Dieblesberg 46 P
Zeliberg 47 P

– Ortsteil Eschenau
Paradies 48

– Ortsteil Eichelberg
Hundsberg 49 P

– Ortsteil Weiler
Hundsberg 49 P
Schlierbach 50

Löwenstein
Altenberg 51
Wohlfahrtsberg 52

– Ortsteil Hößlinsülz
Dieblesberg 46 P
Zeilberg 47 P

**GROSSLAGE
SCHOZACHTAL**

Löwenstein
Sommerberg 53 P

**Untergruppenbach
Ortsteil Unterheinreit**
Sommerberg 53 P

Abstatt
Sommerberg 53 P
Burgberg 54 P
Burg Wildeck 55

Ilsfeld
Rappen 56

– Ortsteil Auenstein
Burgberg 54 P
Schloßberg 57

**GROSSLAGE
WUNNENSTEIN**

Beilstein
Wartberg 58
Steinberg 59

**– Ortsteil
Hohenbeilstein**
Schloßwengert 60

Oberstenfeld
Forstberg 61 P
Lichtenberg 62 P
Harzberg 63 P

– Ortsteil Gronau
Forstberg 61 P

Ilsfeld
Lichtenberg 62 P

Großbottwar
Lichtenberg 62 P
Harzberg 63 P

**– Ortsteil
Winzerhausen**
Lichtenberg 62 P
Harzberg 63 P

**– Ortsteile Hof and
Lembach**
Lichtenberg 62 P
Harzberg 63 P

Steinheim
Lichtenberg 62 P

**– Ortsteil
Kleinbottwar**
Lichtenberg 62 P
Oberer Berg 64 P
Süßmund 65
Götzenberg 66

**Ludwigsburg
Ortsteil Hoheneck**
Oberer Berg 64 P

**GROSSLAGE
KIRCHEN-
WEINBERG**

Heilbronn
Sonnenberg 67 P
Altenberg 68 P

Flein
Sonnenberg 67 P
Altenberg 68 P
Eselsberg 69

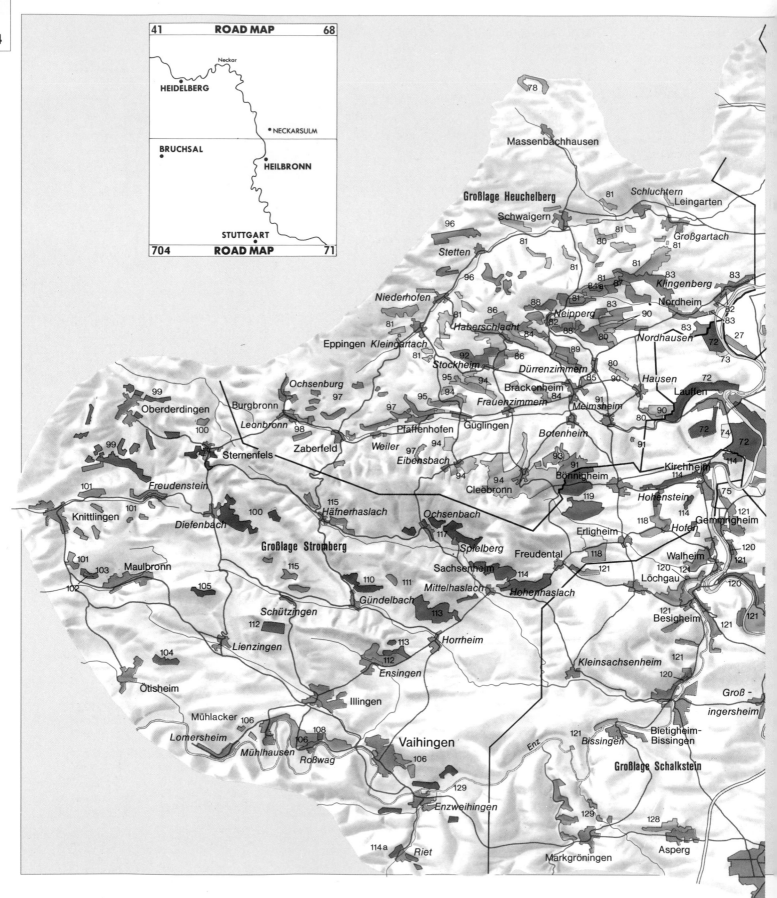

ROAD MAP

41   68

Neckar

HEIDELBERG

● NECKARSULM

BRUCHSAL
●

HEILBRONN
●

STUTTGART
●

704   ROAD MAP   71

Massenbachhausen

Großlage Heuchelberg

Schwaigern   81   *Schluchtern*

Leingarten

96

Großgartach

Stetten   81   80

81

81

81

83   83

Klingenberg

96

81   84   87

Niederhofen   88   81

83

Nordheim

81   86   Neipperg   90

81   82

82   83

Haberschlacht   84   88

Eppingen   *Kleingartach*   80   Nordhausen   27

81   92   86   89   83   73

Ochsenburg   Stockheim   95   80   72

97   95   94   *Dürrenzimmern*   90

99   95   94   Brackenheim   85   90   Hausen

Oberderdingen   Burgbronn   97   *Frauenzimmern*   84   91   Lauffen

97   *Meimsheim*   72

Leonbronn   98   Pfaffenhofen   Güglingen   *Botenheim*   91   80   90

100

Zaberfeld   *Weiler*   94   91   72   74

99   97   *Eibensbach*   93   91   Kirchheim   114

Sternenfels   94   91   Bönnigheim   114

Freudenstein   115   94   Cleebronn   *Hohenstein*   75

101   *Häfnerhaslach*   119   114

101   *Ochsenbach*   118   *Hofen*   121

Knittlingen   100   117   Erligheim   Gemmingheim

Diefenbach   **Großlage Stromberg**   *Spielberg*   Freudental   118   120

101   115   Sachsenheim   121   Walheim

103   Maulbronn   110   111   114   121   120   Löchgau   120

102   105   *Gündelbach*   *Mittelhaslach*   *Hohenhaslach*   120   121

Schützingen   113   121   Besigheim   121

112   113   Horrheim   121

104   *Lienzingen*   112   121   Kleinsachsenheim

Ensingen   120

Ötisheim   Illingen   *Groß-*

ingersheim

Mühlacker   106   121   *Bissingen*   Bietigheim-

Lomersheim   108   Bissingen

106   Vaihingen   Enz   **Großlage Schalkstein**

Mühlhausen   *Roßwag*   106

129

114a   *Riet*   *Enzweihingen*   129   128

Markgröningen   Asperg

Oedheim

Untereisesheim

Brettach 20

Neuenstadt am Kocher
Cleversulzbach 22

Langenbrettach

Neckarsulm

Langenbeutingen

Neuenstein
Kesselfeld

23 22

39

40

37

Großlage Lindelberg

Eschelbach
30

Großlage
Haufenberg

23

40 40

Siebeneich

33

Obersöllbach

30

Gellmersbach

39

Verrenberg 35

Öhringen
Michelbach am Wald

Neckar

Erlenbach 22

26

39

Eberstadt

39

Schwabbach

33

Windischenbach

33

Oberohrn

32

27

43

42

Dimbach

Bretzfeld

Pfedelbach

33

32

31

Heilbronn

25

24

42

Wimmental

Grantschen

39

Sülzbach

46

Waldbach

Adolzfurt 36

36

32

Heuholz

32

28

Weinsberg

43

Ellhofen Obersulm

46

48

Eschenau

Geddelsbach

36

32

24

42

46

Unterheimbach

Unterheimbach

Untersteinbach

29

27

Willsbach Affaltrach

44

46

48

36

Lehrensteinsfeld

44

Hößlinsulz

46

49

Weiler

36

Wüstenrot
Maienfels

67

68

44

50

Großlage
Eichelberg

67

Großlage

67

46

51

52

Salzberg

70

53

Löwenstein

Untergruppenbach

53

71

76

54

Unterheinriet

53

Großlage

56

Abstatt

64

55

58

Schozach

77

Ilsfeld

Schozachtal

59

Neckarwestheim

Auenstein

57

58

Großlage

76

56

58

Beilstein

60

Wunnenstein

58

Hohenbeilstein

61

Gronau

63

61

Winzerhausen

Oberstenfeld

62

124

62

62

123

Hof

63

Mundelsheim

Lömbach

131

132

Allmersbach

124 125

62

Großbottwar

63

133

123

Höpfigheim

62

65

62

Kleinaspach

Aspach

Rietenau

125

62

64

66

Kleinbottwar

Meiningersheim 126

Steinheim

131

Murr

130

Rielingshausen

126

131

Benningen

126

Erdmannhausen

Kirchberg

Marbach
/Neckar

126

Großlage
Wunnenstein
64

126

Neckarweihingen

Affalterbach

126

Poppenweiler

Neckar 126

Talheim
Sonnenberg 67 P
Schloßberg 70 a
Hohe Eiche 71

Untergruppenbach
Schloßberg 70

Lauffen
Katzenbeißer 72
Riedersbückele 73
Jungfer 74

Neckarwestheim
Hernesberg 75

Ilsfeld
Ortsteil Schozach
Schelmenklinge 76
Roter Berg 77

**GROSSLAGE
HEUCHELBERG**

Massenbachhausen
Krähenberg 78

**Leingarten
Ortsteil
Schluchtern**
Leiersberg 80 P
Grafenberg 81 P

**– Ortsteil
Großgartach**
Grafenberg 81 P

**Brackenheim
Ortsteil Neipperg**
Grafenberg 81 P
Schloßberg 82 P
Steingrube 88

**Eppingen
Ortsteil Kleingartach**
Grafenberg 81 P

**Heilbronn
Ortsteil Klingenberg**
Schloßberg 82 P
Sonntagsberg 83 P

Nordheim
Grafenberg 81 P
Sonntagsberg 83 P
Ruthe 84 P
Gräfenberg 87

**– Ortsteil
Nordhausen**
Sonntagsberg 83 P

Brackenheim
Schloßberg 82 P
Zweifelberg 84
Wolfsaugen 85
Dachsberg 86 P
Mönchsberg 89 P

– Ortsteil Hausen
Jupiterberg 80

**– Ortsteil
Haberschlacht**
Dachsberg 86 P

**– Ortsteil
Dürrenzimmern**
Mönchsberg 89 P

**– Ortsteil
Meimsheim**
Katzenöhrle 91

– Ortsteil Stockheim
Altenberg 92

– Ortsteil Botenheim
Ochsenberg 93

Cleebronn
Michaelsberg 94 P

Güglingen
Michaelsberg 94 P
Kaiserberg 95 P

**– Ortsteil
Frauenzimmern**
Michaelsberg 94 P
Kaiserberg 95 P

**– Ortsteil
Eibensbach**
Michaelsberg 94 P

Schwaigern
Grafenberg 81 P
Ruthe 84 a P
Sonnenberg 96 P

– Ortsteil Stetten
Sonnenberg 96 P

**– Ortsteil
Niederhofen**
Grafenberg 81 P

Pfaffenhofen
Hohenberg 97 P

– Ortsteil Weller
Hohenberg 97 P

Zaberfeld
Hohenberg 97 P

– Ortsteil Leonbronn
Hahnenberg 98 P

**– Ortsteil
Ochsenburg**
Hahnenberg 98 P

GROSSLAGE
STROMBERG

Oberderdingen
Kupferhalde 99

Sternenfels
König 100 P

**– Ortsteil
Diefenbach**
König 100 P

Knittlingen
Reichshalde 101 P

**– Ortsteil
Freudenstein**
Reichshalde 101 P

Maulbronn
Reichshalde 101 P
Eilfingerberg 102

Klosterstück 103

Ötisheim
Sauberg 104

**Mühlacker
Ortsteil Lienzingen**
Eichelberg 105

**– Ortsteil
Lomersheim**
Halde 106 P

**– Ortsteil
Mühlhausen**
Halde 106 P

Vaihingen
Halde 106 P

– Ortsteil Roßwag
Halde 106 P
Forstgrube 108 P

**– Ortsteil
Gündelbach**
Wachtkopf 110
Steinbachhof 111

– Ortsteil Ensingen
Schanzreiter 112 P

– Ortsteil Horrheim
Klosterberg 113 P

– Ortsteil Riet
Kirchberg 114 a

Illingen
Halde 106 P
Forstgrube 108 P
Schanzreiter 112 P

**– Ortsteil
Schützingen**
Heiligenberg 115 P

**Sachsenheim
Ortsteil
Hafnerhaslach**
Heiligenberg 115 P

**– Ortsteil
Hohenhaslach**
Klosterberg 113 P
Kirchberg 114 P

**– Ortsteil
Ochsenbach**
Liebenberg 117 P

– Ortsteil Spielberg
Liebenberg 117 P

**– Ortsteil
Kleinsachsenheim**
Kirchberg 114 P

Freudental
Kirchberg 114 P

Kirchheim
Kirchberg 114 P

Bönnigheim
Kirchberg 114 P
Sonnenberg 119

**– Ortsteil
Hohenstein**
Kirchberg 114 P

– Ortsteil Hofen
Lerchenberg 118 P

Erlingheim
Lerchenberg 118 P

GROSSLAGE
SCHALKSTEIN

Gemmrigheim
Wurmberg 120 P
Felsengarten 121 P

Walheim
Wurmberg 120 P
Felsengarten 121 P

Besigheim
Wurmberg 120 P
Felsengarten 121 P

Hessigheim
Wurmberg 120 P
Felsengarten 121 P
Käsberg 122 P

**Bietigheim-
Bissingen
Ortsteil Bietigheim**
Wurmberg 120 P

– Ortsteil Bissingen
Felsengarten 121 P

Löchgau
Felsengarten 121 P

Mundelsheim
Käsberg 122 P
Mühlbacher 123
Rozenberg 124

**Steinheim
Ortsteil Höpfigheim**
Königsberg 125

Murr
Neckarhälde 126 P

**Freiberg/Neckar
Ortsteil Beihingen**
Neckarhälde 126 P

Benningen
Neckarhälde 126 P

Marbach
Neckarhälde 126 P

Erdmannhausen
Neckarhälde 126 P

**Ludwigsburg
Ortsteil Hoheneck**
Neckarhälde 126 P

**– Ortsteil
Neckarweihingen**
Neckarhälde 126 P

**– Ortsteil
Poppenweiler**
Neckarhälde 126 P

Affatterbach
Neckarhälde 126 P

**Ingersheim
Ortsteil
Kleiningersheim**
Schloßberg 127 P

**– Ortsteil
Großingersheim**
Schloßberg 127 P

Asperg
Berg 128 P

Markgröningen
Berg 128 P
Sankt Johännser
129 P

**Vaihingen
Ortsteil
Enzweihingen**
Sankt Johännser
129 P

Steinheim
Burgberg 130

Kirchberg
Kelterberg 131 P

**Marbach/Neckar
Ortsteil
Rielingshausen**
Kelterberg 131 P

**Aspach
Ortsteil Kleinaspach**
Kelterberg 131 P

**– Ortsteil
Allmersbach**
Alter Berg 132

– Ortsteil Rietenau
Güldenkern 133

BEREICH
REMSTAL-
STUTTGART

GROSSLAGE
WEINSTEIGE

Gerlingen
Bopser 134
Ehrenberg 134 a

Stuttgart
Mönchshalde 135 P
Kriegsberg 136

**– Ortsteil
Bad Cannstatt**
Mönchhalde 135 P
Berg 137 P
Steinhalde 139 P
Zuckerle 140 P
Halde 141
Herzogenberg 142 P
Mönchberg 143 P

– Ortsteil Feuerbach
Berg 137 P

**– Ortsteil
Zuffenhausen**
Berg 137 P

**– Ortsteil
Hohenheim**
Schloßblick 138 a*

– Ortsteil Münster
Berg 137 P
Steinhalde 139 P
Zuckerle 140 P

– Ortsteil Degerloch
Scharrenberg 138

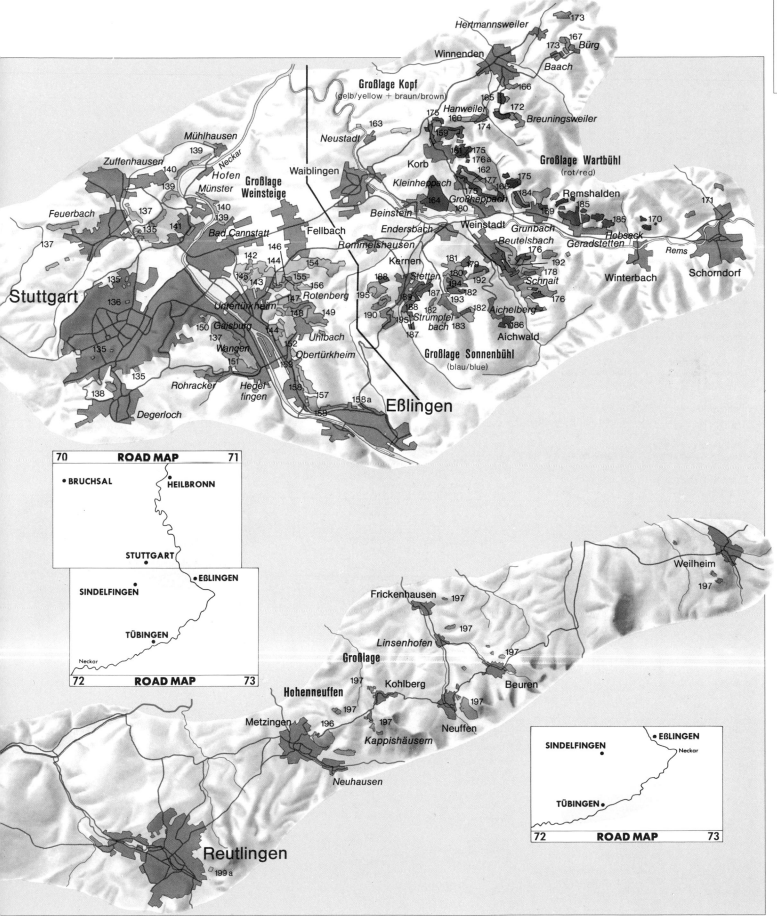

Hertmannsweiler 173
Winnenden 173 167 Bürg
Baach
Großlage Kopf
(gelb/yellow + braun/brown) 166
Neustadt 163 165
Hanweiler 172
Mühlhausen 175 160 Breuningsweiler
139 174
Zuffenhausen Neckar 159
140 Korb 161 175 Großlage Wartbühl
Hofen 176a (rot/red)
139 Großlage Kleinheppach 162
Münster Weinsteige 177
Feuerbach 140 164 175 168 184 Remshalden
137 139 Großheppach 180 169 185
141 Beinstein 178 185 170
137 135 Bad Cannstatt Endersbach Weinstadt Hebsack 171
146 Grunbach Geradstetten
Fellbach Beutelsbach Rems
142 Rommelshausen 176
144 154 181 Schnait Winterbach Schorndorf
145 143 155 Kernen 179
135 Rotenberg 156 Stetten 180 192
136 147 188 187 194 182
Untertürkheim 148 149 195 189 193 176
Stuttgart 150 Gaisburg 190 188 182 182 Aichelberg
137 Wangen 144 195 Strümpfel- 183 186
152 Uhlbach 187 bach Aichwald
151 Obertürkheim
135 Großlage Sonnenbühl
Rohracker Hedel- (blau/blue)
138 135 fingen 157 158a
Degerloch 158 Eßlingen

ROAD MAP
70 71
• BRUCHSAL • HEILBRONN
• STUTTGART
SINDELFINGEN •
• EßLINGEN
TÜBINGEN •
Neckar
72 ROAD MAP 73

Weilheim
197
Frickenhausen 197
197
Linsenhofen 197
Großlage
Kohlberg Beuren
197 Neuffen
Hohenneuffen 197
197
Metzingen 196 197
Kappishäusern
Neuhausen

SINDELFINGEN • • EßLINGEN
Neckar
TÜBINGEN •
72 ROAD MAP 73

Reutlingen
199a

88

– Ortsteil Mühlhausen
Steinhalde 139 P
Zuckerle 140 P

– Ortsteil Hofen
Zuckerle 140 P

– Ortsteil Untertürkheim
Herzogenberg 142 P
Mönchberg 143 P
Altenberg 144
Gips 145 P
Wetzstein 146 P
Schloßberg 147 P

– Ortsteil Rotenberg
Schloßberg 147 P

– Ortsteil Uhlbach
Schloßberg 147 P
Steingrube 148
Götzenberg 149

– Ortsteil Galsburg
Abelsberg 150

– Ortsteil Wangen
Berg 137 p

– Ortsteil Hedelfingen
Lenzenberg 151 P

– Ortsteil Rohracker
Lenzenberg 151 P

– Ortsteil Obertürkheim
Kirchberg 152 P
Ailenberg 153 P

Fellbach
Herzogenberg 142 P
Mönchberg 143 P
Gips 145 P
Wetzstein 146 P
Goldberg 154
Lämmler 155
Hinterer Berg 156

Eßlingen Ortsteil Mettingen
Kirchberg 152 P
Ailenberg 153 P
Lerchenberg 157 P
Schenkenberg 159 P

Eßlingen
Lerchenberg 157 P
Schenkenberg 158 P
Burg 158 a

GROSSLAGE KOPF

Korb
Sommerhalde 159
Berg 160 P
Hörnle 161 P

– Ortsteil Kleinheppach
Greiner 162

Waiblingen
Hörnle 161 P

– Ortsteil Neustadt
Söhrenberg 163

– Ortsteil Beinstein
Großmulde 164

Winnenden
Berg 160 P
Holzenberg 165 P
Roßberg 166

– Ortsteil Hanweiler
Berg 160 P

– Ortsteil Breuningsweiler
Holzenberg 165 P

– Ortsteil Bürg
Schloßberg 167

Weinstadt, Ortsteil Großheppach
Wanne 168

Remshalden Ortsteil Grunbach
Berghalde 169

Winterbach
Hungerberg 170

Schorndorf
Grafenberg 171

GROSSLAGE WARTBÜHL

Winnenden
Haselstein 172 P

– Ortsteil Hertmannsweiler
Himmelreich 173 P

– Ortsteil Baach
Himmelreich 173 P

– Ortsteil Breuningsweiler
Haselstein 172 P

– Ortsteil Hanweiler
Maien 174

Waiblingen
Steingrüble 175 P

Korb
Steingrüble 175 P

– Ort. Kleinheppach
Steingrüble 175 P
Sonnenberg 176 a

Weinstadt Ortsteil Großheppach
Steingrüble 175 P
Zügernberg 177

– Ortsteil Beutelsbach
Sonnenberg 176 P
Altenberg 178 P
Käppele 179

– Ortsteil Schnait
Sonnenberg 176 P
Altenberg 178 P

– Ortsteil Endersbach
Wetzstein 180
Happenhalde 181

– Ortsteil Strümpfelbach
Gastenklinge 182
Nonnenberg 183

**Remshalden
– Ortsteil Grunbach**
Klingle 184

– Ortsteil Geradstetten
Sonnenberg 176 P
Lichtenberg 185 P

– Ortsteil Hebsack
Lichtenberg 185 P

Aichwald Ortsteil Aichelberg
Luginsland 186

Kernen Ortsteil Stetten
Pulvermächer 187
Lindhälder 188
Brotwasser 189
Häder 190 P

Ortsteil Rommelshausen
Häder 190 P

GROSSLAGE SONNENBÜHL

Weinstadt Ortsteil Beutelsbach
Burghalde 192 P

– Ortsteil Schnait
Bürghalde 192 P

– Ortsteil Strümpfelbach
Altenberg 193

– Ortsteil Endersbach
Hintere Klinge 194

Kernen Ortsteil Stetten
Mönchberg 195 P

– Ortsteil Rommelshausen
Mönchberg 195 P

GROSSLAGE HOHENNEUFFEN

Metzingen
Hofsteige 196 P
Schloßsteige 197 P

– Ortsteil Neuhausen
Hofsteige 196 P

Neuffen
Schloßsteige 197 P

– Ortsteil Kappishäusern
Schloßsteige 197 P

Kohlberg
Schloßsteige 197 P

Frickenhausen
Schloßsteige 197 P

– Ortsteil Linsenhofen
Schloßsteige 197 P

Beuren
Schloßsteige 197 P

Weilheim
Schloßsteige 197 P

BEREICH OBERER NECKAR Tübingen and Ortsteile Hirschau and Unterjesingen
Sonnenhalden 198

Ammerbuch Ortsteil Breitenholz
Hinterhalde 198 a

– Ortsteil Entringen
Pfaffenberg 198 b

Rottenberg and Ortsteile Wurmlingen and Wendelsheim
Kapellenberg 199

Reutlingen
Sommerhalde 199 a

GROSSLAGENFREI

Ravensburg
Rauenegg 200*

BADEN · NORTH BADEN

Baden is the new force in German wine – at present only domestically, but soon no doubt on the world stage. Its vineyards have undergone no less than a revolution in recent years: they have been almost entirely rationalized and remodelled by Flurbereinigung, have increased in size and output and now lie fourth in yield in Germany, behind Rheinpfalz, Rheinhessen and the Mosel-Saar-Ruwer.

Baden faces Alsace across the Rhine. It is Germany's warmest (although not necessarily its sunniest) wine region, with correspondingly ripe, high-alcohol and low-acid wines: the diametric opposite of Mosels in style and function. The best Mosel wines are for analytical sipping. Baden makes mealtime wines with a warm vinosity that approaches the French style. It is the choice of grape varieties and the taste for a trace of sweetness that distinguishes them from Alsace wines.

Eighty per cent of Baden's vineyards lie in a 150-kilometre (80-mile) strip running from northeast to southwest, from Baden-Baden to Basel, in the foothills of the Black Forest where it meets the Rhine valley. The combination of dark forested-topped hills skirted by fresh green vineyards is not unique to Baden, but it reaches a picturesque poignancy along that ridge that makes it an unforgettable region to visit. Baden-Baden, the most stylish of spas, is an excellent natural centre for exploration for the main Baden vineyard areas. The balance is of purely local importance. The other areas lie southeast on the banks of the Bodensee (alias Lake Constance), north of Baden in the regions of the Kraichgau and Badische Bergstraße, respectively south and north of Heidelberg (but now united in one Bereich with both names – the Badische Bergstraße/Kraichgau), and far north on the border with Franken, a region known logically enough as Bereich Badisches Frankenland.

Baden has no powerful preference for one grape variety. Relics of local tradition in this most diverse and extended region are not so important today as well-judged selections for particular sites. The Müller-Thurgau is the main grape, Spätburgunder for red and light rosé comes second. Then comes Ruländer, alias Pinot Gris, which makes one of Baden's most striking wines: dense, broad in flavour, low in acid but high in extract and potentially the best wine of the region to accompany its often richly savoury food. In order of popularity Gutedel (or Chasselas) comes next, followed by Riesling, then Silvaner, Weißburgunder and Gewürztraminer. Baden's taste is clearly not for the highly aromatic new varieties; it conjures flavour and harmony out of relatively neutral grapes, regarding wine as first and foremost an accompaniment to food. Nearly 90 per cent of all Baden's crop goes to cooperative cellars for processing.

NORTH BADEN: The two Bereiche in the northern part of Baden have quite distinct characters. The remote little enclave known as Badisches Frankenland in viticultural logic is truly part of Franken. Only a political boundary allies its Tauber valley wines to Baden at all. The Bereich Badische Bergstraße and Kraichgau, although clearly another political compromise, is truly Baden in feeling, its best wines deriving from Ruländer and Riesling, particularly south of Heidelberg round Wiesloch, where remarkably fine and harmonious wines are made. Müller-Thurgau outnumbers all other grapes, but Riesling still occupies one-fifth of the vineyards of the Bereich. A certain amount of red wine is produced but little of it is exported.

VINEYARDS

DARMSTADT

GROSS-UMSTADT

Rhein

WORMS   • BENSHEIM

FRANKENTHAL   • WEINHEIM

MANNHEIM   Neckar

NEUSTADT   HEIDELBERG

LANDAU

BRUCHSAL

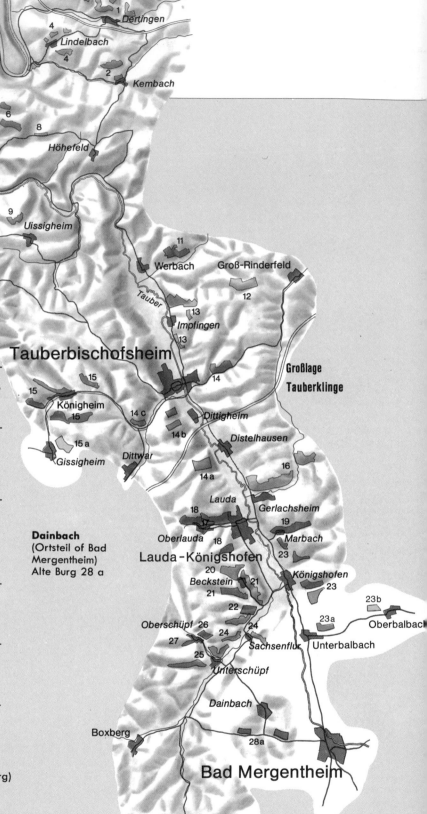

**BEREICH
BADISCHES
FRANKENLAND**

**GROSSLAGE
TAUBERKLINGE**

Dertingen
(Ortsteil of Wertheim)
Mandelberg 1
Sonnenberg 2 P

Kembach
(Ortsteil of Wertheim)
Sonnenberg 2 P

Lindelbach
(Ortsteil of Wertheim)
Ebenrain 4

Wertheim
Schloßberg 5

Reichholzheim
(Ortsteil of Wertheim)
Josefsberg 3 P
First 6
Satzenberg 7
Kemelrain 8 P

Bronnbach
(Ortsteil of Wertheim)
Josefsberg 3 P

Höhefeld
(Ortsteil of Wertheim)
Kemelrain 8 P

Uissigheim
(Ortsteil of Külsheim)
Stahlberg 9

Külsheim
Hoher Herrgott 10

Werbach
Hirschberg 11
Beilberg 12 P

Großrinderfeld
Beilberg 12 P

Impfingen
(Ortsteil of
Tauberbischofsheim)
Silberquell 13

Tauberbischofsheim
Edelberg 14

Distelhausen
(Ortsteil of
Tauberbischofsheim)
Kreuzberg 14 a

Dittigheim
(Ortsteil of
Tauberbischofsheim)
Steinschmetzer 14 b

Dittwar
(Ortsteil of
Tauberbischofsheim)
Ölkuchen 14 c

Königheim
Kirchberg 15

Gissigheim
(Ortsteil of Königheim)
Gützenberg 15 a

Gerlachsheim
(Ortsteil of Lauda-
Königshofen)
Herrenberg 16

Oberlauda
(Ortsteil of Lauda-
Königshofen)
Steinklinge 17
Altenberg 18 P

Lauda
(Ortsteil of Lauda-
Königshofen)
Altenberg 18 P
Frankenberg 19 P
Nonnenberg 20 P

Marbach
(Ortsteil of Lauda-
Königshofen)
Frankenberg 19 P

Beckstein
(Ortsteil of Lauda-
Königshofen)
Nonnenberg 20 P
Kirchberg 21 P

Königshofen
(Ortsteil of Lauda-
Königshofen)
Kirchberg 21 P
Walterstal 22 P
Turmberg 23

Unterbalbach
(Ortsteil of Lauda-
Königshofen)
Vogelsberg 23 a

Oberbalbach
(Ortsteil of Lauda-
Königshofen)
Mühlberg 23 b

Sachsenflur
(Ortsteil of Lauda-
Königshofen)
Walterstal 22 P
Kailberg 24

Unterschüpf
(Ortsteil of Boxberg)
Mühlberg 25

Oberschüpf
(Ortsteil of Boxberg)
Altenberg 26
Herrenberg 27

Krautheim
Heiligenberg 28 P

Klepsau
(Ortsteil of
Krautheim)
Heiligenberg 28 P

Dainbach
(Ortsteil of Bad
Mergentheim)
Alte Burg 28 a

Laudenbach 29
Hemsbach 30
Sulzbach
31
Weinheim
32

| 66 | ROAD MAP |
Main
BAD
MERGENTHEIM •

Lützelsachsen
33 *Hohensachsen*
Großsachsen 34
35
eutershausen 36 **Großlage Rittersber**
KÜNZELSAU
38 39
NECKARSULM •

| 68 | ROAD MAP |

40
Schriesheim
38

Dossenheim
41

41

Neckar
Handschuhsheim
42
43

Heidelberg

**BEREICH
BADISCHE
BERGSTRASSE/
KRAICHGAU**

**GROSSLAGE
RITTERSBERG**

Laudenbach
Sonnberg 29

Hemsbach
Herrnwingert 30 P

Sulzbach
(Ortsteil of Weinheim)
Herrnwingert 30 P

Weinheim
Hubberg 31
Wüstberg 32

Lützelsachsen
(Ortsteil of Weinheim)
Stephansberg 33 P

Hohensachsen
(Ortsteil of Weinheim)
Stephansberg 33 P

Großsachsen
(Ortsteil of Hirschberg)
Sandrocken 34

Leutershausen
(Ortsteil of Hirschberg)
Kahlberg 35
Staudenberg 36 P

Schriesheim
Staudenberg 36 P
Kuhberg 38
Madonnenberg 39
Schloßberg 40

Dossenheim
Ölberg 41

Heidelberg
Heiligenberg 42
Sonnenseife
ob der Bruck 43

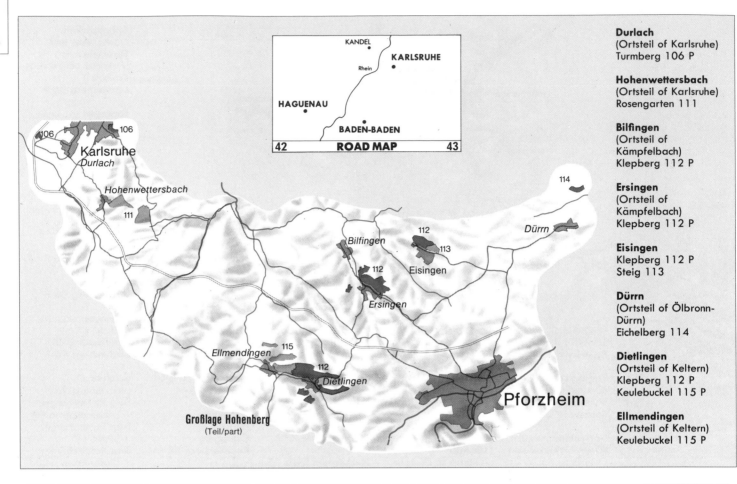

Durlach
(Ortsteil of Karlsruhe)
Turmberg 106 P

Hohenwettersbach
(Ortsteil of Karlsruhe)
Rosengarten 111

Bilfingen
(Ortsteil of
Kämpfelbach)
Klepberg 112 P

Ersingen
(Ortsteil of
Kämpfelbach)
Klepberg 112 P

Eisingen
Klepberg 112 P
Steig 113

Dürrn
(Ortsteil of Ölbronn-
Dürrn)
Eichelberg 114

Dietlingen
(Ortsteil of Keltern)
Klepberg 112 P
Keulebuckel 115 P

Ellmendingen
(Ortsteil of Keltern)
Keulebuckel 115 P

TRAVELLING THE VINEYARDS

Some German vineyards are easy to visit, as they follow closely the slopes of the river that holds the region together. Pick up the Mosel at Trier and you can discover all the well-known wine villages without any further help by simply travelling downstream to Koblenz. The vineyards of the Ahr and the Mittelrhein are similarly confined, and only now and again are vines allowed to establish themselves in attractive side valleys.

Other regions are more spread out and lack the reference point provided by a dissecting river. For them, a well signposted wine road is ideal. Probably the best known of these is the *Deutsche Weinstraße*, dating from 1935, that runs 80 kilometres (50 miles) from the north to the south of the Rheinpfalz, ending at the French border. Here at Schweigen, in the 1920s, the first Weinlehrpfad (instructional wine path) was

constructed in the vineyards. It set a trend that has since been enthusiastically followed, particularly in Baden and Württemberg.

Country walking in Germany is made easy by a comprehensive network of public footpaths, but the instructional wine path with its well-sited notice boards offers guidance in German on such matters as the vine varieties grown, the methods of training, the type of soil and the layout of the Einzellagen. It will always include in its tour one or more Weinstuben (wine bars), so that the effect on the wine of the

vineyard from which it comes can be judged on the spot.

Efforts to build up a clear identity for the wine-growing regions have been linked with the reconstruction (Flurbereinigung) of the vineyards, and the value of tourism has not been forgotten. The new Weinlehrpfade help to explain and therefore to sell German wine, and by the end of the 1970s practically all the eleven wine regions had their own Weinstraßen.

A natural adjunct to the wine roads are the Winzerfeste — the wine festivals — that fill the calendar from late April until October (details can be found in the Travel Information sections that accompany the introduction to each region).

These simple exercises in selling are natural tourist attractions, but they offer a chance to enjoy wine, without being too serious about it. Details of when and

where they take place can be obtained from:
Deutsches Weininstitut GmbH
Haus des deutschen Weines
Gutenbergplatz 3–5,
6500 Mainz 1.
(Tel: 06131-28290)
Office hours are usually 9–12 a.m. and 2–5 p.m. Monday to Friday.

TRAVEL INFORMATION

The northern part of the Baden wine region includes one of Germany's major tourist centres, Heidelberg.

Places to visit
Heidelberg has Germany's oldest university, a superb castle, many historic buildings in the town centre and the vast Heidelberger

Fass (cask), dating from 1751, with a capacity of 220,000 litres (314,286 bottles). In summer there is a drama festival and open-air concerts.

The beauty of the Neckar valley, running east from Heidelberg, can perhaps best be seen from a boat. The lower Neckar valley has a number of castle hotels.

Wine roads
The *Badische Weinstraße* starts

◄ Hand-picking is still the rule in Germany. The quality vineyards are too steep for machines.
▼ Both the old narrow terraces and broad new ones can still be seen in Baden's Kaiserstuhl.

north of Heidelberg and threads through the Bergstraße vineyards and on towards the Ortenau district (see South Baden).

Wine festivals
See South Baden

Food and drink
It is here that the climate becomes more benign and southern, with asparagus among the market-garden crops. Schwetzingen, near Heidelberg, is noted for asparagus; another local delicacy is *Hopfensprossen* — tiny hops dressed with butter or cream. Fruits such as wild raspberries (*Himbeeren*) and currants (*Johannisbeeren*) are also Baden specialities. Many towns

have markets where local produce can be bought. In the Black Forest look out for *Bauernspeck*, country-smoked bacon, and anything involving kirsch, cream and cherries. Black Forest venison is famous: one noted dish is *Rehrücken* or saddle of venison with pears and cranberries.

Regional Wine Information Office
Weinwerbezentrale Badischer Winzergenossenschaften e.G.
Keßlerstraße 5
7500 Karlsruhe 1
Tel: 0721-557028/29

VISITING ESTATES AND WINE CELLARS

Tasting wine
There are plenty of opportunities to taste the local wines in every German wine district. Indeed, some estates rely on visitors, either tasters or those who come to eat in restaurants and bars, for much of their sales. Tastings are usually arranged on a more organized — though convivial — basis than in other wine countries.

Most estate and cooperative cellars are happy to welcome interested visitors during business hours — usually between 9 a.m. and 5 p.m. on week days — although most do appreciate advance warning, either by letter or by telephone. Some cellars set a firm maximum and minimum to the number of persons they will receive in any one party. If a tasting is provided free of charge, it is courteous to buy a few bottles when leaving. Most tastings, especially the organized ones, are charged for.

The Germans are, by nature, very hospitable, but the visitor to a small estate should remember that although tasting in a producer's cellar is one of the most enjoyable aspects of visiting a wine region, it may be occupying a large part of the estate owner's working day and the welcome should not be overstayed. The local wine promotion bodies in the regions have lists of the estates where visitors are most welcome to taste the wines. Alternatively, travel along one of the wine roads or *Weinstraßen* — not many kilometres will go by before a tasting cellar is spotted. In some of the main wine towns there are central cellars where the wines of several growers can be sampled. This is a good way to get the flavour of a region. Many restaurants in wine districts will have a list of local wines which can be bought by the glass.

Buying wine
Flaschenweinverkauf (sale of wine in bottle) is the message that is hung outside many cellars in Germany.

Many estates sell almost all their wines directly to the consumer and have a wine bar or tasting room set aside for this purpose. While customers sit around tables the wines are served to them. Facilities for spitting at "sitting" tastings are not normally offered. General comment on the wines is made, after each has been introduced by the cellar master (Keller-meister) or by the estate owner (Weingutsbesitzer). Such tastings quickly become a social occasion, although the wines still receive proper attention. Their relatively low alcohol content makes it possible to taste many wines in this way and remain clear headed. (In the course of his duties the professional taster will

willingly tackle 70 or more German white wines in one session. For wines with a higher alcohol content this would hardly be possible.)

Some useful terms
Ansprechend Attractive
Aromatisch Aromatic
Ausdrucksvoll Characterful
Ausgeglichen Well balanced
Bukett Bouquet
Fruchtig Fruity
Harmonisch Balanced
Herb Austere
Herzhaft Hearty
Jung Young
Lebendig Lively
Leicht Light
Rassig Racy, with pronounced but pleasant acidity and style
Reif Ripe, full, mature
Reintönig Clean
Säure Acidity
Sortencharakter Character of the vine variety
Süsse Sweetness

SOUTHERN ZONE

98

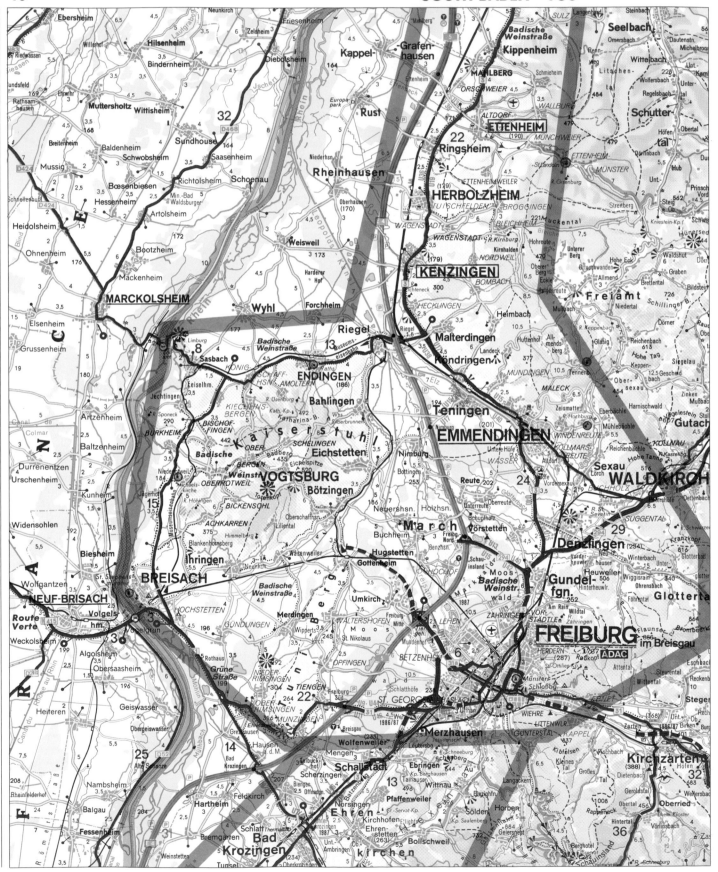

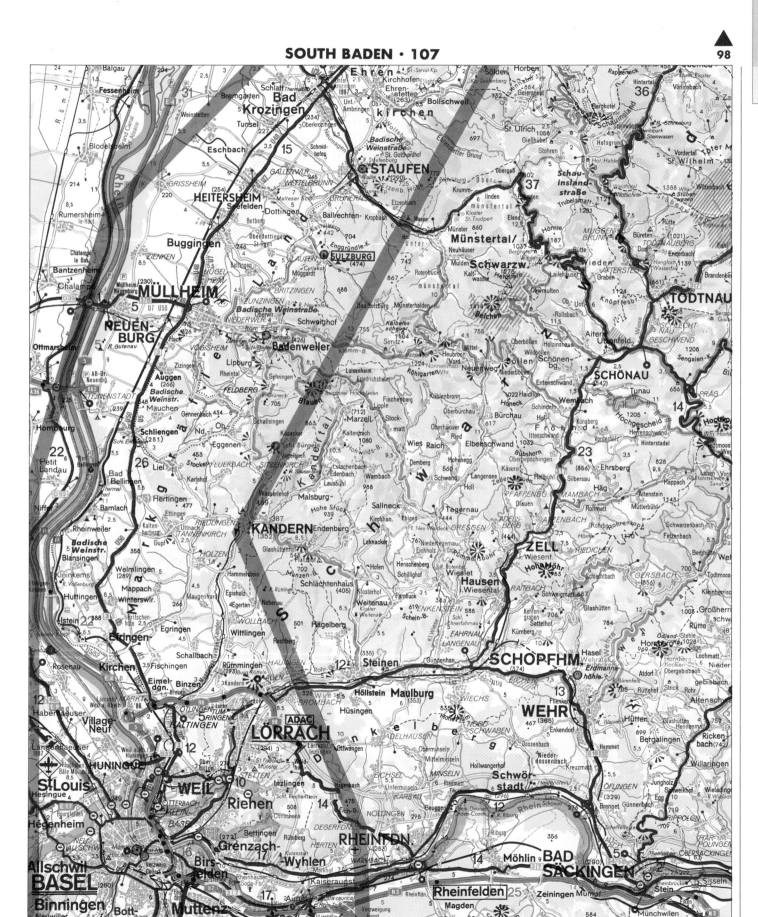

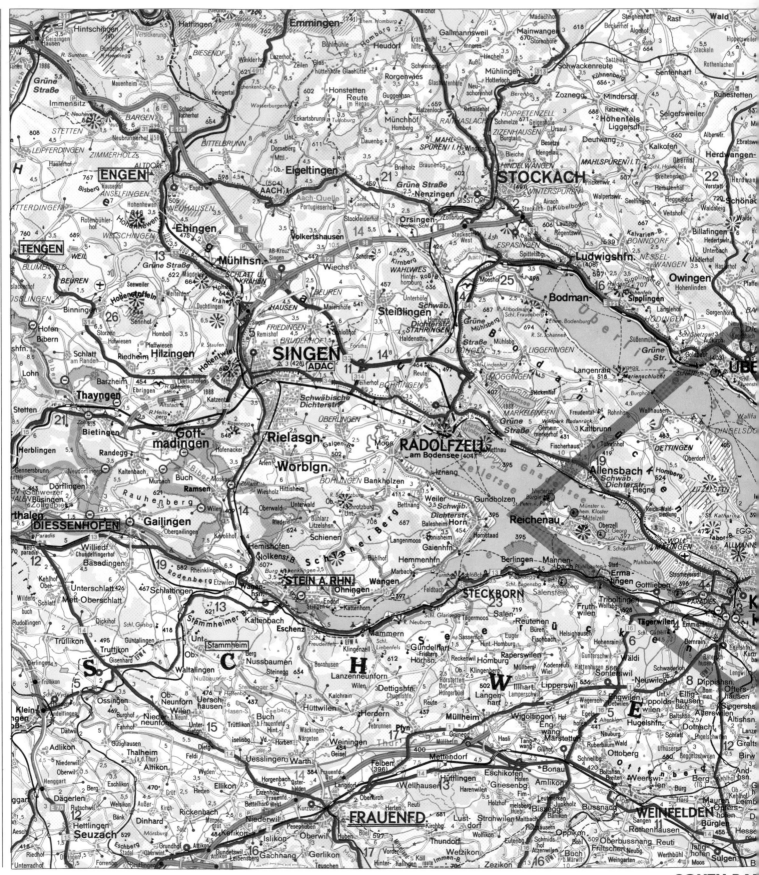

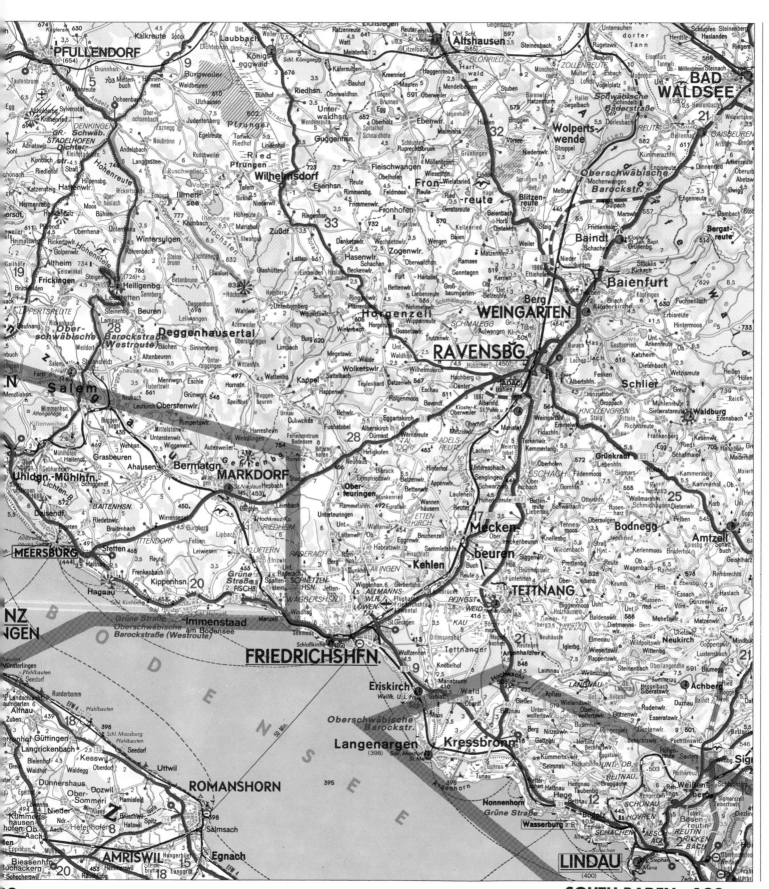

BADEN · SOUTH BADEN

The Baden vineyards really begin in earnest south of Baden-Baden with the Bereich Ortenau, which in turn shades without a perceptible break into the Bereich Breisgau. Ortenau has a privileged climate that allows it to specialize in red and rosé wines: its red Spätburgunders have good colour and are very much to the local taste. Even more so are its pale pink Weißherbst and its curious and original Rotgold, made by fermenting the juices of Spätburgunder and Pinot Gris together.

Undoubtedly the finest Rieslings of the Ortenau are from the steep hillsides at Ortenberg and Durbach (where they are called Klingelberger). Gewürztraminer (here known as Clevner) is the other Durbach speciality. These wines have the "breed", the length and the balance to put Baden on the international map.

The Bereich Breisgau starts south of Offenburg, producing rather weighty dry white wines, largely of Müller-Thurgau and the superior Ruländer. Weißherbst is also popular here.

Considerably more important, and indeed the climax of Baden wine-growing, is the "island" Bereich of Kaiserstuhl-Tuniberg, an old volcano standing out in the Rhine valley, detached from the Black Forest, one of nature's pre-ordained vineyards whose climate and soil can give remarkable character to a wide range of wines. Müller-Thurgau is the main grape grown but there is also a large proportion of Spätburgunder and Ruländer, which performs exceptionally well on these iron-rich slopes. Low acid, always a characteristic of this grape, is compensated for here by fiery concentrated flavours and density of texture, qualities that mature extremely well. Silvaner can also be splendid in warm corners of the Kaiserstuhl. Bereich Markgräflerland, stretching south to the Swiss border, specializes in gentle dry wines. Its Gutedel is often attractively *spritzig*, and an interesting wine is made of the Nobling, a cross between Gutedel and Silvaner with much more aroma than either.

To the visitor to the Bodensee the tiny Bereich on the north shores of the lovely lake is of consuming interest. The lake, Germany's largest, counteracts the considerable altitude to produce a mild climate in which Spätburgunder and Müller-Thurgau both give refreshing, lightly fruity wines. The whites are often *spritzig*, the Spätburgunder usually either pale red or (its most attractive form) made into Weißherbst, the often very lively pale rosé which is the true local speciality.

TRAVEL INFORMATION

▲ Meersburg on the Bodensee (Lake Constance in English) is Germany's nearest approach to a southern port. The climate has attracted famous gardeners as well as winegrowers.
▶ Freiburg im Breisgau is noted for the charm of its ancient streets and the liveliness of its university.

This large region has everything from the sophisticated spa of Baden-Baden to cuckoo-clock-making villages deep in the Black Forest.

Places to visit
Baden-Baden: Germany is a country still much given to visiting – and using – spas, and Baden-Baden is the chief of them. It is both opulently nineteenth century and up-to-date: the waters are pronounced good for "diseases of modern civilization" as well as traditional over-indulgence. Gambling, culture and countryside are on offer as well as the waters. Freiburg: one of Europe's finest gothic spires towers over a medieval marketplace. Kaiserstuhl: range of volcanic hills with walking and fine views west to France and east to the Black Forest. Schwarzwald (Black Forest): well-tended forest paths, farm holidays and folklore. Bodensee (Lake Constance): one of Europe's biggest lakes, with boating, swimming and historic towns such as Meersburg.

Wine roads
The *Badische Weinstraße* runs from north to south along the edge of the Black Forest, passing through Freiburg and ending at

► The beautiful baroque edifice of Kloster Birnau at Oberuhldingen, just north of Meersburg on the Bodensee, overlooks the 32-hectare Einzellage Kirchhalde, planted with a typical regional selection of Müller-Thurgau and Spätburgunder, with an unusual proportion of the aromatic new Bacchus.

the Swiss frontier. A wine path — the *Breisgauer Weinwanderweg* — starts at Freiburg and threads the vineyards as far as Friesenheim, a walk of 97km which is split into 23 stages. The signpost is a goblet on a diamond shape.

Wine festivals

Bubbingen (mid-June), Freiburg (mid-June), Müllheim (end June), Reicholzheim (mid-July), Schloß Ortenberg & Durbach (early Aug), Affental (mid-Aug), Breisach (end Aug), Meersburg (mid-Sept), Heidelberg (end Sept); in October the festivals are too numerous to list.

Food and drink

Baden celebrates food as heartily as its neighbour across the Rhine, Alsace. Game, fruit and all manner of farm produce abound. The area is a popular one for holidaymakers, both German and foreign, and the *Fremdenzimmer* and *Zimmer Frei* signs hang thick in towns and villages. Such places, and the small guest houses and inns, offer good value. In the vineyard districts, they will often be run by winemaking families.

Regional Wine Information Office

Weinwerbezentrale Badischer Winzergenossenschaften e.G.
Keßlerstraße 5
7500 Karlsruhe 1
Tel: 0721-557028/29

VINEYARDS

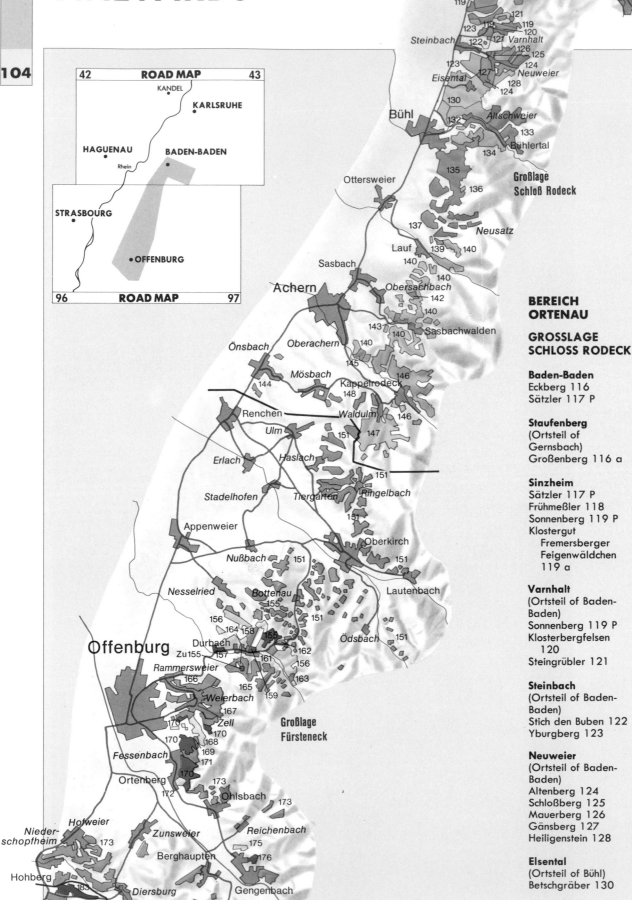

ROAD MAP 42 · 43

KANDEL

KARLSRUHE

HAGUENAU

BADEN-BADEN

Rhein

STRASBOURG

OFFENBURG

ROAD MAP 96 · 97

Baden-Baden

Gernsbach

Staufenberg

Sinzheim

Obertsrot

Hilpertsau

Weisenbach

Steinbach

Varnhalt

Neuweier

Bühl

Eisental

Altschweier

Bühlertal

Großlage Schloß Rodeck

Ottersweier

Neusatz

Lauf

Sasbach

Achern

Obersasbach

Sasbachwalden

Önsbach

Oberachern

Mösbach

Kappelrodeck

Waldulm

Renchen

Ulm

Erlach

Haslach

Tiergarten

Ringelbach

Stadelhofen

Appenweier

Nußbach

Oberkirch

Lautenbach

Nesselried

Bottenau

Ödsbach

Offenburg

Durbach

Zu 155

Rammersweier

Weierbach

Großlage Fürsteneck

Zell

Fessenbach

Ortenberg

Ohlsbach

Hofweier

Zunsweier

Reichenbach

Niederschopfheim

Berghaupten

Gengenbach

Hohberg

Diersburg

Oberschopfheim

Bermersbach

BEREICH ORTENAU

GROSSLAGE SCHLOSS RODECK

Baden-Baden
Eckberg 116
Sätzler 117 P

Staufenberg
(Ortsteil of Gernsbach)
Großenberg 116 a

Sinzheim
Sätzler 117 P
Frühmeßler 118
Sonnenberg 119 P
Klostergut
  Fremersberger
  Feigenwäldchen
  119 a

Varnhalt
(Ortsteil of Baden-Baden)
Sonnenberg 119 P
Klosterbergfelsen
  120
Steingrübler 121

Steinbach
(Ortsteil of Baden-Baden)
Stich den Buben 122
Yburgberg 123

Neuweier
(Ortsteil of Baden-Baden)
Altenberg 124
Schloßberg 125
Mauerberg 126
Gänsberg 127
Heiligenstein 128

Elsental
(Ortsteil of Bühl)
Betschgräber 130

Altschweier
(Ortsteil of Bühl)
Sternenberg 132 P

Neusatz
(Ortsteil of Bühl)
Sternenberg 132 P
Wolfhag 135 P
Burg Windeck
  Kastanienhalde
  136

Bühlertal
Engelsfelsen 133
Klotzberg 134

Ottersweier
Wolfhag 135 P
Althof 137

Lauf
Gut Alsenhof 139
Alde Gott 140 P

Obersasbach
(Ortsteil of Sasbach)
Alde Gott 140 P
Eichwäldele 142

Sasbachwalden
Alde Gott 140 P
Klostergut
  Schelzberg 143

Önsbach
(Ortsteil of Achern)
Pulverberg 144

Oberachern
(Ortsteil of Achern)
Alde Gott 140 P
Bienenberg 145

Kappelrodeck
Hex vom Dasenstein
  146

Waldulm
(Ortsteil of Kappelrodeck)
Pfarrberg 147
Kreuzberg 148 P

Renchen
Kreuzberg 148 P

Mösbach
(Ortsteil of Achern)
Kreuzberg 148 P

Obertsrot
(Ortsteil of Gernsbach)
Grafensprung 149

Weisenbach
Kestellberg 150 P

Hilpertsau
(Ortsteil of
Gernsbach)
Kestellberg 150 P

GROSSLAGE FÜRSTENECK

Ulm
(Ortsteil of Renchen)
Renchtäler 151 P

Erlach
(Ortsteil of Renchen)
Renchtäler 151 P

Haslach
(Ortsteil of
Oberkirch)
Renchtäler 151 P

Stadelhofen
(Ortsteil of
Oberkirch)
Renchtäler 151 P

Tiergarten
(Ortsteil of
Oberkirch)
Renchtäler 151 P

Ringelbach
(Ortsteil of
Oberkirch)
Renchtäler 151 P

Ödsbach
(Ortsteil of
Oberkirch)
Renchtäler 151 P

Bottenau
(Ortsteil of
Oberkirch)
Renchtäler 151 P

Nußbach
(Ortsteil of
Oberkirch)
Renchtäler 151 P

Oberkirch
Renchtäler 151 P

Lautenbach
Renchtäler 151 P

Nesselried
(Ortsteil of
Appenweier)
Renchtäler 151 P
Schloßberg 155 P

Durbach
Schloßberg 155 P
Plauelrain 156
Ölberg 157
Josephsberg 158
Steinberg 159
Kapellenberg 161

Bienengarten 162
Kasselberg 163
Schloß Grohl 164
Kochberg 165

Rammersweier
(Ortsteil of
Offenburg)
Kreuzberg 166

Zell-Weierbach
(Ortsteil of
Offenburg)
Abtsberg 167

Fessenbach
(Ortsteil of
Offenburg)
Bergle 168
Franzensberger
169 P

Ortenberg
Franzensberger
169 P
Freudental 170
Andreasberg 171
Schloßberg 172

Ohlsbach
Kinzigtäler 173 P

Zunsweier
(Ortsteil of
Offenburg)
Kinzigtäler 173 P

Gengenbach
Kinzigtäler 173 P
Nollenköpfle 176

Reichenbach
(Ortsteil of
Gengenbach)
Kingzigtäler 173 P
Amselberg 175

Bermersbach
(Ortsteil of
Gengenbach)
Kinzigtäler 173 P

Berghaupten
Kinzigtäler 173 P

Diersburg
(Ortsteil of Hohberg)
Kinzigtäler 173 P
Schloßberg 181

Hofweier
(Ortsteil of Hohberg)
Kinzigtäler 173 P

Niederschopfheim
(Ortsteil of Hohberg)
Kinzigtäler 173 P

BEREICH BREISGAU

GROSSLAGE SCHUTTER-LINDENBERG

Friesenheim
Kronenbühl 183 P

Oberschopfheim
(Ortsteil of
Friesenheim)
Kronenbühl 183 P

Oberweier
(Ortsteil of
Friesenheim)
Kronenbühl 183 P

Heiligenzell
(Ortsteil of
Friesenheim)
Kronenbühl 183 P

Lahr
Kronenbühl 183 P
Herrentisch 184

Hugsweier
(Ortsteil of Lahr)
Kronenbühl 183 P

Mietersheim
(Ortsteil of Lahr)
Kronenbühl 183 P

Sulz
(Ortsteil of Lahr)
Haselstaude 185 P

Mahlberg
Haselstaude 185 P

Kippenheim
Haselstaude 185 P

Schmieheim
(Ortsteil of
Kippenheim)
Kirchberg 186 P

Wallburg
(Ortsteil of Ettenheim)
Kirchberg 186 P

Münchweier
(Ortsteil of Ettenheim)
Kirchberg 186 P

GROSSLAGE BURG LICHTENECK

Ettenheim
Kaiserberg 189 P

Altdorf
(Ortsteil of Ettenheim)
Kaiserberg 189 P

Ringsheim
Kaiserberg 189 P

Herbolzheim
Kaiserberg 189 P

Tutschfelden
(Ortsteil of
Herbolzheim)
Kaiserberg 189 P

Broggingen
(Ortsteil of
Herbolzheim)
Kaiserberg 189 P

Bleichheim
(Ortsteil of
Herbolzheim)
Kaiserberg 189 P

Wagenstadt
(Ortsteil of
Herbolzheim)
Hummelberg 192 P

Kenzingen
Hummelberg 192 P
Roter Berg 193

Nordweil
(Ortsteil of
Kenzingen)
Herrenberg 194

Bombach
(Ortsteil of
Kenzingen)
Sommerhalde 195

Hecklingen
(Ortsteil of
Kenzingen)
Schloßberg 196

Malterdingen
Bienenberg 197 P

Heimsbach
(Ortsteil of Teningen)
Bienenberg 197 P

Köndringen
(Ortsteil of Teningen)
Alte Burg 198 P

Mundingen
(Ortsteil of
Emmendingen)
Alte Burg 198 P

GROSSLAGE BURG ZÄHRINGEN

Hochburg
(Ortsteil of
Emmendingen)
Halde 199

Sexau
Sonnhalde 200 P

Buchholz
(Ortsteil of
Waldkirch)
Sonnhalde 200 P

Denzlingen
Sonnhalde 200 P
Eichberg 203 P

Heuweiler
Eichberg 203 P

Glottertal
Eichberg 203 P
Roter Bur 205

Wildtal
(Ortsteil of
Gundelfingen)
Sonnenhof 207

Freiburg
Schloßberg 208

Lehen
(Ortsteil of Freiburg)
Bergle 209

BEREICH KAISERSTUHL-TUNIBERG

GROSSLAGE VULKANFELSEN

Nimburg
(Ortsteil of Teningen)
Steingrube 210 P

Neuershausen
(Ortsteil of March)
Steingrube 210 P

Riegel
St. Michaelsberg 211

Bahlingen
Silberberg 212

Eichstetten
Herrenbuck 213
Lerchenberg 214
(The two sites 213
and 214 cannot be
shown separately, as
213 is situated
above 214 on a
steep slope)

Bötzingen
Lasenberg 215
Eckberg 216

Wasenweiler
(Ortsteil of Ihringen)
Lotberg 217

Kreuzhalde 218 P

Ihringen
Kreuzhalde 218 P
Fohrenberg 219
Winklerberg 220
Schloßberg 221 P
Castellberg 222 P
Steinfelsen 223 P

– Ortsteil Blanken-
hornsberg
Doktorgarten 224

Achkarren
(Ortsteil of
Vogtsburg im
Kaiserstuhl)
Schloßberg 221 P
Castellberg 222 P

Bickensohl
(Ortsteil of
Vogtsburg im
Kaiserstuhl)
Steinfelsen 223 P
Herrenstück 226

Oberrotweil
(Ortsteil of
Vogtsburg im
Kaiserstuhl)
Schloßberg 221 P
Käsleberg 227
Eichberg 228
Henkenberg 229
Kirchberg 230

Oberbergen
(Ortsteil of
Vogtsburg im
Kaiserstuhl)
Pulverbruck 231
Baßgeige 232

Schelingen
(Ortsteil of
Vogtsburg im
Kaiserstuhl)
Kirchberg 233

Bischoffingen
(Ortsteil of
Vogtsburg im
Kaiserstuhl)
Enselberg 234 P
Rosenkranz 235
Steinbuck 236

Burkheim
(Ortsteil of
Vogtsburg im
Kaiserstuhl)
Feuerberg 237
Schloßgarten 238

Jechtingen
(Ortsteil of Sasbach)
Enselberg 234 P
Steingrube 239
Hochberg 240
Eichert 241
Gestühl 242 P

Leiselheim
(Ortsteil of Sasbach)
Gestühl 242 P

Sasbach
Scheibenbuck 243
Lützelberg 244
Rote Halde 245
Limburg 246

Kiechlinsbergen
(Ortsteil of Endingen)
Teufelsburg 247
Ölberg 248

Königschaffhausen
(Ortsteil of Endingen)
Hasenberg 249
Steingrüble 250

Amoltern
(Ortsteil of Endingen)
Steinhalde 251

Endingen
Engelsberg 252
Steingrube 253
Tannacker 254

Breisach
Augustinerberg 255
Eckartsberg 256

**GROSSLAGE
ATTILAFELSEN**

Gottenheim
Kirchberg 257

Merdingen
Bühl 258

Waltershofen
(Ortsteil of Freiburg)
Steinmauer 259

Opfingen
(Ortsteil of Freiburg)
Sonnenberg 260

Niederrimsingen
(Ortsteil of Breisach)
Rotgrund 261

Tiengen
(Ortsteil of Freiburg)
Rebtal 262

Oberrimsingen
(Ortseil of Breisach)
Franziskaner 263

Munzingen
(Ortsteil of Freiburg)
Kappellenberg 264

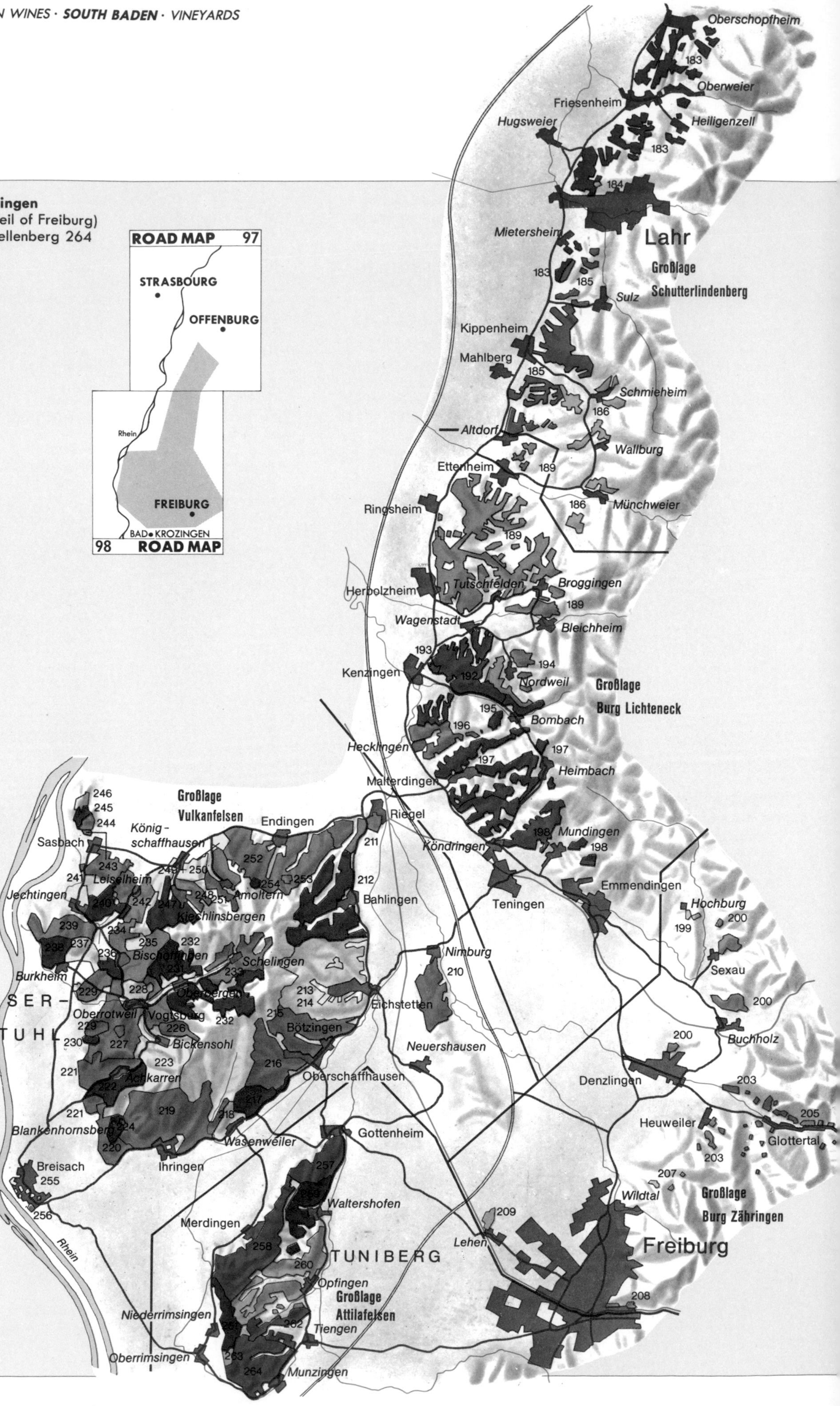

ROAD MAP 97

STRASBOURG

OFFENBURG

Rhein

FREIBURG

BAD · KROZINGEN

98 ROAD MAP

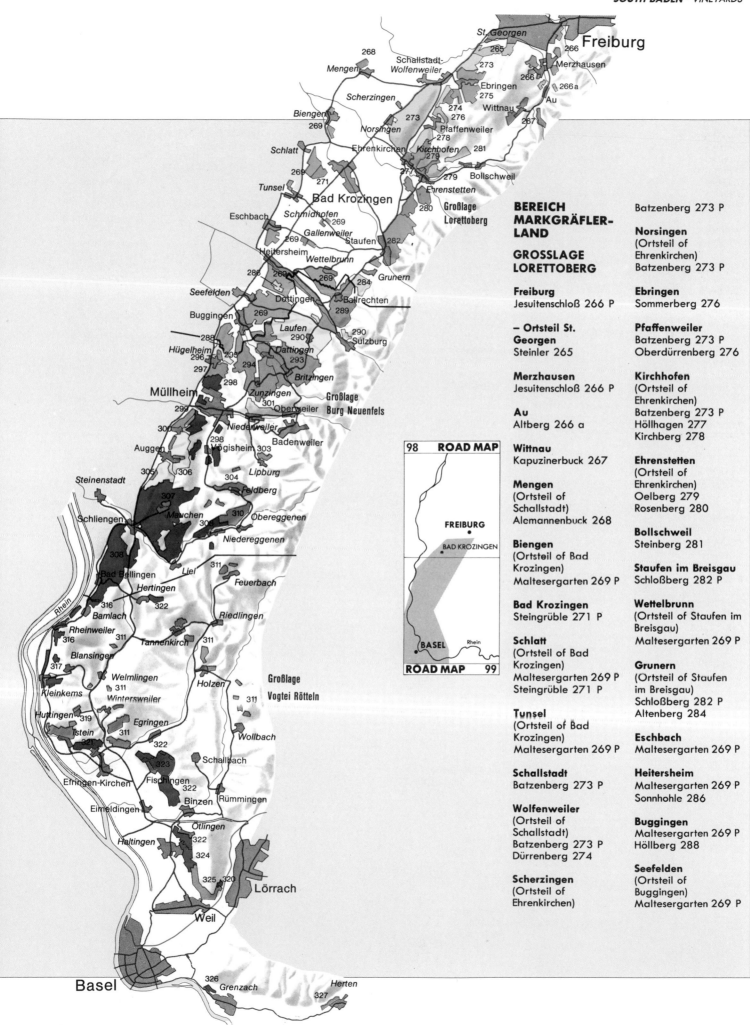

BEREICH MARKGRÄFLER-LAND

GROSSLAGE LORETTOBERG

Freiburg
Jesuitenschloß 266 P

– Ortsteil St. Georgen
Steinler 265

Merzhausen
Jesuitenschloß 266 P

Au
Altberg 266 a

Wittnau
Kapuzinerbuck 267

Mengen
(Ortsteil of Schallstadt)
Alemannenbuck 268

Biengen
(Ortsteil of Bad Krozingen)
Maltesergarten 269 P

Bad Krozingen
Steingrüble 271 P

Schlatt
(Ortsteil of Bad Krozingen)
Maltesergarten 269 P
Steingrüble 271 P

Tunsel
(Ortsteil of Bad Krozingen)
Maltesergarten 269 P

Schallstadt
Batzenberg 273 P

Wolfenweiler
(Ortsteil of Schallstadt)
Batzenberg 273 P
Dürrenberg 274

Scherzingen
(Ortsteil of Ehrenkirchen)
Batzenberg 273 P

Norsingen
(Ortsteil of Ehrenkirchen)
Batzenberg 273 P

Ebringen
Sommerberg 276

Pfaffenweiler
Batzenberg 273 P
Oberdürrenberg 276

Kirchhofen
(Ortsteil of Ehrenkirchen)
Batzenberg 273 P
Höllhagen 277
Kirchberg 278

Ehrenstetten
(Ortsteil of Ehrenkirchen)
Oelberg 279
Rosenberg 280

Bollschweil
Steinberg 281

Staufen im Breisgau
Schloßberg 282 P

Wettelbrunn
(Ortsteil of Staufen im Breisgau)
Maltesergarten 269 P

Grunern
(Ortsteil of Staufen im Breisgau)
Schloßberg 282 P
Altenberg 284

Eschbach
Maltesergarten 269 P

Heitersheim
Maltesergarten 269 P
Sonnhohle 286

Buggingen
Maltesergarten 269 P
Höllberg 288

Seefelden
(Ortsteil of Buggingen)
Maltesergarten 269 P

ROAD MAP 98
ROAD MAP
FREIBURG
BAD KROZINGEN
BASEL
Rhein
ROAD MAP 99

GROSSLAGE BURG NEUENFELS

Ballrechten-Dottingen
Castellberg 289
Altenberg 290 P

Sulzburg
Altenberg 290 P

Laufen
(Ortsteil of Sulzburg)
Altenberg 290 P

Britzingen
(Ortsteil of Müllheim)
Altenberg 290 P
Sonnhole 293 P
Rosenberg 294 P

Dattingen
(Ortsteil of Müllheim)
Altenberg 290 P
Sonnhole 293 P
Rosenberg 294 P

Zunzingen
(Ortsteil of Müllheim)
Rosenberg 294 P

Hügelheim
(Ortsteil of Müllheim)
Höllberg 295
Gottesacker 296
Schloßgarten 297

Müllheim
Sonnhalde 298
Reggenhag 299
Pfaffenstück 300

Vöglsheim
(Ortsteil of Müllheim)
Sonnhalde 298 P

Niederweiler
(Ortsteil of Müllheim)
Römerberg 301 P

Badenweiler
Römerberg 301 P

Lipburg
(Ortsteil of Badenweiler)
Kirchberg 303

Feldberg
(Ortsteil of Müllheim)
Paradies 304

Auggen
Letten 305
Schäf 306 P

Mauchen
(Ortsteil of Schliengen)
Frauenberg 307

Sonnenstück 308 P

Schliengen
Sonnenstück 308 P

Steinenstadt
(Ortsteil of Neuenburg am Rhein)
Schäf 306 P
Sonnenstück 308 P

Niedereggenen
(Ortsteil of Schliengen)
Sonnenstück 308 P
Röthen 310 P

Lief
(Ortsteil of Schliengen)
Sonnenstück 308 P

Bad Bellingen
Sonnenstück 308 P

Obereggenen
(Ortsteil of Schliengen)
Röthen 310 P

GROSSLAGE VOGTEI RÖTTELN

Feuerbach
(Ortsteil of Kandern)
Steingässle 311 P

Tannenkirch
(Ortsteil of Kandern)
Steingässle 311 P

Riedlingen
(Ortsteil of Kandern)
Steingässle 311 P

Holzen
(Ortsteil of Kandern)
Steingässle 311 P

Wollbach
(Ortsteil of Kandern)
Steingässle 311 P

Welmlingen
(Ortsteil of Efringen-Kirchen)
Steingässle 311 P

Huttingen
(Ortsteil of Efringen-Kirchen)
Kirchberg 319 P

Istein
(Ortsteil of Efringen-Kirchen)
Kirchberg 319 P

Wintersweiler
(Ortsteil of Efringen-Kirchen)
Steingässle 311 P

Efringen-Kirchen
Steingässle 311 P
Kirchberg 319 P
Oelberg 321
Sonnhohle 322 P

Bamlach
(Ortsteil of Bad Bellingen)
Kapellenberg 316 P

Rheinweiler
(Ortsteil of Bad Bellingen)
Kapellenberg 316 P

Blansingen
(Ortsteil of Efringen-Kirchen)
Wolfer 317 P

Kleinkems
(Ortsteil of Efringen-Kirchen)
Wolfer 317 P

Lörrach
Sonnenbrunnen 320

Egringen
(Ortsteil of Efringen-Kirchen)
Sonnhohle 322 P

Hertingen
(Ortsteil of Bad Bellingen)
Sonnhohle 322 P

Schallbach
Sonnhohle 322 P

Fischingen
Weingarten 323

Rümmingen
Sonnhohle 322 P

Eimeldingen
Sonnhohle 322 P

Binzen
Sonnhohle 322 P

Ötlingen
(Ortsteil of Weil am Rhein)
Sonnhohle 322 P
Stiege 324 P

Haltingen
(Ortsteil of Weil am Rhein)
Stiege 324 P

Weil am Rhein
Stiege 324 P
Schlipf 325

Grenzach
(Ortsteil of Grenzach-Whylen)
Hornfelsen 326

Herten
(Ortsteil of Rheinfelden)
Steinacker 327

BEREICH BODENSEE

GROSSLAGENFREI

Rechberg
(Ortsteil of Klettgau)
Kapellenberg 347 P*

Erzingen
(Ortsteil of Klettgau)
Kapellenberg 347 P*

Nack
(Ortsteil of Lottstetten)
Steinler 348*

Gallingen
Ritterhalde 349*
Schloß Rheinburg 350*

Hohentengen
Ölberg 351*

GROSSLAGE SONNENUFER

Singen (Hohentwiel)
Elisabethenberg 345 P*
Olgaberg 346*

Hilzingen
Elisabethenberg 345 P*

Reichenau
Hochwart 328

Bodman
Königsweingarten 328 a*

Überlingen
Felsengarten 329

Oberuhldingen
(Ortsteil of Uhldingen-Mühlhof)
Kirchhalde 330

Meersburg
Chorherrenhalde 331
Fohrenberg 332 P
Rieschen 333
Jungfernstieg 334
Bengel 335
Haltnau 335 a
Lerchenberg 336 P
Sängerhalde 337 P

Stetten
Fohrenberg 332 P
Lerchenberg 336 P
Sängerhalde 337 P

Hagnau
Burgstall 340 P

Kirchberg
(Ortsteil of Salem)
Schloßberg 339

Kippenhausen
(Ortsteil of Immenstaad)
Burgstall 340 P

Immenstaad
Burgstall 340 P

Bermatingen
Leopoldsberg 341

Markdorf
Sängerhalde 337 P
Burgstall 340 P

Konstanz
Sonnhalde 344

The yellow area on this map represents the vineyards not registered as Einz.

BEREICH REMSTAL-STUTTGART

GROSSLAGENFREI

Kreßbronn/ Bodensee
Berghalde 201

BEREICH BAYERISCHER BODENSEE

GROSSLAGE LINDAUER SEEGARTEN

Nonnenhorn
Seehalde 202
Sonnenbüchel 203

Lindau
Spitalhalde 204 P

Wasserburg
Spitalhalde 204 P

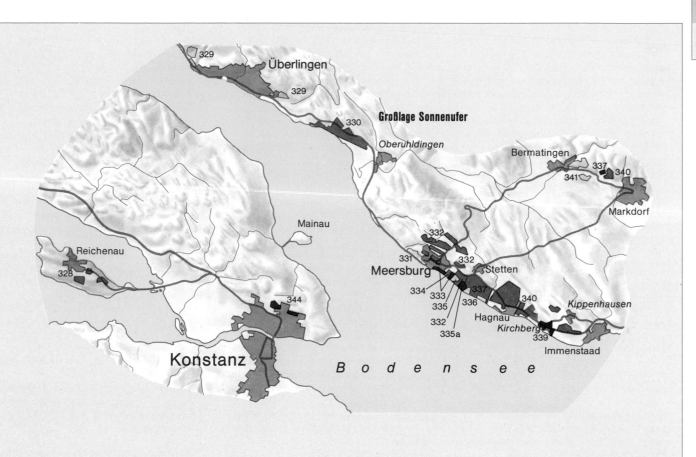

329
Überlingen
329
Großlage Sonnenufer
330
Oberuhldingen
Bermatingen
337
341 340
Markdorf
Mainau
332
Reichenau
331 332
328 Meersburg Stetten
334 337
333
335 336 340 Kippenhausen
332 Hagnau
335a Kirchberg 339
Konstanz Immenstaad
B o d e n s e e
344

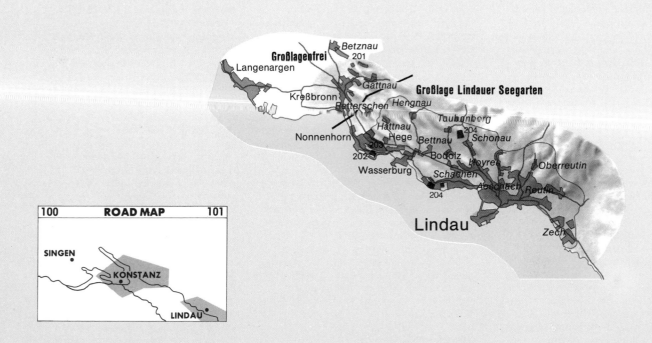

Betznau
201
Großlagenfrei
Langenargen Gattnau **Großlage Lindauer Seegarten**
Kreßbronn Hengnau
Retterschen Taubenberg
Hüttnau 204
Nonnenhorn Hege Bettnau Schönau
202 Bodolz Hoyren
Wasserburg Schachen Oberreutin
204 Aeschach Reutin
Lindau
Zech

ROAD MAP

100	**ROAD MAP**	101

SINGEN
KONSTANZ
LINDAU

UNDERSTANDING GERMAN WINE

Under German labelling laws, German wines are identified in two main ways: by the ripeness of the grapes at harvest, which determines the quality level of the wine, and by geographical origin (region, district, vineyard site), which indicates a great deal about the style of the wine.

Ripeness is the key to the large variety of German wines. Unlike France and Italy, for example, where the classification of quality wines is largely geographical, German wine law is based on the measure of sugar in the grapes at harvest time. The grower must report each batch of grapes as it is picked, and all quality (QbA and QmP) wines are officially tested and tasted before they can be sold. When the wine has passed these tests, it is awarded an "AP" Number (see page 53).

No other country has quality control approaching this, and in no other country is there a stronger guarantee that the wine described on the label will be exactly what will be found in the bottle.

THE QUALITY LEVELS
German wine, like other wines of the European Economic Community countries, is divided into two categories: table wine and quality wine (in German, Tafelwein and Qualitätswein). In Germany, the crux is ripeness – and the care of the vintner. The quality levels listed below are in ascending order of grape sugar concentration at harvest.

TABLE WINES
Tafelwein may be a blend from several regions or from other European Common Market countries (Euroblends). If produced from grapes grown in Germany, the label will identify the wine as Deutscher Tafelwein.
Deutscher Tafelwein can be made only from approved grape varieties in four Tafelwein regions (Rhein-Mosel, Bayern, Oberrhein and Neckar). No vineyard name is allowed on the label.
Deutscher Landwein ("German regional wine") is a designation created in 1982 for dry or semi-dry wine with more body and character than normal Tafelwein, from one of 15 official Landwein regions (e.g. Landwein der Mosel, Rheinischer Landwein, Pfälzer Landwein).

QUALITY WINES
Qualitätswein bestimmter Anbaugebiete or **QbA** ("quality wine from a specified region"), the category that includes the largest quantity of German wine. QbA wines are light, refreshing wines from one of the 11 designated wine regions (Mosel-Saar-Ruwer, Rheingau, etc), made from approved grape varieties, and will have met all the requirements to receive an official control number ("AP" Number, see page 53). They are meant to be enjoyed young.

Qualitätswein mit Prädikat or **QmP** ("quality wine with special distinctions, or attributes"), the category that includes the finest wines of Germany. Each carries one of six special attributes on its label. They are, in ascending order of quality and of ripeness at the time of harvest:
1. **Kabinett** ("normal harvest"), the lightest and most delicate of German wines, made from normally ripe grapes. Generally the driest of QmP wines.
2. **Spätlese** ("late harvest"), balanced, well-rounded wines from grapes harvested at least seven days after the normal harvest, and thus more intense in flavour and concentration.
3. **Auslese** ("harvest of selected, very ripe bunches"), elegant, often slightly sweet wines, rich in flavour, from specially selected bunches of grapes that were particularly ripe and, in exceptional years, affected by botrytis cinerea or "noble rot".
4. **Beerenauslese** or **BA** ("harvest of individually selected, overripe grapes"), rare, remarkably rich, sweet wines with the unmistakable honey-like aroma of botrytis, from overripe grapes individually picked by hand from the bunches. Beerenauslese wines are usually possible only two or three times in a decade.
5. **Eiswein** ("ice wine"), very rare wines from grapes of Beerenauslese quality that have been left on the vine into mid-winter and picked and pressed while frozen. The result is a unique concentration of sweetness and fruity acidity.
6. **Trockenbeerenauslese** or **TBA** ("harvest of individually selected dried grapes"), intensely rich, sweet, honey-like wines from hand-picked grapes that have been left to shrivel on the vine until they have become "raisined". The crowning achievement of German viticulture.

DRY OR SEMI-DRY?
As the demand for drier German wines increases, the designations "trocken" and "halbtrocken" are seen more often on labels. Both trocken and halbtrocken wines can be made at quality levels as high as Auslese.
Trocken (dry) can be used on the label of a wine that has no more than 9 grams per litre of residual sugar. At this level the wine has no perceptible sweetness. Trocken wines in the QbA and Spätlese (QmP) categories are often good with food.
Halbtrocken (half-dry) wines may have no more than 18 grams per litre of residual sugar and frequently have an ideal balance of sweetness to accompany food, especially if of Kabinett status.

SPARKLING WINES
Sekt (pronounced "zeckt") is the familiar term for sparkling wine in Germany – a shortened form of Schaumwein (foaming wine). Usually less austere and lower in alcohol than French sparkling wines. Under the new (1986) German Wine Law, the quality categories of Sekt are:
Sekt, simply the sparkling equivalent of a Tafelwein and may be a "Euroblend".
Deutscher Sekt, sparkling wine from 100 per cent German-grown grapes.
Deutscher Sekt bA, sparkling wine from 100 per cent German grapes, from one of the 11 designated wine-growing regions.

OTHER STYLES OF GERMAN WINE
Badisch Rotgold, quality rosé wine made in Baden exclusively from mixing Ruländer (Grauburgunder) and Spätburgunder grapes (not wine).
Rotling, a rosé wine produced by blending red and white grapes or their pulp – not a blend of wine or must (grape juice).
Schillerwein, Rotling QbA or QmP produced in Württemberg. The name arises from the wine's varying shades of rosé colour ("Schillern" means to change colour). In the past, red and white grape varieties were grown together in the vineyards and both were harvested and vinified together.
Weißherbst, rosé wine made from red grapes, of a single variety, unblended, only at QbA and QmP levels and of most wine-growing regions.

THE GEOGRAPHY OF GERMAN WINE
In classifying German wine, the rule is: the more specific the information concerning the origin of the wine, the more individual in character and flavour the wine will be.
Anbaugebiet, the widest permitted designation for quality wine. All QbA and QmP wines must indicate from which of the 11 specified wine-growing regions (Anbaugebiete) they come (e.g. Rheinpfalz, Rheinhessen). If there is not a more specific designation on the label, then the wine will simply be typical of that region. Wines produced in the northern regions are usually light, fruity, fragrant and described as being "elegant" because of their fresh acidity. The regions further south produce wines with generally more body, fuller fruitiness and sometimes a more powerful flavour.
Bereich, a sub-region or district within an Anbaugebiet. A Bereich includes many wine-growing villages and usually takes its name from the main village or geographic location in its area, e.g. Bereich Bernkastel, in the Mosel-Saar-Ruwer; Bereich Nierstein in the Rheinhessen. Wine that carries a Bereich name can best be described as a regional wine. Wine from Bereich Nierstein, for example, will have a slightly different character from wine from other Bereiche in the Rheinhessen. There are 34 Bereiche in the 11 specified wine regions, made up of 152 collective vineyard sites (Großlagen).

Großlage ("collective vineyard"): each Bereich is composed of collections of vineyards that share a similar geological character and climate. Wine from a Großlage will bear the name of the collective vineyard site preceded by the name of a village, e.g. wine labelled Niersteiner Gutes Domtal is from the collection of vineyards known as Gutes Domtal around the village of Nierstein. On German wine labels, almost all vineyards, both Großlagen and Einzellagen, are coupled with the name of a village (Gemeinde) which in turn is usually identified by the suffix "er". Thus wine from the village of Nierstein is a Niersteiner (as in Londoner or New Yorker). There are 152 Großlagen made up of individual sites (Einzellagen).

Einzellage ("individual site"), the smallest geographical unit. The smaller the unit in the organization of the German wine-growing area, the more specific are the characteristics that distinguish its wine. Thus wine labelled Niersteiner Hipping, from the vineyard site Hipping in the village of Nierstein, is more individual in character and taste than wine from the Großlage Niersteiner Gutes Domtal. There are 2,600 Einzellagen, and each Einzellage is officially registered and in most cases its boundaries are precisely established.

Gemeinde, town or village: the village name always comes before the vineyard on German wine labels (see Großlage, Einzellage).

Ortsteil, a suburb or part of a larger community, e.g. Erbach in the Rheingau is an Ortsteil of the town of Eltville.

BOTTLING TERMS

Abfüller Bottler.

Abfüllung Bottling. When grapes or wines are purchased from the producer and bottled at a winery the term is "Abfüller" followed by the name of the company.

Erzeugerabfüllung Estate-bottled; assurance that the grapes were grown and the wine was produced and bottled by the same grower or a cooperative of growers.

Erzeugergemeinschaft A producers' association, usually for joint marketing purposes, of several smaller or medium-sized producers.

Kellerei Wine cellar; by inference, a merchant's rather than a grower's establishment (which would be called a Weingut).

Weingut Wine estate. The term may only be used by growers who grow their own grapes.

Weinkellerei Commercial wine cellar that buys grapes, must or wine but does not necessarily own vineyards. Weingut-weinkellerei indicates that a company owns vineyards from which it makes its own wine and also buys from other growers or merchants.

Winzergenossenschaft,
Winzerverein Growers' cooperative.

1 The specified growing region.
2 The year in which the grapes were harvested.
3 The town and vineyard from which the grapes came. (In this case, a hypothetical example.)
4 The grape variety.
5 The taste or style of the wine. In this case, semi-dry.
6 The quality level of the wine, indicating ripeness of the grapes at harvest.
7 The official testing number: proof that the wine has passed the tests required for all German quality wines.
8 Wines grown, made and bottled by the grower or a coop-

① RHEINPFALZ

② 1985

③ Winzerdorfer Rebberg
④ Müller-Thurgau
⑤ Halbtrocken
⑥ Qualitätswein b.A. A.P.Nr. 516 987 83 ⑦
⑧ Erzeugerabfüllung Winzer Bacchus, Winzerdorf

erative of growers may be labelled "Erzeugerabfüllung."

Other wineries and bottlers are identified as "Abfüller."

OTHER USEFUL TERMS

Amtliche Prüfung See "AP" page 53.

Anreichern To "enrich": the addition of sugar to must before fermentation to increase the alcohol content and thus produce a balanced wine; the equivalent of the French chaptalization. However, in Germany the addition of sugar is allowed only for Tafelwein, Landwein and QbA wine. In making wine, yeast acts on the sugar of the grape and converts it to both alcohol and carbon dioxide, which escapes. If there is not enough sugar, for example in years of poor weather when the grapes cannot fully ripen, the alcohol level will be too low, the wine will have little staying power and will taste unbalanced. The amount of enrichment is strictly regulated: only as much as is needed to bring the wine to a minimum alcohol level is allowed. Wines in the QmP category, i.e. wines of Kabinett quality and upwards, may *not* be enriched.

Aus eigenem Lesegut "From his own harvest": from the estate; estate bottled.

Bocksbeutel Flagon-shaped Franconian wine bottle.

Botrytis cinerea "Noble rot" or, in German, Edelfäule. A mould that appears in northern climates such as Germany's, coming late in the season when the nights are cool and heavy with dew, the mornings have fog and the days are warm. When botrytis attacks, the grapes begin to shrivel and the water in their juice evaporates, concentrating the sugar and flavour. The longer the grapes stay on the vine, the sweeter they become. But to delay picking also means risk: the grapes may be lost to bad weather. Wine from botrytised grapes, such as Beerenauslese and Trockenbeerenauslese wines, are extraordinarily rich, sweet and elegant.

Bundesweinprämierung See DLG page 53.

Deutsches Weinsiegel See DLG page 53.

Diabetikerwein Must contain no more than 4 grams per litre of residual sugar, 40 mg/l free sulphur dioxide and 12% alcohol, and should be drunk by diabetics only after medical approval is given. The DLG awards its yellow seal to diabetic wines that meet its standards.

DLG See page 53.

Domäne "Domain" – in Germany a term used mainly to describe the estates owned by Federal German States (e.g. in the Rheingau, Franken, Nahe).

Edelfäule See Botrytis cinerea.

Flurbereinigung Term for the Government-sponsored "consolidation" and reallocation of vineyard holdings by remodelling the landscape, a process that has revolutionized the old system of terracing in most parts of Germany, making the land workable by tractors and rationalizing scattered holdings.

Landespreismünze Regional wine prizes, which act as "heats" for the national Bundesweinprämierung (see DLG page 53).

Liebfraumilch See page 49.

Noble rot See Botrytis cinerea.

Perlwein Slightly sparkling Tafelwein.

Restsüße "Residual sugar": the sugar remaining in a wine as a result of incomplete fermentation or the addition of Süßreserve.

Spritzig Effervescent.

Süßreserve "Sweet reserve": unfermented grape juice that the winemaker is allowed to add to his wine in judicious amounts just before bottling to give the wine a harmonious balance and enhance its bouquet. Süßreserve must be of the same quality and is usually from the same grape variety and vineyard as the wine.

THE GRAPES OF GERMANY

White-wine grapes account for 88 per cent of wine production in Germany; only 12 per cent of production is red or rosé. The three most widely planted varieties are Müller-Thurgau with 26 per cent of Germany's vineyard area, Riesling with some 20 per cent and Silvaner with just over 8 per cent. The other main white-wine varieties, in descending order of area planted, are Kerner, Scheurebe, Bacchus, Ruländer, Morio-Muskat, Faber, Huxelrebe, Gutedel, Ortega and Elbling. The leading red-grape varieties are Spätburgunder with between 4 and 5 per cent, Portugieser with just over 3 per cent and Trollinger with just over 2 per cent. If at least 85 per cent of a wine is from one grape variety, it can be labelled with the name of that variety.

Auxerrois Shy-bearing white variety with good sugar level, low acidity, grown in very small quantities in Baden. Not to be confused with the red Auxerrois of Cahors, a synonym of Malbec.

Bacchus A large yielder that makes pleasant, fruity, low-acid wines with good body and a subdued Muscat flavour. Best as Auslesen and should be drunk young. Grown mainly in Rheinhessen, Rheinpfalz, Mosel-Saar-Ruwer, Franken.

Clevner Synonym for Traminer in Baden, but of Frühburgunder in Württemberg.

Domina Red (Portugieser × Spätburgunder) cross and a good yielder. Grown in tiny quantities in the Ahr (where red wine is particularly valued) and in Franken.

Dornfelder Successful red grape producing dark wine with good acidity, mainly in Rheinhessen and Rheinpfalz.

Ehrenfelser A good new cross, between Riesling and Müller-Thurgau in quality. Small quantities in Rheinhessen, Rheinpfalz, Rheingau and Hessische Bergstrasse.

Elbling Once the chief grape of the Mosel, now grown mainly in the Obermosel. Neutral, acidic, clean. Good in sparkling wine.

Faber An early ripening grape that produces refreshing, fruity wine with good bouquet, average acidity, full body and a light Muscat taste. Mainly Rheinhessen, Rheinpfalz, Nahe.

Frühburgunder An early ripening form of Spätburgunder, also called Clevner in Württemberg.

Gewürztraminer ("Spicy Traminer"): pink, spicy grape that makes highly aromatic wine, mainly in Baden and Rheinpfalz.

Gutedel South Baden name for the Chasselas of France (in Switzerland "Fendant"). Light, refreshing but short-lived wine. Good *spritzig*.

Huxelrebe Prolific, very aromatic, early ripening variety (easily achieves Auslese level), popular in Rheinhessen, Rheinpfalz.

Kanzler Rare cross giving a small yield with good ripeness. Rheinhessen, Rheinpfalz.

Kerner One of the most successful of the new crosses (Trollinger × Riesling), now the fourth most widely planted grape in Germany. Early ripening, it has good acidity, fruit and body and a mild Muscat flavour.

Klingelberger Synonym for Riesling in Durbach (Baden).

Limberger Also known as Lemberger (in Austria as Blaufränkisch). Late-ripening red grape grown in Württemberg; often blended.

Morio-Muskat Very prolific producer whose wines have a strong, rich bouquet. Grown mainly in Rheinhessen and Rheinpfalz, it is often blended with a more neutral variety (e.g. Silvaner).

Müllerrebe Alias Schwarzriesling, alias Pinot Meunier. Makes a little dark red wine in Württemberg and elsewhere.

Müller-Thurgau Germany's most widely grown grape, named after Professor Müller of Thurgau, Switzerland, who created it in 1882, probably by crossing Riesling and Silvaner. Produces heavy crops and ripens early. The wine is generally mild and soft in texture, often described as carrying a hint of Muscat in its flavour. It can be excellent as sweet wine.

Muskat The highly aromatic Muskat-Ottonel and Gelber Muskateller are grown in small quantities in Baden and Württemberg.

Nobling A Silvaner × Gutedel cross with a fine aroma, found mainly in south Baden.

Optima A cross of (Silvaner × Riesling) × Müller-Thurgau, delicately spicy. Particularly good for late-harvest wines. Grown mainly in the Mosel and Rheinhessen.

Ortega Very early ripening, aromatic and spicy variety grown in Mosel-Saar-Ruwer, Rheinhessen and Rheinpfalz.

Perle Very aromatic pink grape in Franken.

Portugieser, Blauer Germany's second red grape after Spätburgunder. Gives light, acidic red wines and good Weißherbst in the Ahr, Rheinhessen, Rheinpfalz and Württemberg.

Reichensteiner A "Eurocross" with antecedents from France, Italy and Germany. Most noticeably resembles its Müller-Thurgau lineage but is slightly higher in sugar and acidity. Grown mainly in Rheinhessen and Rheinpfalz, with small plantings in Mosel-Saar-Ruwer.

Rieslaner A rare Franken variety (Silvaner × Riesling) capable of making excellent Auslesen.

Riesling Germany's second most-planted grape variety (after Müller-Thurgau) and indisputably its most noble. Gives wines of crisp, fruity acidity capable of indefinite ageing. It demands a good site (it ripens late) but repays with unrivalled character, finesse and "breed". Surely the world's greatest white grape variety.

Ruländer Alias Pinot Gris (France), Pinot Grigio (Italy). Blue grapes giving full-bodied, robust, very clean and striking white wines, especially in Baden.

Scheurebe Silvaner × Riesling cross well established in Rheinhessen and Rheinpfalz. Potentially magnificent as Auslesen and even sweeter, with good acidity and a bouquet and taste reminiscent of black currants.

Siegerrebe A sweet aromatic variety, mainly used to add richness to blends in Rheinhessen and Rheinpfalz.

Silvaner Germany's third most popular grape (behind Müller-Thurgau and Riesling), a mild variety that was once the most important grape in Germany. A reasonably abundant producer, it ripens about two weeks earlier than Riesling and at its best (especially in Franken and Rheinhessen) has unsuspected depths. Often produced in a dry or semi-dry style, or blended with spicier varieties.

Spätburgunder, Blauer Alias Pinot Noir, the red Burgundy grape, concentrated in Baden with small amounts in Württemberg, Rheinhessen, Rheinpfalz, Rheingau and the Ahr. Its wine is often made as Weißherbst.

Traminer The usual German name for Gewürztraminer.

Trollinger A popular red grape in Württemberg but a late ripener. Its wine is usually light with a distinct fruity acidity.

Weißburgunder Alias Pinot Blanc. Little planted in Germany but gives a smooth, rather neutral wine in Baden and the Nahe.

WINE AND FOOD

The following chart is a guide to choosing a German wine for everyday enjoyment, for dinner or for a special occasion.

	Wine Characteristics	What to look for on the Label	Serving Suggestions
BODY	light	Deutscher Tafelwein Deutscher Landwein	casual entertaining – picnics, informal parties, outings
		Qualitätswein b.A. esp. from northerly regions such as Mosel-Saar-Ruwer	good all-purpose wines – entertaining and/or with light foods, esp. seafood, cold meats, poultry, veal or pork
		Kabinett	because of low alcohol, good for business functions; refreshing as an apéritif; accompanies seafood and light meat dishes, incl. stir-fried
	medium	Qualitätswein b.A. esp. from central or southern regions such as Rhine area	good all-purpose wines – entertaining and/or with most foods (the more body the wine has, the more substance the food should have, e.g. roast turkey)
		Spätlese	richer, more flavourful foods, incl. pork, pâté, dishes prepared with cream sauces
	full-bodied, rich	Auslese types	very special occasions, as an apéritif or with, after or in place of dessert
AROMA	neutral	Silvaner, Gutedel, Burgunder types	serve with light, delicate foods which are not too aromatic
	delicate/fruity	Riesling, Kerner	
	flowery	Müller-Thurgau, Scheurebe, Bacchus	
	pronounced/spicy	Gewürztraminer, Morio-Muskat	serve with spicy foods or those with a fair amount of seasoning
ACIDITY	mild	Silvaner, Müller-Thurgau, Gutedel, Ruländer	serve with light, delicate foods which are not too acidic
	pronounced	Riesling, Kerner, Scheurebe, Gewürztraminer	serve with foods with a marked degree of acidity; more robust dishes
FLAVOUR	neutral	Silvaner, Müller-Thurgau, Gutedel, Burgunders	serve with light, delicate foods which are not highly seasoned or spicy
	fruity	Riesling, Kerner, Scheurebe, Bacchus, Burgunder types	appropriate foods depend on other factors – the wine's body, aroma, acidity, dryness
	spicy	Gewürz., Morio-Muskat, sometimes Scheurebe	serve with spicy foods or those with a fair amount of seasoning
DRY TO SWEET	very dry	"trocken" QbA, QmP to Auslese level	hearty, robust dishes without sauces; shellfish; grilled meat; beef; game
	semi-dry	"halbtrocken" QbA, QmP to Auslese level	dishes with a touch of sweetness; cream sauces; "fatter" fish types; pork dishes
	slightly to medium sweet	QbA, QmP to Auslese level	dishes with a definitely sweet taste and/or richer, full-bodied foods; pâté
	lusciously sweet	Auslese, Beerenauslese, Trockenbeerenauslese	with, after or in place of dessert, served in small quantities

AGEING GERMAN WINES

Good-quality German wines have a much longer lifespan, and benefit much more by being kept in bottle, than fashion suggests or most people suppose. Almost all the superior-grade (QmP) wines, delectable as they may taste in their flower-and-fruity youth, have the potential to put on another dimension of flavour with maturity. When they are first offered for sale they are at their most brisk and lively, with acidity and fruitiness often tending to cancel each other out in a generally tingling and exciting effect. Some fine wines (particularly Rieslings) at this stage have remarkably little aroma.

Sometimes after a year or two in bottle the first rapture goes without maturer flavours taking its place; the wine you bought with enthusiasm seems to be letting you down. Be patient. The subtle alchemy takes longer. It may be four or five years before the mingled savours of citrus and spice and oil emerge.

Each vintage has its own timespan, but as a generalization Kabinett wines from a first-rate grower need at least three years in bottle and may improve for seven or eight, Spätlesen will improve for anything from four to ten years, and Auslesen and upwards will benefit from five or six years up to 20 or even more.

STORING AND SERVING

Like all fine wines, German wines should be stored in a cool, quiet place where the temperature is a constant 50–55°F (10–13°C). When such conditions are not possible, the most important consideration is that the temperature does not fluctuate wildly. It is less harmful to store wines where the temperature is five to ten degrees warmer than ideal than where there are sudden dramatic changes. Wines should be stored horizontally so that the liquid is in contact with the cork, preventing any air from entering the bottle.

Sometimes harmless deposits of tartaric crystals (Weinsteine) form in finer wines during a prolonged period in a cold environment. These in no way detract from the flavour of the wine and are considered in Germany to be a sign of quality and distinction. Simply pour the wine carefully so that the crystals remain in the bottle and are not decanted into the glass.

The ideal storage temperature is also the ideal serving temperature. If served too chilled, the wine will not immediately reveal its full flavour and complexity.

INDEX TO VILLAGES, GROSSLAGEN AND BEREICHE

116

ILLUSTRATIONS
Jonathan Field

KEY MAPS
John Laing

PHOTOGRAPHS
Bildagentur Mauritius, Frankfurt: pages 18, 20, 22, 26, 32, 33, 44T, 44B, 54T, 55, 60, 74, 95BL, 95BR, 102, 103; Jon Wyand: 26BL, 45, 48, 49, 55, 81; ZEFA, London: 19, 95C